Enjoy your passion
for fishing!

Jim C. Chapman

Fishing Passion

a lifelong love affair with angling

Other books by Jim C. Chapralis

World Guide to Fly Fishing

Fishing Escapes (with co-author Paul Melchior)

Fishing Passion

a lifelong love affair with angling

by Jim C. Chapralis

Illustrations by Charles B. Mitchell and John Tianis

AnglingMatters® Press
Evanston, Illinois 60203

Printed in the United States of America

10 9 8 7 6 5 4 3 2 1

Publisher's Cataloging-in-Publication
(Provided by Quality Books, Inc.)

Chapralis, Jim C., 1932-
    Fishing passion : a lifelong love affair with angling
/ by Jim C. Chapralis ; illustrations by Charles B.
Mitchell and John Tianis. -- 1st ed.
    p. cm.
    Includes index.
    LCCN: 2001117916
    ISBN: 09708653-3-3
    1. Fishing--Anecdotes. 2. Chapralis, Jim C., 1932-
I. Title.

SH441.C43 2001   799.1
                                   QBI01-200878

Table of contents

PART SIX Regrets, hopes & dreams

@mitchell

For our love of fishing

We trade a comfortable room for a tent next to a remote stream to take advantage of the late evening hatch or early morning rise. We fish in the rain, often ignoring lightning as we wave our 9-foot graphite fly rods for a few more casts. We endure peanut butter sandwiches or we watch our guide prepare shorelunch when we know darn well he never washed his hands, but heck, we're too busy shooing away mosquitoes and deer flies or inhaling no-see-ums to meekly protest. We may forsake our daily hot shower, or perhaps bathing quickly in a cold lake or river, sometimes accidentally. The amazing thing is that we may pay $300, $500, or a $1,000 a day for the "privilege," and we think this is fun, and, you know, it probably is!

Introduction

ONE OF LIFE'S PROBLEMS is that we must choose a career at an early age; by the time we're sophomores or juniors in high school, we're expected to know what we're going to do for the rest of our lives. Preposterous! How can we make a lifetime decision when as teenagers we aren't sure of our skills or what's involved in the various professions or vocations?

This was a lesser problem in my day: the girls wanted to become stewardesses, nurses or teachers, while most of the guys wanted to be firemen, policemen, or pilots (except for Clarence who, in 3rd grade, said he wanted to become an undertaker and later became one).

Most of us picked an occupation, tested it out on our families, and if we received a few nods of approval we usually pursued it.

Aunt Dena gave me a Gilbert Chemistry Set for Christmas when I was in 4th grade and I became so interested in chemistry that, by the time I was in 6th grade, I assembled quite a laboratory in our living room. I placed a small table near a window for my experiments and used a built-in book case in our living room to store my chemicals and other apparatus. I delivered two daily newspapers to earn money to purchase the equipment.

Unfortunately, I burned our expensive Oriental rug in the living room by accidentally dropping sulfuric acid on it. My grandmother was enraged but gave me a pass.

Cousin Ernie, who was also interested in chemistry, and I conducted various experiments. For example, we made "laughing gas" (nitrous oxide) but because neither one of us wanted to inhale it, we bribed my grandfather by giving him a quarter.

"What's suppose to happen?" he inquired in Greek.

"It's supposed to make you laugh," we replied.

So he inhaled the laughing gas that we produced and stored in a jar, faked a laugh, and insisted on his money. We reluctantly paid him 25 cents, because we wanted to use him for future experiments. He pocketed the quarter, laughed heartily, mumbled something about "easy money" and headed for Talman Drug Store to buy a banana split.

One day, when I was home from school for lunch, I showed grandpa some "chemistry magic." I put a few drops of glycerine on potassium permanganate (don't try this at home!). After a few seconds the mixture started to bubble, smoulder, smoke and then, *presto*, burst into brilliant flames.

He was impressed.

After I left for school grandpa tried to recreate the experiment. Something went wrong because the chemicals didn't burst into fire. Disappointed, he left the house and went for a walk. Apparently there was a delayed reaction, and eventually the compounds flared into flames which ignited the curtains, billowing in the breeze from the open window.

To make a long story somewhat shorter, my grandparents' three-flat building was in flames. Fire engines raced to the house, and firemen, carrying axes, hoses and other equipment quickly extinguished the flames, but all the apartments were damaged, mostly from the smoke. We and the families that occupied the building had to live at a hotel for about a week until the units were restored and decorated.

Grandma was so furious that she dumped all my chemicals and equipment into the alley.

That ended my chemistry lab at 4842 N. Talman Avenue.

I pursued chemistry in high school even though I no longer had a home lab. When I read A. J. McClane's *Field and Stream* article on parabolic fly rods in Mrs. Brabec's English class, I realized that he made a living from fishing. Maybe I could do that. The seed was planted in my mind, but I didn't dare tell my parents about my career fantasy; actually, I didn't seriously consider the possibility myself.

It was only a dream.

I enrolled as a chemistry major at Northwestern University. N.U.'s location on Lake Michigan's beach was spectacular. So were the glamorous, gorgeous coeds. Between classes, Nick Chandler, Jack Shillestad, Bob McFarland and other friends were spending meaningful hours on the beach perfecting a tan or lining up a Friday night date, while I spent three to four consecutive hours in the lab or listening to a professor in a white smock, droning on and on about valences and atomic weights of various elements.

After a couple of weeks I realized I wasn't "chemistry material." I switched to Liberal Arts, as an English Lit major, where I discovered I wasn't "English Lit material" either. Read James Joyce's *Ulysses* (one sentence is several pages long) or his nonsensical *Finnegans Wake* and you'll know what I mean. Or read e e cummings, who didn't believe in using punctuation or caps in some of his poems or in his name, for that matter. My professor called me "the most unEnglish English Lit major I've had in my classroom."

I eventually ended up in the N.U.'s Medill School of Journalism, but the fishing seed implanted in me continued to grow. I worked at a tackle shop, wrote for fishing publications, guided in Canada, started a rod manufacturing company and later booked international fishing trips.

Somehow, I survived. I accomplished my goal of earning a living through fishing.

I'm sure I would have been richer had I pursued a career in chemistry, or marketing, or banking or anything else. Financially, that is.

I don't think I could be any richer in terms of the experiences I've had through the years.

FISHING PASSION: A lifelong love affair with angling is not a book about catching fish after fish. Or where to fish. There are many fine books on those subjects.

This is a book, or odyssey, about chasing wonderful dreams: some that actually materialized, others that shattered into fractured nightmares. But that's part of the territory. No regrets.

I believe there is a similarity between the passionate attraction to fishing (or other interests) and romantic love. I've divided the book into six sections, which show the parallel between romantic love and addicted angling. There are *The innocent years*, *Early flirtations*, *Flings and infatuations*, *Lifelong commitments*, *Feelings, emotions & relationships*, and *Regrets, hopes and dreams*.

It happens in love; it happens in passionate fishing.

In this magical time capsule, called FISHING PASSION, I'm going to take you back six decades, introduce you to some fascinating people, visit a few interesting places, share some of the bizarre experiences, relive the formative days of international fishing and fish with a few special friends.

Fasten your seat belts. We've got a lot of travelin' to do. I hope you enjoy the ride.

JIM C. CHAPRALIS

Dedication

This book is dedicated to sunfish, smallmouth bass, muskies, trout,
steelhead, walleyes, Arctic char, Arctic grayling,
mekousna trout, carp, Pacific salmon, Atlantic salmon,
northern pike, lake trout, barracuda,
wahoo, snapper, jacks, marlin, sailfish,
swordfish, bonefish, permit, snook, tarpon, shark,
dorado, payara, peacock bass, tuna, queenfish, barramundi,
mahseer, zubatec trout, mackerel, crappie, cobia, huchen,
trevally, tigerfish, roosterfish, whitefish, Nile perch,
kingfish, taimen, bluefish, inconnu, largemouth bass,
and all other wonderful species of fish,
for the countless hours of pleasure (and frustration)
they've provided us, and if it were not for them,
our wonderful world of angling would not exist.

-- J.C.C

Acknowledgments

There are too many camp owners, managers, guides, fishing friends and outdoor writers to acknowledge individually: thanks for all your help. However special thanks to Sally, my wife, for the encouragement and reading the basic manuscript ("You're not going to put **that** in the book, are you?"); to Tracy Blair for her tremendous patience, suggestions, encouragement and editing; and, to Elaine Fiedler for final copy editing.

. . . about the illustrators

Charles B. Mitchell studied at the School of Art Institute of Chicago and the Vogue Academy of Design. He is the recipient of numerous awards, including winning trout stamp competitions and his work has appeared in many publications and books. He is an avid angler and a superb trout fisherman.

John Tianis

studied in Europe and at the Chicago Academy of Fine Arts. For several decades he operated his own design studio, and worked extensively for advertising agencies and was the recipient of many awards. He came out of retirement briefly to help illustrate this book.

PART ONE

The innocent years

First recollection of fishing: trolling across the Atlantic;
the Green Lake monster;
baseball, the Pimp, Christmas trees and the
"unauthorized" fishing trip;
the casting club days;
and, about a fishing trip to Canada where
everything went wrong!

In the beginning...

I BECAME ADDICTED to fishing at a young age. I think I was six
or seven. Although I was born in the United States, my parents decided to move to Athens, Greece. At age four, I had few alternatives
but to go with them. I only spoke English, but young kids can pick up
foreign languages easily and soon I was fluent in Greek. Anyway, at six
or seven I read a story about Nikos and Takis, two young boys who lived
near a river in northern Greece. Every day after school they would go to
the river, prepare their bait, rig up carefully, test the lines and fish the
deep hole at the big bend. According to a wise old shepherd who knew
everything about the region, the largest trout in northern Greece lived
there. "You need good bait, but you need patience," he advised.

Understand that they never expected to hook the huge trout—they seldom hooked any fish—but they would go there nearly every day and they would fantasize that they hooked the big fish and how they would play this *therio* or animal, as they nicknamed this ghostly trout. In a way, Takis and Nikos were the Greek versions of Huck Finn and Tom Sawyer.

One day they set out their lines and began their daily chatter while they munched on walnuts. Suddenly Takis' cane poles arced and bucked violently. The boys were shocked when they realized that they had hooked something huge. Was this the *therio*?

"*Voithia! Voithia!*" Takis cried out for help.

The beast made its way downstream slowly, as both boys hung on to the pole.

"We've hooked the *therio*! We've hooked the *therio*!" They shouted exuberantly, although they could not see it in the inky deep water. The monster pulled them a few yards downstream to an eddy, as they held the straining pole with all their strength. Just as they were about to give up the cane pole to the giant trout and the river, their valiant efforts brought the fish closer to the bank.

They could barely distinguish the big dark-brown shape, but when they worked it closer to the surface they saw they had not hooked the *therio,* but a big black, waterlogged branch from the bottom of the pool. They wallowed in disappointment as they trudged home, but they would return the next day and every day after that to try for the *therio*.

"We must be patient. A good fisherman above all must be patient. Use good bait, but be patient," one would tell the other. It became their motto.

This little story made an impression on me. I wanted to fish.

I didn't get a chance to fish until 1939. My father was being exiled from Athens to a small obscure Greek island for his political editorials against the Greek government. My mother, who was born in the United States, my sister and I would have to return to America. We disposed of everything in 48 hours. Fine expensive furniture that we brought from the States sold for a few dollars. Worse, the Greek drachma spiraled in a free fall and we barely had enough money for passage. We traveled from Greece to Italy by boat and train.

World War II was about to escalate. The train was half-filled with Italian soldiers because Italy was mobilizing for the war. My mother was terrified when we appeared to be hopelessly lost near the dock just prior to scheduled boarding; she asked people for help but no one spoke English or Greek, it seemed, and we had no idea where the boat was. We had little money left and lots of baggage. Luckily we found and boarded the American ship *Manhattan* in time and began to sail for United States.

Now, recalling the adventures of Takis and Nikos, I wanted to fish. We would be sailing for a number of days, and surely the ocean had huge fish, much bigger than their *therio*. To keep me entertained, my mother found a spool of heavy thread and then helped me shape a hook out of a hairpin. I tried different types of bait—leftovers from lunch or dinner—just like Takis and Nikos did, but I had trouble keeping the bait on. So I attached a safety pin (to hold the meat or other bait) to the hairpin hook. I would troll across the Mediterranean and then the Atlantic. What an opportunity! As I reflect today, how many anglers have trolled across the ocean? Lefty Kreh? Joe Brooks? McClane? Wulff? None of these icons.

But suddenly something was wrong. The *Manhattan* came to a halt. The loud speakers immediately summoned all passengers to the deck. Even at age eight, I could gauge everyone's nervousness and anxiety. My mother tried to hide her fear from my sister Angela and me. A German submarine surfaced, and our lifeboats were prepared to be lowered. An elderly woman became hysterical, suffered a heart attack and died on the deck.

Years later, my mother explained that the German submarine was preparing to torpedo the boat, because the sub crew thought our boat was carrying troops under the guise of a civilian ship. But our captain finally convinced the sub that his ship carried only nonmilitary passengers (which is why he wanted everyone on deck, especially women and children) and that the *Manhattan* was a registered American ship (the United States had not entered the war at that time). I'm not sure of the details. We survived. We escaped.

I was eight years old at the time and didn't quite grasp the severity of this event, so I continued to troll across the ocean. When I wasn't holding the spool of thread, I attached it to a boat rail. No hits. Seldom could I keep the bait on for very long, but I know I trolled many, many miles of ocean.

Like Takis and Nikos often told each other, "We must be patient. A good fisherman above all must be patient. Use good bait, but be patient."

I was hooked on fishing.

WE RETURNED TO CHICAGO to live with my grandparents. I had forgotten most of my English. While in Greece, I had been very ill for a few months and my skin was yellowish. I was thin. Confused. Why was my dad being punished? He was a good person. He stood for what was right. We received one letter from him stating that he was the only person on this small island, but he was fine, not to worry, and that once a week they brought him food and he was learning to swim.

Aunt Dena and Uncle Jim Nichols and their daughters were kind enough to invite me for a month to their summer cottage at Green Lake, Wisconsin. Uncle Jim gave me a Gephardt steel tubular rod with a pistol grip, and Mike Chirigos—a neighbor who loved bass fishing—contributed a nifty South Bend Anti-Backlash casting reel. I bought a few lures; my favorite was Helin's Flatfish because it wobbled frantically even when it was barely retrieved.

I learned to catch perch, bluegills and rock bass with worms from the pier. Dorothy, Elaine and Cal, my cousins, taught me to row a boat and later I was permitted to take it out by myself.

I was introverted, bashful and sad, and fishing gave me great pleasure. Trolling back and forth from the "Greek cottages" to Sugar Loaf produced a few small bass and several huge bluegills, but I found comfort in my special make-believe world. Like Takis and Nikos, I fantasized that a very big fish lurked in these waters, and with patience I'd connect with this monster.

After two weeks of trolling I hooked it. The big fish grabbed the Flatfish (U-20 model) and took off with amazing speed. The reel whined its melodic high pitch as yards of 15-pound test Ashaway line melted from the spool. I could not stop the big fish. To be honest, I was scared. This was a powerful fish. There were only a few yards of line left on the spool; I must not give them up. I thumbed the reel as best as I could but the fish would not stop. I was at the end of my line.

POP!

Gone.

But wait; the fish had stopped. The granny knot that I used to tie the line to the reel spool was near the first guide. I reached quickly and I grabbed the knot and held it as tight as I could with my thumb and forefinger. I dropped the rod and grabbed the line above the tip-top.

I recovered a few inches, then a couple of feet and then I gained a few yards, but the fish would run again and the line was cutting my hands.

I yelled for help. The big kids playing near the pier heard me, and the Ganas brothers got in a boat and rowed swiftly toward me. I had hardly spoken to them before because of my poor English. Milton "Babes" Ganas jumped into my boat while his brother Teddy remained in his.

"Are you sure it's a fish? You're not hooked on the bottom?" Babes asked, and then he felt the throbbing of the fish at the end of the line.

"You might have the biggest fish anyone's ever hooked on this lake!" Babes was very strong and gave me a hand. Now we had the fish coming our way. Faster and faster. Victory could be ours.

"Look at that monster. It must be 30 pounds!" Teddy shouted. "It's a carp and it took a Flatfish lure! Never heard of that before."

We worked the fish to the surface and Babes inserted his hands under the carp's gill covers, hoisted the monster out of the water and heaved it into the boat. "Congratulations, kid. Congratulations!" I felt proud! Very proud.

Milton rowed my boat in, because I was shaking too much with excitement to row. I stared at the fish all the way. It was exhausted. I was exhausted. We both breathed in syncopation.

Takis and Nikos were right: "We must be patient. A good fisherman above all must be patient. Use good bait, but be patient."

IT WAS THE FOURTH OF JULY. Most of the inhabitants of the five Greek cottages came to the dock to see the giant fish.

"Oh, you are going to be a good fisherman someday," Mrs. Ganas told me in Greek.

I didn't know what a carp was. It was not a pretty fish, but it was big and it was powerful. I quickly learned that most people on the lake despised the carp, because "they ruin and dirty the waters."

"How should we get rid of it?" one of the boys asked.

"Let's put firecrackers in its mouth," another suggested. And they did. The big three-inch red firecrackers. Bang! Boom! BAM!

The carp quivered. But it was not dead. Or it didn't appear to be.

BANG! BAM! More firecrackers were placed in its mouth and now under its gill covers.

Its head was blown apart. The boys cheered, almost in unison. When the fish was finally dead, Babes got a shovel.

"We will bury him in our garden. Good for the tomatoes," someone explained. I realized that we weren't going to eat it.

The great fish was buried. There were more cheers. Firecrackers. Roman candles. Sparklers. To celebrate the Fourth mostly, but to celebrate my fish also. Inexplicably, its cruel death seemed to bring much satisfaction to the younger people.

Somehow, some way I was sad. The carp had given me a tremendous, courageous fight. Before I fell asleep, I visualized many times how the firecrackers exploded and shredded the carp's head to pieces.

The carp couldn't help being a carp, could it?

Today, as I write this, I started to chase away a number of blackbirds, and pigeons that came to my bird feeder in our garden because I prefer the colorful cardinals and other "prettier" birds. But I stopped. They deserve the seed as much as the other more attractive birds.

I think of that carp and its exploding head often; it has helped me develop a most tolerant philosophy on all aspects of life.

8

WHILE I WAS ADDICTED to fishing, I also developed a strong love for baseball. Our team was known as the River Park Gremlins, but casual observers never knew this because we couldn't afford uniforms. Heck, we used black electrical tape to wrap up ripped baseballs and even screwed splintered bats together.

We called Don Gustafson "the Pimp," but we didn't know what pimp meant. We were twelve at the time. We thought it meant small. Not big in stature. Don was our third baseman. He could field and throw to first base as well as any preteen-ager. Henry Peterson was Pigface, Martin Johnson was Horseface and Tom Anderson, our pitcher, was Smoke because of his fastball. Someone was called M4 after the Army tank, but I can't recall who that was. Others had less memorable nicknames. When we wanted to get together, we didn't use a phone, because most of our households didn't have one; instead, we stood outside of an individual's apartment building and called out using his nickname.

"Yo-o-o-o Horseface!" We would shout using all our lung power, which, by the way, was considerable. We would wait a minute. Then again: **"Yo-o-o-o Horseface!"** Only louder.

We never rang door bells. I don't know why. All the kids in our neighborhood did it this way in the forties.

Martin Johnson was proud of his nickname. He belonged. If he was home, he would stick out his head from a window or from a door and neigh like a horse.

"*N-e-e-i-g-h-h-h!* I'll be right down, guys."

His mother would shudder. "Can't they use another name? Something like 'Flash' or something else? Or just plain Marty. What's wrong with Marty? Or Martin! What must the neighbors think?" He lived with his mother; we never asked what happened to his father.

Actually, Marty did look like a horse. Somewhat. Just like Pigface looked like a little pig. But Pigface didn't like his nickname although he didn't complain about it for a long time, until one day he took a bat and went after Lee Pedersen. We never called him "Pigface" again (actually, we sort of dropped him from the team).

My love for baseball initially overshadowed my love for fishing. I remember when the *Chicago Daily News* sponsored Lon Warnecke (a famous Chicago Cub pitcher) and the great Rogers Hornsby to visit the city parks, including Welles Park on the north side of Chicago. They would lob the ball over the plate and each of us, maybe there were 50 kids, would bat against these baseball icons. Imagine what a thrill that was: batting against the old Arkansas Hummingbird, as Lon was called, or the fabulous Rogers Hornsby. Batting against them would be comparable today to playing basketball with Michael Jordan. Well, almost.

One solidly built kid—maybe he was 14 or 15—hit the ball so hard, so far, more than 400 feet, that Hornsby ran over to him and pulled him aside, and asked, "What's your name, kid?" And Rogers wrote down his name and address. Boy, were we jealous. We realized that Hornsby—probably working as a scout—would give the kid's name to some baseball club as a splendid prospect. The kid was nonchalant, downright casual about it. Later we heard that he eventually played minor league baseball, but I don't know if he made to the big league. At least two guys from opposing teams made it to the majors: Buster Carlson pitched briefly for the Chicago Cubs and Marv Rotblatt for the White Sox.

We would go and watch the Chicago Cubs whenever we could, especially on Sundays when doubleheaders were the norm. Sometimes, just prior to the first game and between the two games, we would help a Greek hot dog man run his stand across from Wrigley Field. The Pimp opened the buns and placed the hot dogs in them, I put the mustard and fixings on top, while the Greek—no dummy he—collected the money.

"Step right up . . . get your Chicago Cub hot dogs! Best in town!" The Greek's hot dogs were good. He had a secret ingredient, a type of salt that he sprinkled on his hot dogs. Years later I figured out this was celery salt. We were allowed to eat two hot dogs and were paid a couple of dollars. Easy money!

Some of the rich folk who sat in the box seats next to third base would leave after the first game, stop by for a hot dog and would give us their ticket stubs. The stubs would allow us into the second game. Talk about happy kids. There we were, in the most expensive box seats. The Andy Frain ushers would try to chase us out, but we had the stubs.

10

There was Phil Cavarretta over at first base. And Stan Hack at third. Lou Novikoff (the Mad Russian) played left field and my favorite, Bill Nicholson, was the right fielder. Good ol' No. 25. Swish, as Nicholson was called, was a home-run hitter. We would study the players and strategy and try to figure out cutoff plays and who covered what base on a double steal. I wanted to be a professional baseball player. We all did. I was a catcher, so I focused on Clyde McCullough, the Cubs' catcher.

We would wait outside of Wrigley Field after the games for the players to shower and dress. In their civilian clothes they looked like "regular" people; in their baseball togs they appeared invincible. They patiently signed autographs or said a few words to us; if they had a particularly poor game, we would offer words of encouragement or lay off. Bill Nicholson once took my cap off and rubbed my head. What a thrill! What a difference from today's spoiled baseball players who make millions and only sign autographs for money.

I loved the game. We practiced all summer long. Hours at a time. Unlike today's Little Leaguers, we had no adults to teach us, but we were very disciplined. We practiced sliding and bunting on some days. On other days we would shag flies. We played our games on Saturdays.

The Pimp and I were very good friends and enterprising little characters. We went into a number of businesses together. The best was the Christmas tree business, although it had one fault: it was very seasonal. We found a place that wholesaled majestic Christmas trees for only $1 apiece; even in the 1940s, these stately trees would command $4 to $6. The wholesaler was on Western near Addison Avenue, a few miles from our homes. How would we get the trees to my yard? My family didn't own a car—heck, I didn't even have a bike—but the Pimp's family had a Pontiac. He had watched his father drive, and sometimes he would take the car out for a little spin when his parents were away. Obviously he didn't have a license; he was only 12 years old! Because he was so short he had to sit on a couple of phone books while he drove. He actually showed me how to drive on McCormick Boulevard, north of Chicago. "Here's the first gear, now release the clutch slowly and press on the pedal . . . Geez, it's not that difficult . . . " He'd lose patience as we stuttered up the road.

The Gustafson Pontiac was our only solution. His parents were away for the weekend, so we bought a number of trees, tied them to the car and brought them to my back yard, where we displayed them. We would select each tree carefully, so these were the *crème de la crème*. The wholesalers were highly amused by our entrepreneurship and allowed us to inspect each tree. Of course, we had to park the Pontiac out of their sight and carry the trees to the car. We made lots of trips, but we were never stopped by the police. My neighbors bought our wonderful trees within a couple days and we always quadrupled our investment.

After we had transported the Christmas trees to my yard, Don's mother commented that the car's interior smelled like pine, which it did, even though we made sure that we removed every single pine needle from the Pontiac.

"Mom, that's because it's Christmas," Don explained.

She bought it.

THE PIMP INTRODUCED ME to baseball, and I got him interested in fishing. Actually he had fished before on a family summer vacation at Elkhorn Lake in Wisconsin, but now we were really getting into it. We would read Jason Lucas—onetime *Sports Afield* fishing writer—who invariably caught big bass wherever he went. We hung on every word he wrote. If he said he caught his limit of bass from his bathtub, we probably would have believed it.

We decided to fish the Fox Chain of Lakes region in Northern Illinois, an area about 45 miles from where we lived. The only problem was how two 12-year-old boys would get that far with no ride and little cash?

The problem seemed to solve itself one warm summer day. Don's older brother Jim, in charge while their parents were out of town for a few days, left early for his summer job.

We loaded our meager tackle and sandwiches into the Pontiac, and the Pimp drove us up US 41 sitting on two phone books—under age, no license and no permission to drive the family car. Don wore his dad's big golfing cap pulled over much of his face to make himself appear older. He was a good driver. Our only fear was having a police car stop us, but we made it to our destination without incident.

When we arrived at Round Lake, we parked in the lot and casually sauntered with our tackle to the dock to rent a boat from our Christmas tree profits. The owner showed us a good boat and told us it would cost two dollars for the day. We grabbed it.

"Where's your father?"

"He's not here," Don answered.

"Well, how did you get here?"

"The Pontiac, over there," Don hesitated at first but then proudly pointed to "our" car in the parking lot.

"You what? Listen, kids. We never had this conversation . . . ya hear? I know nothing about this."

He took the two dollars, shook his head, but he seemed amused as he

walked away. I think he liked our spirit.

We trolled Flatfishes and Heddon River Runts and mostly got hung up on weeds, but we did manage to catch two bass of about two pounds each. We returned them because we didn't want to put the fish in the car, fearful that the odor could tip our game, so in a way we were practicing catch-and-release back then!

We drove home, and replaced the gas by buying it in small gas containers from a local station. We were worried about the car's odometer, but his parents apparently never checked it. We never got caught.

Next we discovered the wonderful fishing at Montrose Harbor on Chicago's lakefront. This was in the days of streetcars. To fish the lake successfully you needed long cane poles, 12 or more feet in length.

Most of the fishermen had two-piece, ferruled cane poles, but we could only afford the single-piece models. Because of their length, we had to stand in the back and hold them outside the Lawrence Avenue red-and-yellow streetcars. We'd get off at Broadway, then transfer to another streetcar to Montrose. We would stop at Mayer's Bait shop to buy two dozen minnows for a quarter, and then proceed to the harbor or the Horse-shoe Pier.

We caught perch. Some of the fishermen were there every day. We called them "the regulars," and because they were very successful, we always set up near them and emulated them as best as we could. Some-times they would fish one place, other times another, depending on the wind, season, temperatures and other variables that the Pimp and I never fully understood.

We would catch yellow perch and place them on a stringer. If we caught a perch of more than 12 inches, it was the custom to yell, *"JUMBO!"* as loud as we could.

Twice a day, Nick the Greek would come by with his red wagon, selling coffee, donuts and sweet rolls and liberally dispensing good fishing information to some of his favorite clients.

"Try the south side of the Horseshoe. That's good right now."

I don't think there was a limit on perch in those days, and some of the locals kept huge strings of these tasty fish to feed their families. We kept about ten perch apiece because getting them home was not easy. Not only did we have to hold our poles outside the street car, but then the Pimp and I had to carry two stringers of fish. We managed, though. One time, a man boarding the streetcar saw the perch and bought a stringerful for two dollars! Wow! Were we happy.

In the spring, just after the ice left the harbor, there was a solid her-ring run. These fish were 12 to 18 inches, maybe longer. They were very difficult to catch. They were flashy fighters but extremely wary, so you had to go very light: two-pound test line, tiny hooks, small minnies—or you wouldn't hook any.

When fishing was slow, I often gazed at Lake Michigan, and won-dered how marvelous it would be, if one day, there would be more and larger fish, perhaps even different, sportier species out there. These were dreamy thoughts then. Today, through creative stocking programs, Lake Michigan holds Alaskan-sized salmon and huge trout, but in those days they were just dreams.

And fishermen love to dream!

Aftermath: *When Italy and Germany declared war against Greece, the Greek government, realizing that my dad was correct in predicting that Germany would attack Greece, released him from exile and reinstated him as an officer and in command of troops. He rejoined us in Chicago after World War II.*

Behind steel bars

WHAT ARE YOU GUYS? Boy Scouts? Put that crook in jail!" the captain commanded, and the two detectives ushered me into a cell and then slammed the door. **C-L-A-A-N-G!** What a horrible sound that is. A jail door slammed. It seems so final.

So there I was, peering out from behind steel bars at the Summerdale Police Station.

The day had started pleasantly, like most other days. I attended Amundsen High School, and while in Mr. Huddy's math course, I was summoned to Mr. L. Day Perry's office. The principal.

When I arrived, Mr. Perry looked stern, upset. Two men with fedora hats in their hands stood rigidly next to him. He said they were detectives from the Summerdale Police Station and that I was in trouble, but he wouldn't elaborate.

One of the detectives advanced toward me and said that I had to go with them.

"He is a good boy, on my honor roll, a very good student . . . " I heard Mr. Perry solemnly whisper to the other detective.

"What's this about?" I demanded as they drove me to Gregory's Sport Shop, a few blocks away, near the corner of Damen and Lawrence Avenues.

"You will find out soon enough!"

At this point, I need to give you some background. In the late '40s, I worked for Bill Gregory, the owner of Gregory's Sport Store, after school and all day Saturday. I'm going to tell you without any hesitation that I was a super salesman, and although only 15, I sold more tackle part-time than the boss man did full-time, and when I wasn't selling I was polishing glass cases, sweeping floors, washing windows, pricing items, picking up products from the wholesalers, cleaning the toilet—but mostly selling tackle. I knew my stuff. I enjoyed it.

He paid me 50 cents per hour. Whenever we chatted casually for more than a few minutes, he deducted the time from my paycheck. One day he told me about his two fishing trips to Eagle Lake, Ontario, and he went into such detail that it took almost an hour. He deducted 50 cents from my paycheck. If I sound bitter, I was, and as I write this I still am. Furious.

But there's more. Earlier I had made the Amundsen High School baseball team as a catcher, and I was confident that I would be first string. Chuck Hoover, the other catcher, while a nice guy, couldn't throw to second base without bouncing his peg once or twice, and while neither of us was a power hitter, I could at least bunt. Anyway I had made the team, and I felt confident of being its first-string catcher.

I told Bill Gregory that on some afternoons I wouldn't be able to work because of practice and games, but I would work on Saturday and Monday and Thursday evenings when the sales activity was good. I thought he would congratulate me for making the squad.

"Listen, kid! I gave you a great opportunity and taught you the business. How to sell. How to display merchandise. You decide: It's either

Gregory's Sports Store or that baseball team. I'll tell ya, there are a lot of guys out there who'd like to work and earn some money. And learn the business. They ask me for jobs all the time when you aren't here. They're probably your friends, too."

Decision time. I loved baseball. But I wanted to learn all about fishing, and learning about tackle might come in handy. My heart said "baseball," but my mind said "work," and I listened to my mind. I told Bill that I would work for him and reluctantly and sadly I resigned from the team. That was months before the detectives picked me up.

There was another problem. I was very much interested in tournament casting, and the *Chicago Tribune* had sponsored a mega-casting tournament at one of the sport shows. I was casting very well and was in the semifinals in two events. Bill wanted me to wear a jacket that had "Gregory's Sports Store" lettering on the front and on the back.

"And, kid, keep the front of the jacket zipped up so they can read 'Gregory Sports Shop' in case the newspaper takes a picture of you casting." He would sell me the jacket at 40 percent off list price. His cost.

I refused, because this was an amateur casting division and any commercialism, in those days, would disqualify my amateur status and put me in the professional class. There weren't many pros and very few, if any, casting tournaments for professionals in the Chicago area. He was furious when I refused to wear the jacket, and muttered that I would regret this. Gregory's threats, I discovered, were not to be taken lightly.

That's the background.

WHEN THE TWO DETECTIVES and I arrived at the store, we found Bill Gregory nervously pacing back and forth. Bill was in his 50s, with shocking white hair and wire-rimmed glasses. He had been a bachelor all his life, which was easy to understand because at Christmas he gave his girlfriend a pair of nylon stockings. Big deal!

"Bill, what's this about?"

"You stole 50 bucks!" he replied.

"Huh?"

"Yesterday, I gave you a check made out to cash when you went to the bank. You never gave me the money. So I called the police."

"Bill, I can't believe what you are saying! When I returned from the bank yesterday, you left immediately and told me you wouldn't be back and for me to lock up at the end of the night. When I go to school in the morning, you're closed. I was going to give you the 50 bucks when I came to work this afternoon!"

"Well, you should have left a note. I'm not a mind reader, ya know!" Bill Gregory said. "All right, you guys can leave. I'll drop the charges."

And the detectives left.

I gave Bill the 50 bucks back. He counted it, of course. Maybe twice.

"See ya after school," he grumbled.

"No, you won't. I quit! Do you know what you did, Bill? You embarrassed me at school. The teachers, my friends, the class—they'll want to know why the detectives took me away. I quit! And I don't want my pay!"

I left. I was furious.

I went straight home. I had a terrible headache and decided to take a nap. I swallowed two Bayer aspirins and fell asleep.

THE DOORBELL RANG. My grandmother answered it, woke me up and said that there were two men who wanted to talk to me. "They say they are police, but they do not have uniforms," she was very worried.

"Sorry kid, old man Gregory decided to press charges again. We have to take you to Summerdale. Put your shoes on."

The detectives were nice guys. They weren't going to put me in a jail. Instead they played checkers with me outside the cells.

That's when the captain came in and told them to lock me up.

C-L-A-A-N-G!

That evening when my father came home, my worried grandmother related the events. He hurried to Summerdale jail. When he saw me behind bars, he laughed at first, said he would post a bond, and then ordered the policeman to release me. I think dad felt that he was still an officer in the Greek army as he barked his order to the police. It worked because the detectives released me quickly.

"You look so funny behind bars," he teased me on the way home. He had been exiled from Greece on three occasions for his political views, so in comparison, my problem was humorous to him.

My father hired a lawyer and we went to court.

I was so infuriated that I didn't give our lawyer much of a chance to talk. When the judge asked me a question, I began to defend myself. I had saved close to $1,000 and had my savings account book to prove it.

"Why would I take $50, when I have $953 in the bank?" I showed the judge my savings book from the Commercial National Bank. Furthermore, while taking the streetcar to go to school that morning, I chatted with Zack, the conductor. When I opened my wallet to pay for the fare, I saw Gregory's $50. "I have to return it to Gregory's Sport Shop this afternoon," I had told Zack.

"Call Zack as a witness," I offered.

By the time I finished my speech the judge was laughing, especially when I mentioned that I thought the check-cashing scheme was perhaps a scam of some sort, in order to avoid income tax.

Bill Gregory's face turned red. He never said a word. We could have sued him big-time for defamation of character but my dad decided to wash this off the record, which we did, by accepting one dollar from Gregory.

Oh, and I won the casting tournament in spinning accuracy and came in second in the 5/8 ounce plug-casting championship.

Bill Gregory died one year later.

Cancer.

Mr. Seeley and Mr. Payne

MR. WILLIAM SEELEY was a nattily dressed, distinguished gentleman, perhaps in his early 60s. I must admit that as a teen-ager it was difficult for me to tell anyone's age past 30, let alone 60! Mr. Seeley, as I called him, would come to the Lincoln Park Casting Club to practice. He tried spinning, but invariably would end up with a snarl of monofilament that even I had trouble clearing, despite possessing good eyesight, great experience and patience in untangling tangles.

Mr. Seeley preferred fly casting and practiced often. He was not very good at it, but he managed a few dozen good casts in a session. The problem was that he frequently snapped off practice flies, because he didn't always allow the back cast enough time before he began his forward stroke and because he used very fine leader tippets.

"I may go to Montana some day and I hear you need long, fine leaders," he would explain when I would suggest a heavier tippet.

The tournament or practice flies in those days cost 25 cents each, and were tied by Henry Fujita, a wonderful tournament caster and tier.

Mr. Seeley must not have had much money, I assumed, because if he lost a second fly he would quit fly casting for the day.

"What's wrong, Mr. Seeley? Why aren't you casting?" I'd ask.

"Son, I allow myself to lose two flies a day. That's my limit. Then I have to quit."

I felt sorry for Mr. Seeley. And puzzled. Sometimes he drove up with a blue Cadillac, but mostly with his white Cadillac. Cadillacs were expensive, right? I didn't even own a bicycle, but on some days, even if I lost several flies I bought more and kept casting.

I liked Mr. Seeley. "Don't worry, Mr. Seeley. I'll get your fly back!" And so I would open the big storage bin where we kept the oars, unlock the little boat we had for the placement of the casting targets, get in the dinghy and start rowing furiously after the floating dry fly, hoping to reach it before it sank. Usually I was able to recover the fly and return it to Mr. Seeley. I would then lock up the boat, place the oars in the cement storage bin and help Mr. Seeley tie the fly on his fine tippet. On one day, I recovered flies for him three times.

George Applegren, one of the best dry-fly tournament casters of all time, sharpened me up. George was a few years older than me and much wiser. "When I was young, I used to do that for him. You know how rich he is? He is president of a huge corporation. He is very wealthy. He is wealthier than probably all the club members put together and we've got some very wealthy guys."

"Wow!"

From then on, I would occasionally retrieve flies for Mr. Seeley, but mostly I didn't. I would pretend that I hadn't noticed, as he would slowly take down his fly rod, glancing helplessly in my direction.

"See you tomorrow, Mr. Seeley," I would say in my most innocent tone as he disappointedly departed for home.

MR. SEELEY TOOK PRIDE in owning fine tackle. He was a good customer of the fabulous VL&A store (Von Legerke and Antoine) on Wabash Avenue, which later was bought by Abercrombie and Fitch.

Mr. Seeley loved a Payne fly rod and every time he was in the store he would pick it up, carefully inspect the ferrules and windings, shake it a few times and smile wryly, undoubtedly fantasizing that he was fishing on a Montana trout stream.

Paul Stroud was head of the fishing department. "That's a fine rod, Mr. Seeley. Jim Payne's best model. You ought to buy it."

"Yes, but it costs $150. I don't know," Mr. Seeley wiggled it a few more times, but one day he told Paul to wrap it up. "It's a lot of money, but . . . " He took the precious rod home.

Of course, Mr. Seeley had absolutely no intention of using the fly rod. He took it to his office, called in his engineers and ordered them to make a duplicate rod *exactly* like it.

In their spare time!

Perhaps the engineers took it on as a challenge. They miked the tapers as best as they could, photographed it from every angle and perspective and meticulously recorded all the specs.

A couple of weeks later Mr. Seeley went back to VL&A.

"Sorry, Paul, I've decided to return the rod. I don't want to spend that kind of money now because I may never fish in Montana."

Paul took the rod back and made the refund, because Mr. Seeley was a good customer.

I can only imagine what occurred in the laboratory. The engineers had to make everything from scratch. There weren't many books on split-bamboo rods in those days (Claude M. Kreider's book on split bamboo wasn't published until later). The engineers had to manufacture the 28 percent German silver ferrules. Fabricate a reel seat. Obtain similar guides. Lots of things. But the big problem was acquiring the bamboo. They must have been stunned to learn that most bamboo fly rods were composed of six *tapered* strips glued together, and that they had to adhere to the micrometer specs that they had diligently recorded. Then, of course, there was the problem of obtaining Tonkin bamboo from China. I have no idea how they accomplished all of this.

From time to time, Mr. Seeley would update Frank Steel, Clare Bryan and other club members about the progress of the "Payne" rod. Clare Bryan, a superb caster and a talented engineer, would shake his head and turn away to hide his wide smile.

The following spring Mr. Seeley came down to the club. He had a devilish grin on his face as he opened a rod case and pulled out his "Payne" fly rod. What a wonderful job his engineers did. It looked like the original! He put the rod together and shook it. He was very pleased.

Mr. Seeley handed the rod to me. I waved it a couple of times, simu-

lating the casting motion. It felt marvelous. I handed it back to him.

"They did a fantastic job," Mr. Seeley said as he chuckled, proud of his chicanery.

He attached the reel to the rod and I helped him string the line through the guides, attach a leader and finally tie on a practice fly.

He handed the rod to me. "Jim, you're a fine caster. You've always been nice to me. I want you to take the first casts. I want to watch you cast and see the action."

I was honored, but I refused.

"No, Mr. Seeley. You should cast it first. It's your rod. You should make the first casts." I had no reason to say this, but I insisted that he should try it first.

So he headed to the fly targets, stripped some line, and began to false cast, quite well, I must say. Better than ever before. He hit the first target. The rod was responding very well. Then he hit the next one. What a smile on Mr. Seeley's face!

He stripped some more line from his reel in order to reach the yellow target, which I believe was about 40 feet away, and just as he was coming forward with his cast, there was a sickening snap, the rod broke just above the butt ferrule and the limp line plopped around Mr. Seeley as the fly and tippet landed on his hat.

In retrospect, Jim Payne and Paul Stroud would have relished this moment.

When Clare Bryan heard about this, he chuckled. "That rod must've cost fifty times more than what he could've bought it for. Maybe a hundred times!"

I'm sure it did.

Terms of endearment

LUTHER BROWNING WAS HIS NAME. He visited Chicago's Lincoln Park Casting Club sometimes on weekends, but mostly on week days, right after work, I assumed, because he always wore a suit and tie and his shoes were polished to a gloss. Even when he cast he wore his suit jacket and seldom loosened his tie. Weird, I thought, just like the British anglers who wore tweeds and a tie to go fishing. In England, tweeds and tie were standard fishing attire, and to be seen in lesser dress, well, it was simply barbaric, according to the Brits.

Luther, who appeared to be in his mid-40s, was a good fly caster. His weakness was stream-trout fishing, though I noticed that the trunk of his car also included plug-casting tackle along with his waders, fishing vests and an assortment of gear. He was a salesman who often traveled to northern Illinois or southern Wisconsin, and it was certain that he took a few casts at enticing waters when and where convenient. He enjoyed all game fish but he had a special fondness for brook trout. The largest brookie he ever caught was a 14 incher from Upper Michigan. In the Midwest, speckled trout are usually measured in inches rather than in pounds.

Bill Blades, one of the great fly-tying legends and a club member, came to the Lincoln Park Casting Club one evening clutching some photos of huge brook trout that he had caught recently in the Algoma district of Ontario, Canada. The largest brook trout probably weighed three to four pounds. Luther entered a strange, dreamy zone as he studied the photos and then listened to Bill's adventures. He asked the customary questions: What flies? Where did he fish? Where did he stay? When's the best time? The usual stuff.

Luther put away his tackle, got into his car, took a left on Fullerton Drive and headed home, as was his custom every time he visited the casting club.

But he never made it home.

The next day the police came to the casting club and asked many questions. When was the last time we saw Luther Browning? Which direction did he drive? Did anyone follow him? Were we aware of anyone having a reason to kill him?

Later, several people from his office also came to the casting club and they asked similar questions. In Chicago sometimes people disappear forever, and street-wise locals insist that there are bodies buried under certain pavements or encased in cement and dumped into the Chicago River or Lake Michigan.

Four or five days later, Luther suddenly emerged at the casting club. He was unshaven, his trousers were dirty and tattered, and he must have left his suit coat and tie in the car. He was carrying a heavy, soggy carton. He looked exhausted. Weary-eyed. His face was pocked with insect bites. We were stunned.

"Come over here, fellows! Wait until you see what I have!" He opened the box. There were a half-dozen brook trout, the largest probably close to four pounds. The ice had melted long ago. The bottom of the box broke open and several trout slithered across the cement platform. Luther hysterically grabbed them before they slid into the water.

"Luther! Where have you been? The police . . . your office . . . your wife . . . were looking for you!" Dick Westra demanded.

"I drove that night to Algoma, Canada where Bill Blades fished," Luther seemed perturbed that our questions did not center on his fish or fishing. "Aren't these beauties? I caught them on Mickey Finn streamers, because it rained a lot, but I caught some smaller ones on dries, too."

"Yes, they are beauties, but Luther, why the hell didn't you tell your wife or your office that you were going?" Dick asked sternly. "We've had the cops down here several times."

"Actually I was going home that night but I kept thinking of those trout in Bill's pictures. The office is closed at night, and I tried calling my wife several times, but the phone was busy. *Yapi-Yap. Yapi-Yap.* Probably talking to her mother, and there weren't any phones in Algoma where I was fishing. So I gave up calling her. Come on, guys, have you ever seen such big brook trout? I mean, in real life, not in pictures!"

We hadn't. And they *were* beautiful fish!

W E CALLED THEM "the honeymooners" when they weren't around. Terry and Janet had just moved into the Fullerton area and because they both loved to fish, they decided to join the Lincoln Park Casting Club. We called them the honeymooners because they had been married for almost six months now and they were so affectionate to each other. They held hands at every opportunity, and seldom did they utter a sentence without a term of endearment:

"*Honey,* can you bring me the 3/8-ounce outfit?"

"Sure, *sweetheart,* is this the right one?" And Janet would pick up a rod from the green metal rod rack.

"That's it, *darling,*" and then, "Ohh, thank you so much, *hon.*"

"You're welcome, *love!*"

To hear this dribble every evening, and I mean almost *every* evening because they seldom missed coming to the club, was enough to drive most of the members crazy.

Despite their mellifluous talk, they were generally well liked although some of the aged casters were turned off by all this "lovey-dovey" talk. Terry and Janet were becoming good casters. As a matter of fact, some of the lady anglers were starting a women's team and were seriously considering Janet.

The display of affection continued for weeks, and rather than lessen, it seemed to increase.

"*Sweetheart*, I am a little hungry. I think I'll go to the Parkway Restaurant and get a grilled cheese sandwich. Would you like to come along, or do you want me to bring something back for you?"

"No, *honey*, I think I'll practice casting," she said. "Don't eat too much because I have a special dessert for you!"

As Terry walked west on Fullerton Avenue, toward the Parkway Restaurant, he waved affectionately to Janet and she waved too.

He never came back.

Janet called the police and gave a description and a photo of Terry. Days passed, and each evening Janet would come to the casting club and sit down alone, hoping that Terry would return. She did this for two weeks. We never saw her again.

Then Janet received a note, according to Bertha Burns, one of the lady casters who was in touch with her.

The note was from Terry. Yes, he loved Janet very much, and there was no one else in his life, but he didn't want to be married any longer. He wished her happiness and was sorry that it turned out this way. He disappeared somewhere out there in the big world. So did Janet, eventually.

We never heard from them again.

The Lincoln Park Casting Club was my second home. At the time, I was very depressed, because the family doctor advised me to give up playing baseball and football temporarily due to a health problem. I loved competition. I loved camaraderie. Tournament casting and the Lincoln Park Casting Club quickly fulfilled these needs.

Because I was associating with adults I learned a lot about life in general. The consternation, confusion and chaos caused by Luther Browning's selfish disappearance and the grief created when Terry walked out of his marriage without notice were shocking but important lessons learned and applied in my personal and business life.

The great Kishkutena adventure

I CONFESS. It was a con job, right from the start. I flimflammed Bob Feldtman and Wally Bolland even though I was only a teen-ager and they were very successful, sophisticated businessmen. But I wanted to return to Kishkutena Lake, Ontario, Canada and didn't have the funds or transportation.

I had fished at Bergstrom's Camp the previous season when I talked my mother, sister and cousin Dorothy into taking a Canadian vacation. One day, I hired Carl Meline, a Nestor Falls guide, to take me to Bergstrom's outpost camp on Kishkutena Lake on an overnight trip. The smallmouth bass fishing was so incredible, that somehow, some way I had to return the following season, but I couldn't afford it. Paul Brewer, a 17-year-old friend, also wanted to fish Kishkutena but didn't have the money. We both belonged to Chicago's Lincoln Park Casting Club which was composed of a very affluent membership in those days.

One spring day, Clare Bryan was telling Bob Feldtman, Wally Bolland and me about the great smallmouth bass fishing he enjoyed in Ontario in previous years.

"But you have to go early in the season. Otherwise you won't find them. Once the temperatures rise, they go into deep water," he warned.

I grasped the opportunity. "I know a place where you can catch 50 smallmouth on a fly rod in one day, even in the hot weather . . . July . . . August . . . anytime. I'm talking near surface fly fishing."

Clare laughed. "No such place!"

"Yes there is. Really. I can catch 50 smallmouth on a fly rod on a good day." I insisted.

Bob and Wally wanted to know where the place was. After some conversation, I told them that Paul Brewer and I would be happy to go along with them to prove the point. I explained that there was an outpost cabin, we would have to portage in, but we would have the entire lake to ourselves and the fishing would be superb.

"Lots of muskies, too," I added as an enticement.

They were skeptical, so I suggested a bet: "If I catch the 50 bass in a day on flies, you guys (Wally and Bob) pay for the trip. If I don't, Paul Brewer and I will pay for your trip and travel expenses." Naturally, we would use their big comfortable cars for transportation.

They took the bait.

Slam. Dunk.

Clare sensed the con and shook his head.

When I revealed the great news to Paul Brewer, he was very concerned: "Look I don't have the money if we lose . . . "

"Neither do I. Don't worry. I don't plan on losing this bet." Young. Brash. Cocky. Confident. And dumb. Today—many years wiser—I would never bet even on a sure thing in fishing *unless* I could afford to lose the bet.

They agreed on rules for the bet. I would pick a single day and I was the only one allowed to fish, because obviously anyone else would be catching "my" potential fish.

I selected the second day we were in Kishkutena. By noon, I had landed 37 smallmouth on a fly. Wally and Bob, realizing that they would lose the bet, waved the white flag, and declared us the winners, because they wanted to fish. Paul and I were relieved to have won our bet and Wally and Bob were even happier, for indeed they would be fishing one of the great smallmouth places in Canada, and we had the lake entirely to ourselves. We all caught lots and lots of bass. Incredible fishing.

I SHOULD POINT OUT that the trip into Kishkutena Lake, wasn't quite as smooth as I had planned. We arrived in Nestor Falls mid afternoon and Gust Bergstrom said it would be wise to overnight at his main camp and go into Kishkutena the next day.

But no. I insisted that we go in that afternoon. Why waste a day?

"We could be catching smallmouth tomorrow morning, guys. Maybe a muskie or two." I convinced our group to do it.

Okay, we got lost, but only because I thought I discovered a short cut on a big-scale map that would eliminate two portages and about an hour's time, but it turned out to be a swamp. When dusk arrived earlier than I anticipated we had to sleep out. No big deal. We had sleeping bags. Paul, Bob and I weren't worried, but Wally was uneasy; after all, this was his first wilderness trip.

Actually we found out that Wally was hesitant about going on this trip, because he had survived several mild heart attacks earlier in his life. He almost changed his mind about going a few days before our scheduled departure, but his brother, a doctor, urged him to go.

"You need to get away . . . go with Chapralis and the group. It would do you good," the doctor, who was also a fisherman, recommended.

The problem with sleeping on shore was that we had lots of prime steaks and other meats in our coolers. Wally woke me up several times at night, concerned with the animals that were obviously attracted by our food supply. You could hear them rustling in the bush as they were getting closer and closer to our meat-laden coolers.

"Don't worry, Wally," I told him several times. "They're just black bears. They won't attack us. They won't come any closer. They're afraid of us! Go back to sleep!"

"Yeah, and how do you know?" Wally had a point. After all, I was city bred and spent only a few weeks in the north.

We made it through the night, but I don't think Wally slept much.

"Don't worry Wally, we'll be getting into Kishkutena Lake soon . . . and enjoy the greatest smallmouth bass fishing ever." And we did.

WE WERE RUNNING OUT of food supplies–because of our ravenous appetites–and Bob wanted to phone his office, so he and I decided to go into Nestor Falls. The trip from Kishkutena and Nestor Falls is about four hours by boat. It would involve our dragging a very heavy Thompson wooden boat and outboard motor over wooden skids on five arduous portages. But there was also a square-stern canoe at the outpost which would be easy to portage.

To reduce travel time and make the portages easier, Bob and I decided to place one of the outboards on the square stern, and after a trial run or two, whizzing around the outpost camp island at an incredible speed, we decided that this was absolutely the way to go. We not only could fly with that big motor, but portaging the light canoe would also be a snap. We could go into town, procure supplies, Bob could phone his office, and we would be back in Kishkutena in time for supper. We took along sandwiches, some tackle and Bob's brand new Speed Graphic camera.

"See ya at supper time," Bob said as he and I shoved off.

"I'm not so sure," said a worried Wally Bolland. "That canoe wasn't made for a big motor."

Cautious Wally.

When we got to Marl Lake, which is connected by streams, I urged Bob to use his fly rod and try to hook a muskie, as this little lake often contained huge quantities of that elusive species. I was having some success writing for outdoor magazines. An article on muskies via fly fishing—in those days—would be a sure seller.

It didn't take long before Bob hooked a muskie on a streamer and his

35

treasured Edwards split-bamboo fly rod.

As I reached for the camera, I noticed it was a very acrobatic fish. The muskie went under the canoe, and Bob leaned over the gunwale to save his expensive fly rod.

"What a shot this will make!" I said as I also leaned over the same side to get a photo of Bob's wonderful facial expression, with his precious fly rod bent in a dangerous arc.

That's when it happened!

Everything was dark, cold and wet. I could hear aquatic echoes and felt several buckets of water rushing into the hip boots that I was wearing for the portages, and my poplin jacket absorbed water like a sponge. I touched bottom for an instant, an oozy bottom it was, and then automatically I bobbed to the surface.

I wiped the water from my eyes but then started to laugh hysterically. Bob apparently had reached in his pocket for a comb *while underwater* because when he surfaced he was combing his thinning hair. As he realized how foolish this act of vanity was, he too began to laugh wildly. Meanwhile the overturned canoe was floating away at a 45-degree angle because of the heavy motor at the stern.

Bob, a very powerful swimmer, finally caught up with the canoe and

advanced it toward me. I lunged for it and I was immensely relieved that my hand found its target. We both clung to the canoe for a few minutes gasping for air. Camera, rods and sandwiches went overboard with no hope of recovery. The fuel tank was lodged in the overturned canoe. We worked our way to shore near the portage, where we were able to pull up our canoe on solid land and assess the damages. Although it was late July, the weather was cold and we were shivering. No matches to start a fire. We took off all our clothes, except for our underpants and boots, and placed them on a big rock where we hoped that they would dry. Then we carried our canoe, motor and tank to the other side of the portage. We floated down the river for a few yards, to get away from the shallow, rocky bottom, to try to start the outboard, when suddenly an intruder appeared in the narrow stream.

There we were, Bob Feldtman and I, clad only in our underpants and boots, fiercely backpaddling our canoe against the current so that we wouldn't run smack into that huge, ornery moose standing in the middle of the stream huffing and puffing and blocking our course. We were tired, hungry, cold, wet, dejected and too concerned to worry about the swarms of blood-sucking mosquitoes that feasted ravenously on us. The moose looked at us with those baleful eyes, lowering his head to make sure we were aware of his massive antlers and warning us with snorts and grunts. It was a standstill for a while, but then Bob and I could not backpaddle any longer—we were too exhausted—so we gave up and let the canoe drift downstream, with a whatever-happens-happens attitude but never once taking our eyes off the moose.

It was showdown time, and we weren't going to be the first to blink. When we were only a few yards away, the monster turned around and nonchalantly trudged up the bank. We exhaled a sigh of relief, but we still had a long way to go to reach Nestor Falls.

"Let's try to start the engine in deeper water and we can come back later to get our clothes and things," Bob suggested.

He worked on the motor as the current drifted us away from the rocks, but our Johnson outboard wouldn't start. We were shivering. We probably didn't know what hypothermia was then, but I think we were in its early stages. We simply didn't have the energy to paddle back upstream to the rock where our clothes were drying. I don't think we were operating on all mental cylinders.

Bob tried the motor again. *Pttrrrr.* Still the same empty sound.

"Maybe water got into the fuel. I'll put new gas in the motor," he said.

We continued to drift further and further downstream. We had not eaten anything since breakfast and we were completely exhausted. Now, in more open waters, a breeze kept the mosquitoes away—a welcomed relief.

"We'll never make it paddling. We're miles from Nestor Falls," I was dejected. "Try that motor again."

Still the same. Or was it? I thought I heard it cough and then I was sure it turned over. By gosh, we were moving. The motor had started! Surely, it never should have, since it was under water for a long time. Perhaps it was the new gas? We only had a fraction of its power, but we were moving. *Hurrah!* But our clothes were drying on a rock, some distance upstream on the other side of the portage.

"I'm afraid to go back," Bob explained. "There are lots of rocks near the portage and we don't have any shear pins. I don't want to stop the engine. It may not start again, and we don't want to be out here at night with the bugs."

I agreed. We decided to head to Nestor Falls in our underpants. What the heck? We took off.

We had to shut off the engine a couple of times for the remaining two portages, but it started on the other side after a few pulls on the cord. We reached Big Pine Lake in no time and then "sped" at what would be trolling speed across Oar Bay and into Crooked Pine Lake. Soon we could distinguish Bergstrom's Camp at Nestor Falls. The view of the camp silhouetted against the orange-streaked afternoon sky was too beautiful to describe. An oasis, to be sure. The slowly rising puffs of smoke suggested that Mrs. Bergstrom had something warm on the stove.

What a sight we must have made as we crossed the highway from the dock to Bergstrom's camp! Bob and I both in our underpants, he in ankle boots, and I in my hip boots, turned down and up, cavalier-style. A few drivers on the highway honked their horns and laughed, while others swivelled their heads to get another look as they sped by us. Nestor Falls was a small, friendly village in those days: a few camps, stores, and not a lot of people, but it was on the main highway for Kenora.

I thought Gust Bergstrom, the camp owner, liked me but he had nicknamed me "S.B." (short for "Scatter Brain") the previous season for some dumb thing I did that year. He must have been dumbfounded when he saw us trudging across the road from his kitchen window in our underpants and boots. He ran out to meet us.

"Well, S.B., this has to be a good story! I can't wait to hear it. You've outdone even your nickname this time!"

Bob and I went into an empty cabin where we had stored our traveling clothes and other items that we wouldn't need at the Kishkutena outpost.

Back in warm clothes, enjoying Mrs. Bergstrom's fine cooking, we related our story to guests, guides and other employees who had gathered around our table. They laughed and laughed and then Gust Bergstrom brought out a bottle of cognac and poured a drink for Bob and others. He gave me a Coke. Under age.

B OB AND I spent the night at Bergstrom's in Nestor Falls. Surely Paul and Wally must be very worried because we didn't return to the Kishkutena outpost the day before as scheduled. There were very few charter planes flying in the area in those years, and absolutely no one else was on the lake. They would have every reason to be concerned, so after taking care of our errands and replacing our outboard, we zoomed for Kishkutena.

The portages were a snap, we recovered our clothes that we had set out to dry on the rocks and soon we were in Kishkutena. And feeling great.

We could see the outpost cabin as we approached the island. Wally was at the corner of the island waving a white tee-shirt frantically, probably assuming we were another party. On the other side we spotted Paul

Brewer casting relentlessly.

"Why aren't they fishing?" I asked Bob. He shrugged. Soon we were at camp.

"Boy, am I glad to see you guys. I thought you drowned or something," Wally forced a smile.

"Sorry we didn't make it back last night. We had a problem. Hey, where's the other boat and motor?" Bob inquired as we tied our canoe to the makeshift dock.

Paul put down his casting rod. "Well, we went out last evening and had a ball. Smallmouth were hitting top water all over the place. When we came in, we didn't tie up the boat and it drifted away. There were some strong winds last night. And this morning we got up and discovered no boat. You had the other motor so we couldn't look for it. The other boat doesn't have oars."

"No motor. No Bob. No Jim," Wally added. He was obviously flustered.

Unflappable Paul was not as concerned except that their fishing was confined to the island because of the missing boat and motor.

"I raised a nice muskie over there," Paul pointed casually. "What happened to you guys, anyway?"

We explained; Paul seemed amused, but Wally kept shaking his head.

Bob and I unloaded our supplies, refueled and searched for the boat with our souped-up canoe.

According to Paul, the boat should have been on the west side of the lake. We looked there but couldn't find it. We went to the east side and found it despite the numerous islands and extensive bays. Hot dog! That rented boat and motor would have cost us a lot of money to replace.

Wally relaxed and even joked a bit. Paul Brewer said he found lots of muskies at a place that is indicated on a map as Brewer's Point.

"Someone had the foresight to name it after me," he quipped.

Now settled, I walked to the other side of the island where it was my custom to sit on a big rock every day and make some entries into my journal. But this time I scribbled something quickly, tore the page out of the notebook, folded the paper and placed it under a rock.

The day was gorgeous. Azure blue skies. Warm. Great fishing for smallmouth and we saw lots of muskies at Brewer's Point, too. We even hooked a few. Everything was perfect now.

Until that night.

We were all sound asleep when we were aroused by a fierce storm. Thunder. Lightning. Strong winds. A bolt of lightning struck our island. The cabin, which had no foundation, stood at the edge of a small cliff and began to rock.

"Good grief! Lightning has set the big tree outside the cabin on fire!" Bob Feldtman announced as he peered out the window. He opened the cabin door and we went outside, but the wind was so powerful we could hardly stand upright.

"Look over there!" Paul pointed to a corner of the island. There was a small fire starting up. "And over there, too." Sparks from the burning tree were flying about everywhere, it seemed.

"Geez! We have a choice of staying on the island and burning to death or getting into the boats and drowning." I thought I was being humorous, you know, to break the tension. Mistake.

Wally felt a pain in his chest. He reached for some medicine. We could not attend to him except to tell him to relax and that we would put out the fires.

Because of the powerful winds, we had to crouch as low as possible, and even our flashlights had trouble discerning the vague path that led to the lake. We filled our buckets with water. Luckily the tree that was struck by lightning was now merely smoldering, and we were able to put out the small fires elsewhere on the island.

We returned to the cabin. Wally seemed okay. This had not been the type of vacation that his brother, the doctor, had prescribed. The strong winds subsided and the lightning was now so far away we could barely hear the thunder.

The great storm was over.

We settled in our sleeping bags again, when suddenly I got up and reached for the flashlight. I urged Paul and Bob to follow me to the other side of the island. They did.

"Paul, turn over that rock," I said when we arrived. There was a piece of paper under it. "Read it."

"It says, *'Tonight—Thursday—there will be a tremendous storm!'* It's in your handwriting, Jim."

That's the note that I had scribbled earlier in the day when I was making entries in my journal. I don't know what possessed me to write this particular message, because the day was gorgeous. All I know is that I wrote it, put it under a rock and forgot about it until after the storm.

We returned to the cabin.

"What was that all about?" Wally inquired.

"Oh, nothing. Nothing at all. We'll tell you tomorrow," Bob said, but we never did, and Wally never asked again.

A number of years later Wally Bolland heard that another friend, Bob Kukulski, and I were planning a fishing trip to Ireland. "When are you going to Ireland?"

"We're thinking about mid July, Wally. Want to join us?" I asked.

"No! I am going to Ireland this summer and I want to make sure I'm not there at the same time you are." He considered me bad luck. "I think I'll go in August."

And then he laughed uncontrollably.

PART TWO

Early flirtations

Joe Godfrey: one of the most creative people ever;
to Paris for the international casting championship and to meet
Monsieur Charles Ritz;
about a fisherman with a very unusual occupation;
and, a new fishing companion named Paul Freeman.

"Me and Joe" and publishing

IT SEEMS as if I always worked on a newsletter. When I was in my teens, 15 or 16, I began to write and produce a quarterly newsletter for the Lincoln Park Casting Club. This was no big deal, except for the winter issue. It gets very, very cold in Chicago. Not only would I shiver, while waiting for the right streetcar connections, but then I had a long walk in the snow from Clark and Fullerton to the Lincoln Park Casting Club. The clubhouse was a one-story, brick building, with lockers for about 120 members, fly-tying tables, a workshop, washroom, and a small kitchen.

The problem in the winter was the big, six-foot-wide steel gate leading to the clubhouse. I would have to clear a lot of snow and sometimes ice from the ground, to allow the gate to swing open. Often there would be two-foot drifts that had to be removed by gloved hands because there was no shovel.

There was no heat in the casting club, but it was slightly warmer inside than outside. Just a little. Thankfully, there was a big, potbellied stove near the center of the main room, and some wood and coal. After I got a hungry fire going, the clubhouse was warm enough so that I could take off my gloves, coat and hat, and sit over by the mechanical L. C. Smith typewriter and begin to "cut" a mimeograph stencil. Perhaps only the over-50-year-old crowd might remember what a tortuous job it was to cut a stencil. You switched a lever on the typewriter so the cloth ribbon would remain out of the way, and the sharp, metal typewriter keys could strike hard on a dark blue paper form that looked like carbon paper. If you made a mistake, you might be able to use some correcting fluid, but if it was a major error, you were better off ripping the stencil out of the typewriter and starting all over.

The Lincoln Park Casting Club Newsletter was eight pages, so it took some time to cut the stencils, but there was no sense in hurrying. The A. B. Dick mimeograph machine wouldn't even begin to work—to ooze out a thick, almost syrupy ink—until the room temperature was at least 60 degrees for about a half hour.

When the room and the machine were warm enough, I'd insert the stencil on the mimeograph machine, load it with paper, and start turning the handle vigorously until page by page the newsletter would be printed. Actually, I would have to print pages 1, 3, 5 and 7 and let them dry sufficiently in order to print pages 2, 4, 6 and 8 on the back of the first set, in order to save on paper and postage. This pagination was critical because if you goofed up the back-to-back printing, well, you'd have to start all over again.

When everything was done and dry, I would collate, staple and fold the pages, insert them into the addressed, stamped envelopes and take them to the post office. Our circulation was about 150 copies.

The newsletter provided information on upcoming casting tournaments, new tackle that might improve a caster's score, perhaps an item or two on nearby fishing hot spots, introduction of any new members and short fishing book reviews. That sort of thing.

I produced the casting club newsletter for more than four years. At times I questioned why I was doing this, but then my ambition was to make a living from sportfishing and one day this experience could be helpful. As my dad always preached: "When you do a job, do it to the best of your ability; someone is always watching and noticing, regardless of how menial the task might be." (Actually, he told me this in Greek but I thought it best to translate it here.)

How true this statement turned out to be!

I RECEIVED A CALL from a Mr. O. A. "Dutch" Feldon, who asked me to come to his office on Wabash Avenue. All I knew about him was that he was a successful business man who owned and published a number of magazines. He was distinguished looking—meticulously dressed in his white shirt, tie, dark suit and polished shoes—but at the same time he had the knack of putting an awkward, shy, young person (me) at ease with his informal talk and frequent smiles.

Mr. Feldon told me that he was going to launch a new but different type of hunting and fishing magazine; different because *Midwest Sportsman's News* would only cover a half-dozen states. Today, of course, there are dozens of regional outdoor publications, but back in 1952 this was a unique publishing concept.

"I need an editor. I want you to be that editor," he said.

Whoa!!! Before I could answer he told me the weekly salary would be more than a hundred dollars—that was back in the 1950s!

"If you sell ads, I will give you ten percent of the net, and you will get paid on a word basis for any articles you write."

Was this a dream? This was the kind of a job offer that most young people fantasize about. I would have to visit some of the fishing waters, of course, but this would be on an expense account. It doesn't get better than that, does it?

Of course I grabbed it. I would've even without pay.

I was puzzled.

"Mr. Feldon, how did you decide to contact me for this job?"

"Joe Godfrey. Joe told me if I was interested in a young writer who'll work hard and produce I should consider hiring you. He said you will need some seasoning. 'Salt and pepper' as he calls it. Joe said he never met you, but has seen you at the casting club and likes the newsletter you produce."

Imagine that. Dad was right. "Do the best job you can because someone is always observing you."

I started working and preparing the first few issues. What an ideal job. I worked for a few months and then I got a *Greeting* note from Uncle Sam, explaining that I had been drafted in the U.S. Army. I had to leave my great job and serve in the military. Reluctantly. Yeah, yeah, I know I should have considered this a privilege to serve my country.

In the meantime, *Midwest Sportsman's News* changed its name to *Sportsman's News* and became more national in scope because the big advertisers were reluctant to use regionals in those days, and after a year or so, the publication ceased because it wasn't profitable.

I, of course, got to know Joe Godfrey prior to and after my military service, and despite our age difference, we became very good friends. I found out that he had been the publisher/owner of *Sports Afield* magazine many years ago, started the very successful Sportsman's Club of America and also the original Fishing Hall of Fame. He fished often with Ted Williams and other dignitaries and was right in the middle of the sportfishing mainstream. He also produced a number of successful fishing magazines, including the annual *Goin' Fishin'*. I helped him with several publications after my Army days.

He was easily the most creative salesman I've ever met, and I was hoping that some of his creativity would rub off on me.

My favorite Joe Godfrey story was when he worked as an advertising troubleshooter for *Newsweek* magazine. It seemed that *Time* magazine had a lucrative full-page advertising schedule from Firestone tires. No matter how hard *Newsweek* tried, it could not crack the Firestone account. So the assignment was turned over to Joe Godfrey.

Joe tried to see the account executive (AE) at Firestone's ad agency. No dice. He tried again and again but could not see him. Busy. Out of town. Important meetings. The AE was simply not interested in using *Newsweek* and wasn't going to hear Joe's pitch.

Joe took out a half-page ad in *Advertising Age*. The ad was addressed to the account executive (AE) at the agency that handled Firestone. Joe's message in the ad was along these lines: Since the AE was too busy to see him, but read *Ad Age* in his spare time, Godfrey was going to present the advantages of advertising Firestone tires in *Newsweek*. The ad appeared. People in advertising read it with interest. Still, no response from the account executive. Joe followed it up with additional facts about *Newsweek* in another ad. Then a third ad.

By now the subscribers couldn't wait until the next issue of *Ad Age*. Meanwhile, *Newsweek* was obtaining lots of good publicity among many advertising agencies. *Ad Age* also loved it. It was a stroke of genius.

Vintage Godfrey.

Finally, CEO Harvey S. Firestone, Jr. called his ad agency and asked why the AE wasn't seeing Joe Godfrey. The embarrassed AE called Joe to set up a meeting. He had no recourse but to put *Newsweek* on a solid ad schedule. If he didn't, who knew what Joe would do next? Joe Godfrey and Harvey Firestone Jr. became good friends and, I believe, even fished together.

Many times, in my business life, when an insurmountable problem appeared, I would think of this story and ask: "What would Joe Godfrey do?" Often a solution suggested itself.

I REMEMBER WHEN Joe and I went to the AFTMA tackle trade show in the late 1960s. He was publishing his annual *Goin' Fishin'* magazine and sold ads at the show for his next issue.

We stopped at a major tackle company's booth.

"Joe, I'd like to advertise again with you but I can't. I'm disappointed. We received only five coupons back from our full-page ad in your last issue," the sales manager said.

"If I were you, I would restructure your mail department," Joe countered.

"What d'ya mean?"

"Heck, I filled out more than eight coupons from your ad and mailed them in from various cities with phony names," Joe said. "Something's wrong with you mail department."

The sales manager and Joe laughed and laughed. Advertisers generally suspected that small magazine publishers mailed in coupons with names and addresses from phone books in order to create the illusion that the ad pulled.

He gave Joe an order for a full-page ad for the forthcoming issue.

O N ONE OF HIS NUMEROUS northwoods trips Joe Godfrey met two wardens who had just killed a big black bear because it had broken into a cottage several times. The sow had a cute cub. Somehow, Joe talked the wardens into allowing him to take the baby bear with him, promising to donate it to Chicago's Lincoln Park Zoo.

He brought it home, bottle fed it, and "Blackie" became part of the Godfrey household. Sometimes Joe would take the little cub for a ride in his blue convertible (with the top down, of course). The bear would sit in the front seat next to Joe, who would occasionally drive downtown to visit advertising agencies.

When Joe walked into an agency, followed by the little, obedient cub, office personnel would immediately follow the cuddlesome bear (I don't remember what Joe did about Blackie's toilet training). Joe became a very famous personality.

Unfortunately, many of the kids in his neighborhood would tease and infuriate the animal, which was growing rapidly, so Joe finally donated him to the Lincoln Park Zoo, as he had originally promised the wardens. There are hundreds of Joe Godfrey stories.

Through Joe Godfrey I met many important people in the sportfishing industry, including tackle manufacturers, camp owners and writers. Ironically, while most of Joe's ideas were profit-motivated, he seemed to lose interest once they made money and quickly "invented" new projects.

This was a source of embarrassment to me at times. He started a publication called *The Sportsman and his Family*, and made me its editor. It was well received, subscriptions were coming in, and ad revenues were increasing. After a year, he folded it despite the fact that it was mildly successful. I think he just lost interest.

One day in the late 1950s, Joe and I were having lunch to discuss one of his ideas. It was a national fishing club centered on one species: the black bass.

"There are more U.S. fishermen interested in bass than any other species," Joe explained. "We'll offer a magazine, decals, fishing hats, membership cards and discounts on fishing tackle. We'll have thousands of members. Maybe even fishing tournaments. What do you think?"

"Now, Joe, why would a fisherman want to join something like that?" I replied and gave him some reasons why it wouldn't work. I don't remember what my objections were, but I convinced him to drop the idea.

Of course, years later, someone tried a similar idea, added bass fishing tournaments, and today B.A.S.S. is one of the most successful, potent organizations of this type in the world. It has about 500,000 members.

So much for my feedback!

Casting at the Bois de Boulogne

TO MY MIND, Paris is the most beautiful of all cities. It has everything: Promenades with endless shops; the Champs-Élyseés; the Eiffel Tower; the Arc de Triomphe; the Louvre. The list is endless. It's the greatest walking city in the world; walk in any direction in Paris and you are bound to find a point of interest no matter what your tastes are.

During the mid-50s, I was drafted by the Army and was sent to Orleans, about 60 miles south of Paris. I noticed in a French fishing magazine that the International Casting Tournament was to be held in Paris at Bois de Boulogne, a beautiful sprawling park with lagoons, pathways, cultivated gardens and numerous species of trees.

I had no intention of competing (I had cast in some tournaments in the United States), but I wanted to observe a European casting championship. I found the casting area easily. You get a nose for those things.

I recognized the names of France's Pierre Creusevaut, one of the leading European casters, and Albert Goddard, the famous Belgium caster. There were other skilled competitors getting in their practice casts with the hope of becoming the 1955 international casting champions.

The events were somewhat different from what I was used to. Of great interest were the obstacle accuracy events, where targets were placed under or next to obstructions that simulated actual fishing conditions. I noticed, too, that on the spinning accuracy events, the casters would use an underhand flip or pendulum cast (now employed by the bassin' guys to fish under brush) instead of the standard overhead cast.

I struck up a conversation with some of the casters who spoke English, and I told them that I had cast in some tournaments in the United States. I was introduced to Pierre Creusevaut, who was very fluent in English.

"Why don't you enter the tournament?" Pierre asked. "We will be casting distance fly next."

"My favorite event. But I have no tackle."

"You can use mine. I have a Pezon et Michel rod that [Charles] Ritz and I have developed."

What luck!

The equipment used for fly casting distance at this tournament was different than what was used in the States. It was lighter and more harmonious with actual fishing conditions.

Pierre Creusevaut, Albert Goddard and others scored very impressive distances. Pierre handed me the rod and coached me through a few practice casts.

It was my turn.

"Representing the United States Military from Orleans, Monsieur Jim Chapralis," the man with the bull horn announced. I felt a rush. There was ample polite applause. By now a fair-sized crowd was attracted to the casting area.

The rules allowed you to make five casts and the three longest would be averaged to determine the winner. The trick was that you had to yell, *"score"* just before you unleashed the forward cast. There was a reasonable time limit in which you had to complete your casting.

I felt important because I was representing the "United States Military," but I was not particularly nervous. Ironically, when you're young, competition is not the nerve-wracking experience that it becomes when you are considerably older, at least for many of us.

I had two good casts scored and I needed a third one to attain a high average, but time was running out because I had to untangle my shooting line. One more cast. I thought my next back cast was good, so I yelled *"score"* as I made my final forward cast. It was a satisfying distance. I did not embarrass the "United States Military" or myself.

There was applause. Pierre Creusevaut came up to me and congratulated me.

"You've won! You did exceptionally well." Albert Goddard and others shook my hand and they were all very cordial and genuine. *La Pêche*

Independante, the French national fishing publication, took a photo of some of the champions and they placed me in the center. I was flattered.

An impeccably dressed man with a slight build and a trimmed but pronounced mustache, came up to me, shook my hand with enthusiasm. Repeatedly. It was Charles Ritz. THE CHARLES RITZ.

"Chapralis, you cast well. You have long arms and you are tall. Good double haul." Besides operating the Ritz Hotel, the most famous of all hotels in the world, Charles was on Pezon et Michel's advisory board. Pierre Creusevaut was the pro for this venerable French tackle firm.

"You have a good double haul," he repeated.

I received a fair amount of publicity in various publications including the military's *Stars and Stripes*. I felt good. Real good.

I SAW CHARLES RITZ OFTEN. Sometimes he would lend me a Pezon et Michel prototype rod to try out. One day he invited me to have lunch at his famous *Espadon* dining room, which he had just unveiled for his rich and famous clientele.

We talked about the great fishing places, about the Ritz Hotel, and the Montreal Canadien hockey team. Suddenly an assistant with white gloves brought him a message on a small silver tray.

"*Quel dommage*," Ritz said, and shook his head. "I have to go to a very important meeting. I will assign a car and chauffeur to drive you to your hotel." Ironically, Charles always seemed to use public transportation to get around Paris.

"Where would you like me to drive you, sir?" the driver asked. Man, did I feel important.

"George Cinc . . . Hotel George Cinc." Of course, I didn't stay at Paris's second best hotel, the George V. Not on the $122 a month I made as a soldier. I stayed at a small students' hotel on St. Andre des Arts, Left Bank, near the jazz clubs, and paid only $2 a night. Bed was clean. Not much heat. Bathroom down the hall. Perfect!

But I didn't want the driver or Charles Ritz to know where I stayed. Silly, youthful pride. My plan was to stop at the George V, have a drink at its outdoor café, and then walk to my modest hotel.

The chauffeur pulled up in front of the hotel, got out of the car, opened my door, saluted me with his gloves in hand—very official like—and wished me a good day. Hey, I liked this good life!

I snaked my way to an empty table, sat down, ordered a Pernod. Out of the corner of my eyes, I saw someone get up slowly from his chair and head toward me. At first, I didn't recognize him in his civilian clothes, but it was Major Richard Davenport, my commanding officer.

Uh-oh.

"Chapralis! Did I see what I think I saw?"

"What did you see, sir?" I stood up quickly and saluted him, although it was not necessary as we were in civilian clothes.

"You got out of that limousine . . . and the chauffeur, too!"

"Yes, sir. You are right." I looked down, in my most innocent, sheepish manner.

"Well?" Major Davenport demanded an explanation.

"Okay, okay. Look, my family is rich. Filthy rich. Dad has investments in Europe. But, sir, please do not tell anyone. And please I want to be treated just like any other private!"

Major Davenport promised that he would.

Of course, I was lying about my family's wealth; most of the time we just scraped by financially.

He said he loved Paris and would be retiring in a few years and he would like to work in France as a civilian. I nodded. Major Davenport never found out that my family was financially middle class.

I did find Army life a lot easier and better after that experience.

Monsieur Charles

IN ADDITION TO MANAGING the prestigious Ritz Hotel in Paris Charles Ritz was France's premier angler, and had the contacts and resources to fish many of Europe's classic trout and salmon waters. While fishing in general was his passion, fly casting and fly rods were his lifelong addiction. He was always experimenting with different rod actions and, of course, was famous for his parabolic action rods, mostly produced by the fabulous Pezon et Michel factory, located in the Loire valley, south of Paris. Ritz and Pierre Creusevaut, France's champion caster, were constantly experimenting with rod actions and materials. Charles designed lots of tackle for Pezon et Michel, including a unique collapsible landing net.

After our meeting at the international casting championship at Bois de Boulogne, Charles and I became good friends, not great friends like he and A. J. McClane, Arnold Gingrich and others, but good enough so that he would lend me tackle to try out, and occasionally he would call me at my Army base in Orleans, south of Paris.

"I'm taking up this bloody golf game. Please pick me up a half-dozen golf balls at the PX," he would ask. "They're so bloody expensive here in Paris." And so I would.

One would think that Monsieur Charles was very cheap, and in some ways he was. Once when I met him in New York, he lost his eyeglasses. He was bent on finding a Woolworth's or other variety store that carried inexpensive, ready-to-wear eyeglasses in various magnifications. While they were popular at one time, and they are again today, there was a period of time—1950s and 1960s—when ready-made glasses were almost impossible to find. We walked all over Manhattan searching for stores that might have these inexpensive glasses.

"Charlie, you can go to an optometrist and have the glasses very quickly," I suggested as we walked in and out of many variety stores.

"I know! I know! But I have several pair back in Paris. Why should I pay big money for another?" he reasoned. "Finding a place that sells these eyeglasses is like trout fishing. You can't give up easily. You have to try and try and be patient. Then you succeed. By the way, have you ever fished in Yugoslavia? You should. It is very good there."

He succeeded in finding ready-to-wear eyeglasses in a musty, old variety store. He bought them for a few dollars, and spared me a follow-up of that "you-see-it's-like-trout-fishing" lecture.

In Paris he often rode public transportation, sometimes hanging outside the crowded bus, although there were always hotel limousines and chauffeurs at his disposal, and, of course, taxis.

While we burned shoe leather for almost an entire day looking for a variety store that had the ready-made eyeglasses, he didn't hesitate to fly from Paris to Montreal, see a Montreal Canadien hockey game and fly back to Paris the next day. First class, mind you. Go figure.

HE DIDN'T HAVE AN OFFICE, as such, at the hotel—at least that's what he told me. He had tremendous energy and was always in motion.

"If you have an office, you can't study the staff and inspect everything," he explained.

We went to his room one day to pick up a fly rod, and I expected to see a very elaborate suite, with priceless antique furniture and famous originals on the wall; instead it was a tiny room, very Spartan. Elizabeth, his wife, had died years ago, so there was no necessity to have a big room. He did, however, have another room specifically for his mystery novels and pipes, and a third large suite for his model railroad setup.

Charles was always charming and unique with that special ability of reducing complicated philosophies to a very simplistic 2+2=4 logic, but, at times he could do just the opposite. He could take something simple like fly casting and apply advanced casting theories that few of us understood or practiced and he always gave them tricky names such as HS-HL, which stood for his "high speed, high line" casting theory.

Ritz introduced many angling innovations, and among them, was his Variopower fly rod which was composed of a fiberglass butt with a split-bamboo tip section. It never became very popular.

He did many nice things for me. He introduced me to the Pezon et Michel tackle firm, and, after I completed my Army gig and returned to the States to start Sportackle International, he arranged for me to import its tackle. He also allowed me to use his name on our deluxe fiberglass fly rods, without royalties or other payments.

"Make sure they are good," he said sternly. And they were. The best.

When I met him in New York at his hotel, one of the staff brought him a huge batch of mail, because he had been traveling in the United States for several weeks. He riffled through the mail quickly and placed about a dozen unopened envelops aside and then deposited them in the waste paper basket.

"Aren't you going to open them?" I was curious.

"No! Those are from my mother in Paris. She is up in years and she thinks I'm a little boy. All those letters are about how the Ritz Hotel should be run, on and on."

"Maybe she sent you some money," I teased.

"Are you kidding?" He laughed.

I recalled meeting Charles Ritz's mother in Paris. She was in a wheel chair but even so she had plenty of spunk and was admonishing Charles to "pay more attention to the hotel instead of fishing rods."

WHEN I WAS IN THE ARMY, Charles Ritz invited me to a special event at the Ritz Hotel but didn't go into detail. When I arrived in my best gray flannel suit (the only suit I had when I was in the Army) and my finest white dress shirt (the one with the French cuffs), I thought I looked very sharp. I was quite confident until I entered the hotel from Place Vendôme and saw the rest of the guests attired in tuxedos and designer formal dresses. The "beautiful people." The international set.

I did a 180-degree turn and was about to slither out of the Ritz palace, but I changed my mind. I went back and stood in line with the "beautiful people." Coat checkers took coats but curiously never gave the guests any stubs. Hmmm. They must know every guest and they must remember everyone's coats and hats, I reasoned.

That's the Ritz Hotel for you.

Just as I reached the front of the line, some assistant manager type, undoubtedly checking out my garb and thinking that I was misplaced, grabbed me by the arm and pointed me to the Ritz Bar. I was annoyed at his supercilious attitude. To show him that I indeed belonged with the "beautiful people" I casually handed my coat to one of the checkers and, spotting Monsieur Charles Ritz, I walked right up to him and said hello.

"Jim, I'm glad that you could come, but right now we're on live TV and I'll see you in a few minutes," he said. I turned around and saw several lights on him and a couple of television cameras.

No wonder it was so bright where Ritz was standing. *Yikes!*

It turned out that someone had found some of Ernest Hemingway's writings in the Ritz Hotel. Ernest spent a considerable amount of time there, and, as the story goes, he helped liberate the Ritz Hotel at the end of the war in 1944. This discovery, Hemingway's literature, was the purpose of this special occasion.

As I sheepishly slithered out of camera range, I noted a very attractive woman sitting alone. She was about to light a cigarette, and I seized the opportunity. I dashed over quickly—and I hope smoothly—sat next to her, reached in my pocket and pulled out a matchbox. I was a smoker in those days.

"*Permittez moi,*" I said as I pulled out a match stick and struck it. She placed the cigarette holder to her lips in preparation for the light, closed her eyes sensually, but the match didn't light. I tried another. It too fizzled. A third one broke. *Damn French match sticks,* I thought. She seemed amused by my clumsiness. At least, she smiled.

While I fumbled for another match— it was almost like a bumbling scene from an Inspector Clouseau film—a hand and arm came between us. French cuffs. Manicured nails. Elegant silver, engraved cigarette lighter. The lightest touch on the wheel produced a glowing flame. The lighter and arm moved purposefully to the exact distance so that the gorgeous woman didn't have to lean or move her cigarette more than a centimeter or two.

"*Merci beau coup,*" she said. I looked at the intruder. He was, of course, extremely handsome in his impeccable formal wear, and he gazed at her bluish-green eyes before saying something soothing in French, and then walked off.

Next life, I'd like to look and be just like him.

I learned that this woman spoke only French and German. I spoke English, and only a few words of French, and, oh yeah, Greek, of course.

So we discussed the weather, and how beautiful the event was. Probably several times. She would say something in French, and all I could say is *"Oui, oui, oui . . . "* or *"Certainement"* but, of course, I didn't have a clue about what she was saying.

I felt so uncomfortable that I would have given up two months of Army salary to be back at the military post; instead I asked her if she would like to have a drink in the Ritz Bar, which must have struck her as very unusual, since the drinks flowed freely in the ballroom. But she agreed. Probably curious. Amused.

The famous Ritz Bar was only half filled. She ordered some sort of French drink and I ordered a Scotch and soda with a lemon twist.

It was very awkward. No language communication. We couldn't have been in the Ritz Bar more than a half hour, but it seemed like half a day. When we finished our drinks I called for the bill, paid it and left a generous tip. I tucked the paper francs in my wallet and placed lots of French coins in my pants pocket as we got up to leave.

The coins dribbled through a hole in my pocket onto the black and white marble floor. *Click. Clank. Clink.*

A wave of panic struck me. She placed her hand to her mouth to conceal her laughter. The other patrons looked at me. Some in amusement, but most anxious to see what I would do next.

Should I stoop down to pick up the coins and inconvenience the patrons under whose chairs and tables several coins trickled, twirled and gyrated? Or should I ignore the coins? But then would the patrons think of me as a "spoiled American" who didn't bother to pick up his money?

No time for Socratic dialectics. A quick decision was required and I made it. I picked up those coins that were on my way to the door and left the others under tables and chairs. By now my face was sunburned red with embarrassment, but I managed a forced grin for the patrons.

I wasn't going back into the ballroom. I said "good night" to the beautiful woman, grabbed my coat and left the hotel, and when I was safely on the other side of Place Vendôme I turned around and gazed at the fabulous Ritz.

"Well, Jimbo, you goofed up," I muttered. "You don't belong in the Ritz Hotel. At least not with the international set. Someday? *Naw!"*

But she was ravishing and sensual, that she was.

The man in the tuxedo

I MET CHARLES RITZ at his hotel in Paris, and he handed me a Pezon et Michel fly rod. "This is a very rare Superparabolic model. Only four were made so far, and the Pezon et Michel people and I want you to have this one. It's a gift."

Whoa!

I was honored, of course, thanked him profusely and headed to the Left Bank clutching the precious rod as though it were worth 100 times its weight in gold, but at the same time trying to look casual so as not to alert any unscrupulous being that this was a very, very valuable item.

I stopped at a St. Germain café to order some Pernod—the French aperitif with the licorice scent that gives you a little buzz. It was a time for celebration, I thought. The place was bustling with students, artists, and, I'm sure, musicians. Nearly always you would find lots of good-looking chicks in this café. There were pods of young people at each table, and although they all seemed to be talking at once, it appeared that everyone knew exactly what all the others in the group said. Especially the chick tables. Remarkable.

I sat at a small table away from the buzz-buzz of the other patrons, observing the scene, but still clutching the precious rod. I kept looking at the embroidered red, white and blue Pezon et Michel logo and label on the canvas bag that covered the aluminum case. I recalled reading A. J. McClane's *Field & Stream* article on Pezon et Michel's Parabolic rods in Miss Brabec's high school English class. I had decided right then and there that somehow I would make my living in fishing, just as McClane was doing. Your mind wonders a lot, especially in French cafés, and after a couple of Pernods.

"Oh, I see you have a Pezon et Michel rod. Very fine rod, indeed. I prefer them to Hardy's . . . although I do like Hardy's Casting Club de France model. Have you ever cast a C.C. de France? You are a fisherman, I'm sure?"

"Huh?" I turned around slowly. Behind me was a tall, slim, very good looking Frenchman, a la Louis Jourdan, maybe in his mid-30s. He obviously had noticed the label on the rod case. He was unique in that he was immaculately dressed in a tuxedo.

"Marcel!*"* He commanded before he sat next to me. *"Un Pernod aussi!"*

I explained that I was a fisherman, or trying to be one, and that I was stationed in nearby Orleans with the U.S. Army.

He, too, was a fisherman. Actually he was well traveled and fishing to him was more than a hobby, It was a driving force. He enjoyed trout fishing in Yugoslavia, he told me, but he was particularly enamored with Atlantic salmon fishing on the Driva in Norway.

"There are better rivers than the Driva," he ticked off a half-dozen Norwegian rivers, "but they are ridiculously expensive. The bloody Brits drive the prices up!"

I told him of the French streams I had visited and that I had fished in

Spain with Jacques Meyer, owner of the famous Saint Hubert fishing tackle store in Paris. "Unfortunately we had poor fishing for salmon, but there were many great brown trout streams in Spain."

And we talked more and more on fishing. He was intrigued with muskies. He had never been to North America; he had read about them in *Field & Stream*. "They are very intriguing . . . these muskies. Mysterious. Addictive like certain beautiful women."

"Like Brigitte Bardot?" I offered. Brigitte was steam in those days.

"No, no! Bardot is easy to read. More like, ahhh . . . more like Juliette Gréco!"

He was impressed, I think, that I knew who Juliette Gréco was. Gréco, a French singer/actress, sometimes showed up at Club Saint Germain de Pres, a marvelous jazz club. I think she had a thing for Jacques Distel, a guitarist, considered the sexiest man in Europe at the time. Anyway, she had that certain look in her eyes.

"I am curious, you are dressed in a tuxedo like you are going to some fancy place, yet, you are having a Pernod at this . . . this, ahhh, students' café."

"I live not far from here and I've been coming here since my Sorbonne university days."

"But the tuxedo? Are you going somewhere special?"

"Yeah, I'm going to work!"

"Are you a musician? I bet you are a violinist! Naw, a pianist! A famous pianist?" I offered.

"No! I'm a pickpocket."

"A what?" Quickly I checked to see if my wallet was still in my front inside coat pocket. It was.

"Don't worry. I don't steal from the poor. I assume you aren't rich, although you do have a Pezon et Michel rod. I steal only from the very rich."

That was reassuring.

He explained that he would go to these swanky parties or dances and "practice his art" there.

"Look, it's expensive to fish in Norway or Yugoslavia. I like good things. My family wanted me to be an architect but I lost interest and this is so much fun. My parents don't talk to me. Pickpocketing is a lot like fishing. You spot your quarry. You advance slowly; make a cast, so to speak. There is the danger element that intrigues me, too."

I was startled. I looked around to see if the other patrons had heard about his unusual occupation.

"Ahh, no problem. They all know what I do for a living."

My ill-at-ease feeling began to disappear and I could relax again.

"I don't know how people don't realize that they have been pickpocketed, unless they are drunk," I told him. "I am always very cautious about my wallet, although I never have much money in it—being a soldier—my watch and other things."

"Well, yes. You are very observant! I can tell. You are clutching that Pezon et Michel rod like it's the most precious thing you ever owned. You are sensitive to your surroundings. If you were to come back in life, say, as a fish, you would surely come back as a brown trout. That's it! A wary brown trout. V-e-r-y difficult to fool."

I was flattered. Yeah, he was right. I was very observant. Sensitive to my surroundings, too. I wanted to ask him if he was ever caught, but he changed the subject. Talked about fishing. He told me about a stream south of Orleans that had big trout. "It's a very communistic place there. They don't like Americans very much. Actually, they don't like anyone outside of their region, to be honest, but they have big browns. You have to be very cautious with these trout. Best to approach them from the bank, kneeling, or better yet, crawl on your stomach. You know, like you soldiers practice."

I excused myself to go the washroom. I thought about taking the valuable fly rod with me, but decided against it. Surely, it would offend him. I trusted him. Sort of. But I must say that I did "go" quickly and I didn't bother to wash my hands.

He looked at his expensive gold watch. It was time for him to leave. We shook hands, and he said he enjoyed our conversation.

"I hope to see you again." He seemed sincere.

I wished him Good Luck, and then I was embarrassed when I realized that I was wishing good luck to a pickpocket! Good grief!

As he left, he stopped to acknowledge several of the patrons and then he walked out confidently. Suddenly he turned around and headed toward me. Did he forget something?

"I wanted to teach you a lesson. Remember how you said it would be difficult, no, *impossible* for anyone to pickpocket you? Well, here is your wallet and here is your watch. Maybe you will learn from this. Most people are easy targets for good pickpockets, and I am very, very good. The best!" He laughed loudly and prepared to exit. He stopped, whirled around and added: "Don't let anyone take that Pezon et Michel rod from your case." He wished me good fishing and left.

Some of the students snickered. They all knew what had happened.

"He is very good," one of patrons tried to console me. "He is very good. The best in Paris, I hear. Maybe in Europe."

He must be a great fisherman, too, I thought.

Suddenly I wondered if the Pezon et Michel rod was still in its case. Perhaps he quickly took the rod out of the case when I had gone to the washroom and stashed it somewhere in the café? And only four of these rods existed. What would I tell Ritz? I bet the man in the tuxedo took the rod! I was convinced he took it.

I was not going to look in the case while I was in the café. Surely others in the bar would have noticed.

I walked briskly to the corner and only when the café was out of sight did I loosen the canvas bag that enveloped the aluminum case. I removed the cap, and pulled out the silk red case that held the rod.

It was there. Thank God!

I exhaled, and then I whistled a riff as I headed for my hotel on St. Andre des Arts.

He was surely good.

The best in Paris, I thought, and probably a darn good fisherman, too.

Good ol' Army days

JACQUES MEYER, owner of the famous Saint Hubert hunting and fishing store in Paris, and I became good friends. On one of my visits to his shop he invited me to fish his private trout stream located not far from Paris.

"Come next Saturday," he said. "Don't worry about tackle, because as you see, we have plenty here."

When I arrived at the store the following week, Jacques introduced me to another American: "Meet Paul Freeman," is all he said.

Paul was a tall, dignified man in his early 50s with a pleasant smile. We shook hands and discussed various fly-fishing tactics and I realized that he had read most of the important fishing literature, especially the how-to books. Ted Trueblood was his favorite. This was Paul's first opportunity to fish at Jacques' private trout waters.

Jacques, like many French, drove very fast—I'm sure in his fantasies he wanted to be a race-car driver—and soon we arrived at his private stretch. It was a beautiful stream, well maintained and supervised by his river keeper, whose main job was to prevent poaching and to keep the grounds and the river immaculate.

Soon we had our rods together and Jacques alternately guided first Paul and then me in different sections of the river. We caught only a few small trout, despite the fact that this stretch was fished only by Jacques and a few friends. Chalk stream trout are tough to fool.

"This river has many big trout, but they are highly educated and will not be easily fooled. At sunset, when there's usually a heavy mayfly hatch, you wouldn't believe the size and quantity of trout. The water boils with feeding trout! All over, trout feeding. Unfortunately, the fishing laws prohibit fishing after sunset and we follow this policy. You know, in France, one would probably get less of a jail sentence if he kills his wife than a deer out of season,"

I think Jacques was joking.

The three of us got along very well. At lunch time, Jacques prepared a feast using all kinds of unique kitchen utensils and gadgets that I never saw before or since. It was a sumptuous lunch that included several carefully selected wines, and all courses were elegantly served by Jacques and the river keeper.

I was curious about Paul Freeman. At first, I thought he was in France as a tourist, but judging from some of the conversation it appeared that Paul was living in Paris. He knew that I was in the military because I was wearing my Army fatigues. I had just been promoted to Private First Class a few weeks ago and had earned one stripe.

"Hey, Paul, do you live in Paris?" I asked.

"Yes."

"Do you work in France?"

"Yes, I do," he replied, but he didn't volunteer anything more. When I asked him if he was in business in France, he said no.

"Are you in the military?" It suddenly occurred to me to ask.

"Yes, I am."

"Are you an officer? A lieutenant? A major? A colonel?" I was getting more and more nervous as we ascended up the Army ranks.

" I am General Paul Freeman. I'm head of USAEUR in Europe."

Whoa! I quickly jumped to my feet, saluted him, and apologized for wearing military clothes while fishing (a military taboo).

"No, no! Relax, Jim. Jacques and I decided not to tell you my occupation and rank. I've fished in France before and also in Austria, but all the other officers keep catering to me. When I'm fishing, I want to be considered a fisherman. Jim, I want you to continue to call me Paul while we're fishing, and let's treat each other as anglers on this trip. Of course, in a military setting, I expect the normal procedures."

I was stunned. Fishing with a general! A lowly private fishing with a general that I'd been addressing by his first name! Jacques, of course, found this very amusing. We finished our feast with freshly brewed coffee while the river keeper put things away.

Paul headed for the river and began to wade upstream. He paused for a few seconds and then started to fish

"Ahh, Paul, I think it's my turn," I said.

"You're right," he replied and laughed.

We only caught a few trout, but it was certainly one of the most unusual days I've spent on a stream.

On the drive back to Paris, General Freeman asked me about my Army life and about the base.

"You know, general, I think we have a problem at the base in Orleans. A lot of the men don't have sufficient activities to keep them busy and they go to Paris once a month and spend their entire paycheck on prostitutes and drinking. Then you see them lined up at the medical unit, getting shots for VD and other diseases," I explained. "Many of these guys are interested in hunting and fishing, but there is no opportunity because the lands and most of the waters are private. I know in Germany there are some active U.S. military sportsmen's clubs, but not in France."

General Freeman became very interested in the subject. I received a couple of letters from him in the ensuing weeks, explaining that he discussed this subject with other generals in Europe.

(*Aside:* One of his letters was addressed to me as "Dear Jimmy." Naturally, I left this note, casually, on my desk in Orleans for the eyes of my commanding officers).

I was transferred to Special Services and my new assignment was to help form hunting and fishing clubs in France.

Working closely with several officers and Sgt. Clarence Bizet, who had a strong interest in hunting and fishing, we created several sportsmen's clubs in France for U. S. military personnel.

We even established a fishing tackle store on the Orleans military base. It was my job to order tackle, which we sold at ridiculously low prices and made a profit. For example: The Mitchell 300 spinning reel was selling for $27.50 in the United States, and I believe it was "fair-traded" (it could not be sold for less through normal distribution in the United States). The PX (military stores on the base) did not have to abide by the fair trade laws and was selling this reel for $12.50—a fantastic bargain. But our fishing tackle store on the base sold it for $9! Quite a few soldiers were buying quantities of these reels and sending them to various family members and friends in the States. We sold

HEADQUARTERS
UNITED STATES EUROPEAN COMMAND

To: Dear Jimmy —   Date May 27

Your letter arrived just before I start a 10 day trip. I hope what I have done bears fruit — copy enclosed.

In Austria, introduce yourself to general Charles E. Hoy & Lt. Col. John Tactical Command, G-1, USFA. Both in Salzburg. Hay, G-1, USFA. I don't have time to sorry I wrote a letter for you (show them this.)

Also, see Helmut Dschulnigg, owner of the large sporting goods store. It was a pleasure to have met you last Sunday.

* I did write to Col. Hay about you.

Hastily,
Gen. Freeman

rods, reels, landing nets, line and lures, and each week the club was making hundreds of dollars. Eventually, this money was used to lease fishing and hunting rights in France.

The people who operated the PX at Orleans wondered why suddenly their fishing tackle sales diminished considerably; they had no idea of our fishing club on base. When the PX personnel discovered our tackle store they protested, but our membership included a number of very influential officers who upheld the club's right to sell products for whatever price it wanted to.

We were able to buy French tackle (i.e., the Mitchell and Luxor reels) cheaper than the PX could, because Jacques Meyer introduced me to some of the tackle manufacturers and they liked the idea of the American fishing clubs in France. After all, the soldiers would eventually return to the United States to become civilians and they would have been presold on their products.

We started other military sportsmen's clubs in France that became successful. Jacques thought there was a great opportunity for me to remain in France—after completing my service—and develop the military fishing tackle sales in Europe.

"You could also sell the American military clubs in Germany, Austria and other places." He was very convincing.

I loved Europe. I was able to fish many fine trout steams in France and salmon rivers in Spain. I developed some fine friendships and met some very influential people.

But I decided to return to Chicago. I had an idea. Maybe I could import certain fishing tackle from Europe and start a business in the States.

On the flight back to the United States, I thought of the name for my new company.

Sportackle International.

Yeah, that had a nice ring to it. Sportackle International, it would be.

PART THREE

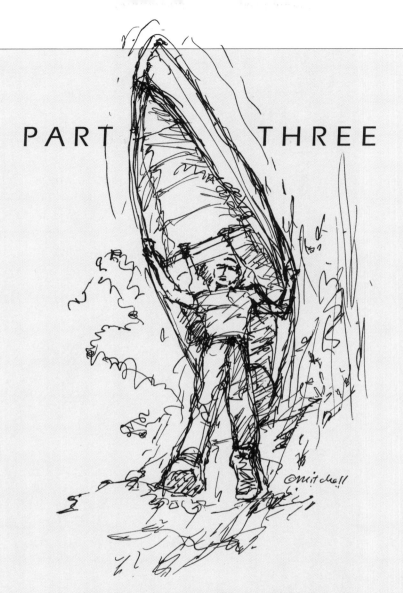

Flings & infatuations

Sportackle International:
harsh lessons learned at 1523 W. Fullerton;
the adventures of "Big Story Jim"
(Psst! There are easier ways of making a living than guiding).

1523 West Fullerton

WHEN I RETURNED to the United States after my military service in France, I started Sportackle International. I imported Pezon et Michel bamboo fly rods and later other products, but the future in the tackle business clearly was in fiberglass rods.

With limited funds, I rented a 2,300-square-foot street level shop at 1523 W. Fullerton, in Chicago, converted it into a factory with a showroom and office in the front. It was a good setup. Close friend Joe Godfrey introduced me to Ken Trisler, a very creative, fabulous rod designer. Ken, in his late 30s or early 40s, had helped to set up Fenwick, the leading rod company at the time. He came to Chicago, was interested in working for my firm, and his salary demands were modest so I hired him. He set up the rod winding machines, drying rooms, storage bins, taught employees to wrap rods and handled just about everything else. Soon, we had a small rod manufacturing company and ran two shifts. To Ken's credit, the fiberglass rods we made were fabulous, as good as any on the market. None better.

I was in charge of sales. I knew very little about business in general and even less about the tackle business, but at the national tackle show we sold a lot of rods.

"Do you have spring dating?" dealers and wholesalers would ask.

"Of course, we do!" I had no idea that "spring dating" meant that, although we would have to ship the rods in the winter, we wouldn't get paid until spring. And, to some accounts, "spring" meant July or August. Sales were good, but cash flow was barely a trickle and profits, of course, nonexistent.

Soon I was in a financial bind. My dad spoke to several of his friends, who were extremely successful businessmen and they became intrigued with Sportackle International. I believe they considered it a challenge. Could four or five men go into a business that they knew nothing about and turn it into a success by applying common sense, experience and all necessary resources? They realized I knew little about business, but this was no major problem for them. They would finance the company, put in their accountants, do the billing, and take care of all the things that were necessary to operate a successful business.

When they met Ken, they quickly grasped the fact that he was an extremely creative rod designer. He knew the industry well, had the proper contacts and was clearly the key to future success. And while they would invest to help me out, they would do so only because they had tremendous confidence in Ken's ability. They were talking about financing Sportackle International in terms of several hundred thousand dollars, and that was in the mid-1950s. They, in return, would take a small share of the business.

What a deal! What a great deal!

One day Ken, a recovering alcoholic, received his final divorce papers. He became so depressed that he almost drank himself into another world. There he was, in the hospital, his eyes fixed on a ceiling fan. He was breathing, and occasionally he would blink, but not much more.

When my potential partners found out about Ken's drinking problem, they visited him in the hospital. They decided that without Ken, there would be no hope of continuing and they advised me to close up Sportackle International. I was depressed. We were so close to establishing a good tackle company, but now we were back to square one. No money. No future. There was no other way but to dissolve Sportackle International. I was about 24 years old, and I owed more than $70,000. I'm talking in the 1950s when you could buy a new house for $35,000.

A few days later I received a call from Van Nomikos, one of the prospective investors. Van liked the business. More than that, he liked helping young, ambitious men of Greek descent.

"I will help you," he told me. "I have plenty of money. Order what you need. Come by the office on the 15th and I will give you a check for $85,000. And if you need more money we will work it out later. My lawyer and accountant will oversee the business. They'll draw up some papers. If it works out, you pay me back. If it doesn't, well, if won't be the first time I lost money. I want to help you."

When I told Ken Trisler about this turn of events, he miraculously recovered, checked out of the hospital and headed for our shop. He ordered lots of rod blanks from Don Green at Grizzly, "extra, extra" select cork from Armstrong, ferrules from Featherweight Products and other components. He begged for immediate delivery and because they knew and respected Ken, they agreed to rush the shipments.

The blanks came in quickly, and since nearly all the rods were two-piece models, Ken measured and cut them in two and began ferruling them. He was whistling again—he always whistled when he was happy—and he worked long, hard hours to reduce our backlog of orders.

We were back in business. And how.

ON WEDNESDAY MORNING I called Van Nomikos' lawyer, who was to have a check for $85,000 for me.

"Jim, I've got very bad news. Very bad news. Van died of a heart attack last night. He was scheduled to come over this morning to go over some papers and to sign the check. I'm sorry."

I was speechless. Stunned. Shocked.

"Jim, I know he promised the money. I've drawn up the papers, but he didn't sign them. He told me all about his plans for Sportackle International, but there is no way I can give you the money now. There's the widow, and the son, you understand."

I was sad. Sad for Van, for he hardly knew me but wanted to help me. What a generous man.

I was sad for me. For Ken.

I had to release Ken because I had very little money left and I had exhausted my sources for loans. We couldn't return the blanks because they had been cut in two, some ferruled. Others had cork and reel seats already glued in.

Ken was stunned. He thought he could get a job in Milwaukee and he did. I kept a several girls working—they wrapped and varnished rods— and by now I had a good idea of how to assemble rods, and the orders were coming in. Abercrombie and Fitch. VL&A. Bon Marche. Marshall Field's. Great accounts. Good friend Gene Badal and cousin Ernie Chiagouris worked for free to help me out.

But our checks were bouncing all over the neighborhood, after our employees cashed them at various local businesses. The grocer came by with one check. Then the hardware guy with another. Other employees banked their checks and wrote personal checks to pay their rent and other expenses. I promised I would make all payments but I needed some time. How did this happen? Two large checks from our customers bounced because of insufficient funds. Thus, ours did, too.

The trickle down theory in reverse.

W E RECEIVED A GOOD ORDER from a jobber in Ohio. I met him at an industry tackle show in Chicago and he was floored when he saw our Luxor Gold Medal rods.

"I'm in a hurry because I have a flight soon. Here's my card. Send me a half-dozen spinning and casting rods—you know, for Ohio fishing—as soon as you can. I want to run them by our dealers for their opinion. I'll pay you right away. Give me a three percent cash discount."

We shipped the rods with our invoice. He paid it immediately.

He called again. "I need two dozen of your six-foot spinning rods as soon as possible. They love them in Ohio. I'll need three dozen of each of four models very soon." He gave us the model numbers.

We shipped the 24 rods and worked day and night to get his next order ready.

His check arrived for the 24 rods a few days later. And so did his new order—for 144 more rods.

We were able to ship them out. Our shop was humming again. We were all happy. The radio in the winding room was blaring a South American tune. We started a conga line and we all snaked our way around the factory.

One-two-three, La Conga! One-two-three, La Conga!

We didn't care that a salesman from Armstrong Cork walked in. He was amused. We asked him to join in our conga line, but he refused.

We waited for the check from the jobber in Ohio.

No check.

After a week, Gene Badal was worried and phoned him. "I just called him and I found out his phone has been disconnected. I think we've been had."

"Don't be silly. He's paid us all the other times. Maybe he has moved into bigger offices." I was trying to keep everything upbeat, but I knew Gene was right.

I called the police in his town.

"How much did he take you for?" the person at the other end asked.

I told him that he owed us about $1500 for the rods.

"Consider yourself lucky. He worked the same deal with lots of companies. He took a golf company for $75,000 by playing that same game."

Gene, Ernie and the girls didn't have to ask when I hung up.

It was a very dismal period of my life. Friends suggested that I consider bankruptcy as an alternative. I dismissed that road immediately. I moved into the shop, in Ken's vacated room, which we put together so he could live in the factory, because he often worked in the middle of the night. I worked long hours.

I woke up one Saturday morning, contemplating what I would do next. I opened the front door, stepped out and marveled at what a beautiful day it was. What a great day to go trout fishing, or catch some bass at Green Lake, Wisconsin, where I began to fish as a kid. It was that kind of a day. Yes, I would call fishing pals Bob Kukulski and Elmer Bergendahl and maybe we could go to Green Lake for the weekend.

I was in the middle of a yawn when suddenly a person came tumbling down in front of me, followed by his scaffold. He barely missed falling on me. He died instantly. Bones. Bloody flesh. The agony on his face. You don't forget that. One minute he was alive, tuckpointing the top of our building, enjoying the beautiful day, perhaps whistling and the next minute, he was a bag of bones. He was in his 60s, I guessed.

I called the police. I called it a day.

W E HAD SHIPPED 80 steelhead spinning rods to Bon Marche in Seattle. A few days after shipment I realized that I had glued the fixed reel seats upside down by mistake. There was no way to correct this without tearing the cork handles apart and the guides on the butt section. Now the fishing buyer was on the phone. Surely he must be furious, I thought, as he had needed the rods right away. It would be impossible to repair them quickly. What to do?

"Jim, I love those new rods. Some of the guys who bought them like the new uplocking reel seats. . ." He then ordered another hundred.

Wow! It's nice to win one, occasionally. Some money was trickling in now so we hired another girl to help wrap rods.

On my way home, I saw that Arden's, a local shoe store, was swamped with business due to another series of "going out of business" sales. Signs plastered all over the windows. Women going in. Women coming out, schlepping boxes of shoes under their arms and flashing smiles on their faces. Everyone loves a bargain, I guess.

"Geez!" I thought. "Old Man Arden has been going out of business for months." In the front of the store a truck pulled up and the delivery man brought in more boxes of shoes.

"If he's going out of business, then why are they delivering more shoes?" I wondered.

Idea.

The next day I affixed a "going out of business" sign on our window. Until now, we only sold our products directly to wholesalers or dealers. Now I was inviting the public to come in and buy rods direct. As an incentive, I offered a 20 percent discount off list price on most models and 40 percent on a few experimental rods.

Business was absolutely fabulous. Fishermen were coming from all over the city to buy these rods. Tempel Smith, the steel industrialist, purchased $2000 worth of rods! Remember, we're talking in the 1950s. He was going to line a fishing den with our rods.

The doctors from Presbyterian St. Luke's hospital became superb customers, and at times there would be five or six doctors in our show-room ordering fishing rods. Money was pouring in. I rehired a couple of girls to wind additional rods. On some days, I would gross a couple of thousand dollars, but on others only several hundred.

"Jim, we're sending over a Doctor Bryan. Take care of him. You know what I mean? We don't like the guy, and he is always looking for a bargain. Give him a little *flimflam*," Dr. George Pasternak told me.

I understood exactly what he meant.

E VEN THROUGH HIS THICK GLASSES, I noticed that Dr. Bryan looked at me suspiciously. He didn't have to tell me who he was; he only nodded when I greeted him warmly. He quickly gazed at the rods in the display room and arrogantly into my office.

I showed him a 6-foot Luxor Ritz Riviera spinning rod. This was the most expensive rod we made and was priced at $29.95. It was on sale for $19.95.

"Is it worth $19.95?" he asked.

"Of course, it is, Dr. Bryan. It's worth a lot more, but we need the cash to pay our bills!"

He tried to haggle on the price. I didn't budge.

"Look, Dr. Bryan this rod is worth at least $29.95 . . . and I'm selling it to you for $19.95. If you buy it, and want to sell it back to me at $29.95, I will buy it for that price!"

"Why would you do that?"

"Because it's worth $29.95!"

Dr. Bryan was very confused. We had to go over this again and again. But the dangling bait (profit) proved irresistible to Dr. Bryan.

Skeptically, if not reluctantly, he gave me a $20 bill. I casually made out an invoice, rubber stamped it "paid" and handed him the rod, invoice and a nickel.

"I thought you said you'd give me $29.95 for the rod," he was irritated.

"Well, you haven't offered to sell it to me."

"Okay. What will you pay for the rod you just sold me?" He was now impatient.

"$29.95!" I replied without hesitation. He nodded, growing more dubious by the second.

"I peeled out his $20 and added another $10. He gave me the nickel and the rod back. I asked for the paid invoice back.

He was very confused. He walked backward out of the office, clutching the $30, never turning his eyes away from me, opened the door slowly but left quickly.

A couple of hours later, Dr. Pasternak called from St. Luke's. His laughter was uncontrollable. "That was a classic, Jim. All the doctors here got a kick out of it. Bryan doesn't know that you put him on."

Although these doctors had purchased many rods in previous days, they came back to the shop and bought many more, each one wanting to hear the conversation I had with Dr. Bryan. It was obvious that he didn't have many friends on the medical staff.

More importantly, I was slowly able to pay back many of my suppliers. Some let me off the hook after I paid back more than half of the amount owed.

"We appreciate your efforts, and the fact that you've paid most of it. We'll wipe off the balance." Hot dog! Nice guys.

The problems however, didn't disappear.

On a Saturday morning I found a business card on my door. It was from the Internal Revenue Service. There was a note scribbled on the card. "Call me Monday morning."

What a terrible weekend that was. I know I had not paid some of the employees' withholding taxes to the IRS, because whatever money came in was used to pay bills, employees or to buy more components to complete additional rods. Good grief! Why was I ever attracted to the sport fishing business, anyway?

Saturday was dreadful. So was Sunday. Would I go to jail? I talked to Joe Godfrey, my good friend and mentor. He lectured me, but gave me about $800, which is what I owed.

"Two things you must always do: pay the government and have plenty of insurance," he said sternly.

Monday morning.

"Mr. Brockenhaus? Ah, this is Jim Chapralis at Sportackle International. You left a card Friday? Asked me to call?" My voice must have cracked several times. I mean, what I really wanted to ask was, should I go home, pack a toothbrush and pajamas and check myself into the nearest jail?

"Yes, yes. Here it is. Hmmm. Well, Mr. Chapralis, I need to ask you a few questions because we're doing a survey on small businesses and how we can make it easier for them to prosper. Do you have a moment? Good. Good. May I ask you several questions over the phone?"

Pheewww! I answered the questions, and he thanked me. Later, I also made arrangements to pay the IRS with the $800 Joe gave me.

Our rods were slowly earning a lofty reputation. Rockland Tackle called. I believe Rockland was importing its wonderful Alcedo spinning reels from Italy and were promoting ultra-light fishing.

"We like your ultra-light rod very much. We'd like you to design and manufacture them for us under our label. We'll probably need 150 to 200 rods per week, and probably increase it to 400 or 500 if they sell."

What an opportunity. Joe Godfrey advised me to do it. "You got all the equipment, trained help . . . you ought to do it."

Although the offer was tempting, I was burned out. Cousin Ernie was worried about my sanity. There were some inexplicable things happening in the shop, like rods moving on their own from one room to another. I know they did. But Ernie insisted that I was hallucinating.

So instead of remaining in the rod business, I continued to pay bills, including several months' back rent, and at the opportune time I closed the shop. The employees were sad and it was a very emotional day. As a matter of fact, Ernie gave them the bad news, as I simply couldn't do it.

The employees understood. Sort of. Yeah, they could get other jobs for more money, but Sportackle International, well, it was like a bud trying to sprout and blossom into a flower against many odds, but it never did. Now the completely remodeled building houses Multimedia Facets, a small movie theater featuring eclectic films and videos.

Today, some 45 years later, I have occasional nightmares of Sportackle International, the shop at 1523 W. Fullerton.

"Big Story Jim" –
Guiding on the Manitou

AFTER I WOUND UP Sportackle International, I got a job as an associate editor at *PTM* (a music trade magazine), and continued to pay off the loans and bills. I knew nothing about pianos, saxophones, drums or guitars, although I had a strong interest in jazz. But, then, I hadn't known much about the tackle business either.

It was a fun job but, unfortunately, two of the six employees committed suicide.

You could always tell when our cheerful accountant was in the area. He usually whistled a single note and if he wasn't whistling, you could hear the aspirin bottle rattling in his pocket when he walked. No wonder they put cotton in aspirin bottles! But he was mostly happy, or so it seemed, until the day he jumped off the fire escape from our 10th-floor offices in downtown Chicago. No explanation. No note. Just like that, he ended it all. He appeared to be no different on his final day than on any other: the rattling aspirin bottle, the same one-note whistle.

Our advertising gal sold many ads because of her superb telephone voice and her tenacity. She, too, appeared to be very upbeat but also ended her life. I can't remember for sure, but I think she jumped from the same fire escape which was adjacent to her office. Except for these two tragedies, I enjoyed working at *PTM* for a couple of years.

But I wanted to get back into fishing.

Jerry Tricomi came to the rescue. "Why don't you spend the whole fishing season at the camp? You could guide, write some articles, help promote the camp and take some time off."

What a splendid idea! I would learn about fishing camps and guides from another perspective. Jerry and his wife Lorine owned Camp Manitou, a wonderful fishing lodge on an island in Ontario, reached only by float plane. It was east of Nestor Falls and north of Fort Frances (the Canadian town across from Minnesota's International Falls).

In fact the idea sounded so good that my cousin Ernie Chiagouris wanted to do the same thing. So we both gave notice and quit our jobs and went to Camp Manitou for the season. Just like that.

"Geez," Tricomi teased, "this is the first time any Ontario camp had two Greeks from Chicago working as guides!" He laughed.

Nearly his entire guiding staff was composed of Canadian Natives (or Indians as they were called in those days).

Ernie and I knew we would be tested before being accepted.

Canadian Native fishing guide Val Perrault looked at me askance. We wrestled. We had canoe races. Lots of competitive things. He won in all these events, of course, but in time we became good friends. I felt accepted when the Indians gave me a nickname: Big Story Jim.

"Don't get carried away with your nickname," Val told me, "we really call you **B.S. Jim**, ya know. You always have a big story, but we can't call you B.S. in front of guests, so we'll call you Big Story Jim."

Marvin Bruyere was the intellectual among the guides and spent most of his leisure hours reading and gobbling up historical novels as fast as he could find them. Ernie and Marvin hit it off and soon we were accepted. In fact, Ernie and I decided to move from a private little log cabin on the island to the crowded guides' shack where Val, Marvin, Sunboy, Willie and a half-dozen other guides lived. The only guide who wasn't a Canadian Native was Foy. He had been guiding for years at Camp Manitou, so as Marvin put it, "Foy is really one of us, a blond, blue-eyed Indian!"

What a difference between the guides in those days and some of the guides today! *Whoa!* Jerry's guides took pride in the fact that they would portage into various lakes and only use the outboards to get to the vicinity. They would scull the AlumaCraft boats, even against the wind, except when they would troll, of course, but they trolled only if guests' casting skills were hopeless. Today, many of the Canadian guides start the big engines to get a lure off a tree branch or to move a boat 50 feet.

The Indians would always set me up for trouble with my clients. They knew I had no idea of how to portage a boat and where some of the outlying lakes were located.

"Hey, tell 'Big Story' Jim to take you to Gates Lake," Val told Bill Wallo and Tom Gable, two of my clients for the week. "There are big pike there. Some more than 20 pounds." I tried to discourage them, but no, they insisted that we fish Gates Lake. I wanted to kill Val.

I had only a rough idea of where Gates Lake was, and then there was the problem of portaging a boat and motor into these lakes. For portages we used an AlumaCraft Model A boat, which was about 12 feet long.

Val must have felt sorry for me, so the night before he took me to the dock to show me how to carry a boat.

"Look, it's easy to carry these boats on your back, if you balance them right. No problem." He demonstrated and explained how to do it, and soon I was prancing back and forth with the aluminum boat on my back. It *was* easy if you balanced it right. He told me how to find the Gates Lake portage (the guides often camouflaged the portages so that neighboring camps wouldn't locate them).

I spotted the portage without difficulty and found it remarkably easy to carry the boat and then the motor. I think the portage was about a quarter-mile long. Tom and Bill carried the tackle and lunches, and they were impressed with my portaging skills. I was, too!

We fished Gates Lake and caught lots of pike but none was more than eight pounds. We decided to troll with big spoons for a change of pace. Bill Wallo hooked a larger pike, which we didn't see, because as he fought it, his mono line touched my cigarette (we all smoked in those days). On the next run, the pike broke the line easily because it was burnt. I was ready to apologize to Bill.

"Holy Cow! Did you see that? That big pike broke my brand-new 20-pound test line. Val was right. There are huge fish here!"

I didn't have the heart to tell him otherwise. I kept my mouth shut and nodded in agreement. We continued to catch lots of small pike until it was time to go back to camp. Then I realized that I was lost!

Although Gates is a small lake, I had no idea where the portage back to the Manitou was. The Indian guides had always cautioned me to look backwards from time to time when running an outboard in new waters because the landscape appears different on the return.

"Ya go one way and it looks like one big piece of water because all the outlets, islands and bays blend together. Then when you return you see different water slots and wonder which one to take," Sunboy told me. "Ya gotta always look back." But I forgot his advice.

I insisted on trolling some more, as I searched the shoreline hoping to locate the portage. I could not find it. How embarrassing. Lost in Gates Lake! Wait until the Camp Manitou guides hear about this.

"Hey, Big Story, you just passed the portage," Bill Wallo said while pointing to it. "Why don't we call it a day and go in? We had a good day!"

"I know, I know, but I want you guys to try for a very big fish by the island!" I said. Of course, I wasn't going to let on that I'd had no idea of where the portage was until Bill pointed it out, and I certainly wasn't aware of any big fish by the island. Remember that I had never been to Gates Lake before.

As it turned out Tom Gable hooked and landed a big pike after an energetic battle. I think it was about 14 to 16 pounds. Maybe less.

Tom was enthralled. "There is an-honest-to-goodness 20-pound pike! The largest I ever caught in my life!" He wanted to bring it into the lodge and weigh it, maybe have it mounted, but I told him that this was a special fish.

"Look, Tom. I only take a few special guests to fish for this pike," I said.

I must have been convincing because Tom instructed me to release it. He felt very special. I felt very lucky. That fish would never have weighed 20 pounds!

At the dinner table Bill and Tom were telling other guests about the great fishing that we had. "You fellas ought to tell your guides to take you into Gates Lake. Big fish there."

I was eating with the guides in the

kitchen and they overheard the conversation and snickered.

"Big Story Jim! Perfect name we gave you." Willie said.

"Yep, perfect name, **B.S.** Jim," Val emphasized the B.S.

G UIDING ON THE MANITOU was a wonderful experience but not without tension and frustration. A guide (especially if he uses Polaroids) often sees fish in the water, because he is used to focusing his eyes *below* the surface. Most of the clients only focus *on top* of the water.

"Look at that muskie!" I said excitedly, pointing to a big fish about three to four feet below the surface.

"Where? I don't see it," Les, a client, said. Surely, he thought I was putting him on.

Or I'd point to a place where I saw a big fish surface, but he couldn't make the cast. Or he would backlash. Then at the dinner table Les complained that he didn't have good fishing, and in hushed tones, he told fellow guests, "Well, they assigned me to one of those Greek guides from Chicago . . . probably knows Rush Street quite well."

I guided another guy for some muskie fishing at Grant Lake. Suddenly I spotted a huge muskie by the island near the shorelunch grounds. "Quick, Joe, change to that Homer LeBlanc musky bait." Joe slowly removed the Johnson Silver Minnow he was using for pike. Then he reached nonchalantly for his Kennedy tackle box but the cover was stuck. He couldn't open it, so he began to pound on it with his fist, not out of anger, but to open it.

"Sometimes, it gets stuck and you have to pound the top," he explained as he continued to bang on the tackle box. You can imagine the reverberating noise he made in our aluminum boat. He opened the tackle box, took out the LeBlanc lure, attached it to his line, and then asked, "Now, where did you see that big muskie?"

"Over there," I said pointing in a general direction. I wanted to add, "but don't bother, because by now that muskie is probably on the other side of the lake." I didn't.

I felt more pressure guiding than I ever did in my working life, with the possible exception of operating Sportackle International. Guiding can be very frustrating. First, the clients may not be able to cast or see the fish, or retrieve or feel the strike; secondly, even if they are good fishermen, you are always at the mercy of the fish's disposition. There are hours or even days when the fish simply won't feed, even at such remote and pristine waters as the Manitou.

I wanted most parties to enjoy wonderful fishing and I knocked myself out to deliver it, but there were also times when I wanted some characters to have poor results because they were jerks or very demanding. But often the opposite occurred. Jasper, for example, told the waitress that he wanted his bread toasted on one side only. Hmmm. There was only one type of toaster in camp and it did both sides.

Although Jasper had never been on these waters before, he would tell me where he wanted to fish, and he insisted that I paddle against the wind. Usually that's the wrong approach, because the slap-slap of the waves against the aluminum bow would alert the fish, but darn it, bass would come out of the most unlikely places and smack Jasper's lure with gusto.

"Listen to me, kid! Pay attention to what I say and you'll be a good guide before the week's over," Jasper boasted.

Grrrr! Of course, after he left, these same places and tactics produced terrible results. Go figure. Where was the Greek God of Justice? I'm sure there was one. The ancient Greeks had one for everything. He was probably hitting on Venus, methinks.

At lunch, Jasper and his partner, Ken, were very demanding, but I'd hustle to make the shorelunch a highlight of the day. They would gobble their lunch in a let's-get-this-over-with-quickly attitude, never commenting on the meals. After feeding them, I would prepare to eat and to relax for a few minutes with a cup of coffee. You need to rest a bit, because paddling a big boat all morning is exhausting.

But as soon as Jasper and Ken finished their lunch they wanted to go. "Okay, Big Story, let's go fishing . . . take your lunch with you and eat while we fish."

So I'd douse the fire, clean the campsite, pack up, place everything into the boat, grab a couple of pieces of fish (no coffee or dessert) and munch on fish while paddling. Thank goodness for Rolaids!

Jasper and Ken were truly unappreciative jerks, but they had superb fishing.

"One time I took a party into Gordon Lake [a fly-out, tent outpost] for an overnight," Marvin recalled, "and they caught many muskies and big walleyes. I think they had the best fishing ever in Gordon. When we came back, Jerry [the camp owner] asked them how the fishing was. 'Oh, it was okay, but the butter was too soft,' they said. Can you imagine that?"

Ernie and I felt we had to work harder than the Indian guides because we were "imported" and had to prove ourselves. Guiding in those days— late 1950s—was hard work, at least at Camp Manitou, where portaging and paddling was standard. Jerry Tricomi was a tough taskmaster, but I'm sure we, as a group, were the best guiding corps in Northwestern Ontario. We worked hard. Very hard.

Often it was a seven-day job, because many of the guests would book a full week in order to take advantage of the cheaper Saturday weekly charter plane service. Guides woke up early to have breakfast before the guests, mix gas and oil for their outboards, prepare the boats, arrange the tackle and double-check the shorelunch utensils and fixings. At noon they had to prepare shore-lunch, start a fire (not that easy if it rained and the wood was wet), fillet and cook the fish, make the coffee, and then back to fishing. After dinner, many of the clients wanted to fish the evening hours. By the end of the week the guests were tired and fished out, but happy and proud of their ice chests full of bragging-sized fillets (these were the days before catch-and-release). Just as the guides exhaled a sigh of relief, a new group would arrive, full of enthusiasm, energy and anticipation. No time for the guides to recoup. Then another group would come in. On and on. By the end of a month, the guiding staff was exhausted.

Cousin Ernie and I spent the whole summer on the Camp Manitou island, never once going into town, not even for haircuts. The guides cut our hair: "Time to be scalped again," they'd say. When Ernie and I had time off, we went fishing. The guides? Every so often they would find it necessary to go to town to get away from the fishing scene.

Camp Manitou could only be reached by float plane, and many of the guides' families lived on the Fort Frances reservation. There were no phones and the mail would only come in with the weekly float plane, unless the pilot forgot to bring it in, which meant we had to wait another week for the mail.

How did the camp receive messages from the outside world? Via radio. I don't mean radio telephone, I mean from a regular radio station that broadcast from Fort Frances, Ontario. Every day at noon, it was *"Message Hour."* The radio station would halt its normal programming and the announcer would read messages for the various camps, guides and other individuals or businesses that could only be reached by float plane. The message hour was very popular, and most camps tuned in, not only for their own messages, but because they were interested in the sometimes gossipy information intended for others. Call it curiosity. A camp owner could gauge how well his competitors were doing from the messages. If another camp's contact person in Ft. Frances relayed that "we rounded up eight guides for next week for the Robinson party," every listener knew that this particular lodge had a big group booked the following week.

The guides used the message hour to their advantage. If they wanted a little R and R, somehow, some way, they would get one of their accomplices in Fort Frances to post a radio message. It might say: "Val, your Aunt Mary is dying and your mother wants you to come in this weekend for the funeral!" Of course, there was no Aunt Mary in the first place.

"Hey, Val, your Aunt Mary is dying again and your mother said you have to go into Fort Frances . . . you know, [*wink, wink*] see her for the last time," Camp owner Jerry Tricomi would say sarcastically. "By the way, how many times has your Aunt Mary died this season?"

"She's good at recovering so far. And besides I have two Aunt Marys," Val would respond. Jerry didn't care if the guides went into town, unless there was a shortage of guides.

Jerry was puzzled. "How do these guides get the messages to their friends in Ft. Frances to place them on radio? There is no phone within 30 miles of our waters." He would sometimes ask the guides directly.

"Hey, Mister Jerry. We send smoke signals in the sky when we make shorelunch. Didn't ya know that? Haven't ya ever seen a Gabby Hayes cowboy and injun movie?"

We never found out. "Maybe there's a little Western Union guy somewhere in the bush telegraphing the messages," Ernie would suggest.

Naw!

FOY, THE ONLY non-Indian guide, except for Ernie and me, was especially clever. He would take parties to Walleye Lake, which required a portage of about two miles. There were boats and motors permanently stashed on the other side of the portage, but Foy and the sports would have to carry their own rods, tackle boxes, lunches and gas.

About halfway through the portage, Foy would ask the guests if they would like to take a break. Of course, they would. They would be exhausted. Most of the days were very warm, and the guys would develop a tremendous thirst. Foy would admit that he, too, was very thirsty and soon they would be talking about how wonderful it would be to have an ice-cold beer or soft drink.

"Well, we're in the middle of nowhere. But when we get to the other side of the portage we can drink the lake water," Foy would say. "Why don't you fellas relax a bit. I'm going to look around here, for moose sign for the next hunting season."

Within five to ten minutes, he would return with a few cold cans or bottles of beer or pop.

" Look what I found!" He'd say.

The clients would be astounded. "*Where* did ya get those? *How* did ya get them?"

"Oh, I found this elf in the woods and he's opening up a little bar, so I bought them from him," he'd reply.

Foy's ploy? At the beginning of the season, he would stash several varieties of canned pop and beer in a very cold spring where he had planned to take a break. Of course, he never let on. Tricks of the trade.

"The guys always increased their tips by a few bucks just because of this and other surprises I arranged."

IT WAS A COLD DAY in late September. "Ernie! Jim! I want you to take two parties to Gordon Lake for an overnight," Jerry commanded.

"But we've never been there," was our response, realizing of course, that in late September the temperatures could dip close to freezing at night. Who wants to sleep in a cold tent when you can have the comforts of a warm cabin with a red-hot potbellied stove?

"You gotta go. All the other guides are booked to fish lake trout in the Manitou, and we're over-booked by four people. We don't have enough beds, and it's only a couple of days."

So we went. Four clients, Ernie and I. We had to set up a canvas tent, split some wood, take care of all the housekeeping chores and then, of course, take them fishing for long hours.

My two clients were pretty nice guys, but impatient; they wanted instant action. I took them to a narrow channel that Jerry had said was very productive for muskies. The problem was that it was too narrow, about 120 feet wide. A muskie swirled next to shore and Angler No. 1 quickly sent out a Pflueger Globe lure in the general direction. Only he overshot the bank and the Globe plug twirled around a pine at least a half-dozen times. High up. Maybe 12 feet high!

"Ohh, we've got to get it back," he said, as he kept pulling on his rod trying to break the branch. "It's my favorite muskie lure and it's my only one."

The Globe was one of my favorites also, but how were we going to get it?

Just then Angler No. 2 dispatches a cast to the other bank and he wraps up a big Heddon plug on a branch. So there we are: Angler No. 1 hooked up on a tree on one bank, and Angler No. 2 snarled on the other bank.

"There's no way we can get the Globe plug," I told Angler No. 1. "It's too high up."

"Can't you climb the tree?" He then realized that the pine wouldn't hold me and followed that with an even dumber statement. "Maybe you can cut the tree down."

"I don't have an axe in the boat," I replied, with my best customer-service smile. "It's back at the tent camp."

"Maybe you could go get it," he suggested.

Now here was a very successful businessman, his buddy is snagged

on a tree on one side and he is hooked to a tree on the other side. How did he propose that I get the axe? Well, yes, I could put Angler No. 1 on one bank and then Angler No. 2 on the other, but both shores were boggy and marshy and one of Jerry Tricomi's Guiding Rules was, *"If you go out with two live guests, you must return with two live guests."*

He was very strict about this rule.

So they finally broke off their lures and we caught a few walleyes for supper.

At day's end I was exhausted. I slept on the floor in one tent with Anglers No. 1 and No. 2, while cousin Ernie did similarly with his two clients in another tent. It was *c-o-l-d!*

In the middle of the night, Angler No. 1 woke me up.

"Sorry, but I can't sleep," he said. "Could you make a fire and some tea?"

I was sound asleep. Ernie had our only flashlight in his tent and there was no sense in waking him and his guests up. So out of the tent I went, shivering, trying to find some wood to start a fire, which I finally did. I got some water from the lake, in pitch darkness. I fumbled, stumbled, and nearly crumbled, but finally I had a blazing fire and a teapot going, and Angler No. 1 seemed pleased.

"Actually, I can't sleep because I have a business problem. As you know, I'm in the furniture business and have done very well, but I'm thinking of expanding . . ." *blah . . . blah . . . blah . . .*

And he went on and on with his business plan.

"What do you think?"

Huh!

"You know what I think? First of all, I have had mostly bad luck in business, and I don't have a clue. Second, it's two in the morning. I'm tired and exhausted, and cold and sleepy. So let's go to sleep and discuss it in the morning."

He agreed.

I doused the fire, cleaned the metal tea cups, and looked skyward. Why me? I wondered. I went back into the tent, stretched out on the cold, damp ground, and was about to fall asleep, when Angler No. 1

starts snoring so loud that I couldn't sleep. His snoring actually woke up Ernie in the other nearby tent. I could hear Ernie giggling.

No, he was laughing out loud.

THE VERN GESTLER party of 16, which we booked from one of the Chicago athletic clubs, was a very entertaining group. I was assigned to guide Vern, the leader, and his fishing partner (he would have a different partner each day). As soon as we began fishing, Vern began his chatter: talking to his lure, encouraging imaginary fish.

Lots of chatter.

"Come on Heddon River Runt . . . do your stuff. Swing those hips. You can do it . . . you can do it . . . " Then he would address the invisible pike: "Come on, Mr. *Esox lucius.* Hit that River Runt. You mean, you're going to let that little runt of a lure prance in your territory? You sissy! Hit it. Damn it. Hit that Runt. You're the boss, king of your neighborhood . . . "

On and on with the chatter. Did he think the lure could hear him?

Okay, Vern had a booming voice, that probably travelled long distances under water, but did he think the lure or the pike could understand him?

"I bet you played baseball and you were a catcher when you were young," I said to Vern.

"Yeah, how did you know?"

"Just guessed," I lied. I didn't tell him that I was a catcher in my youth and was quite good at the chatter myself. You know, the "Swing batter! Swing!" stuff. Or "watch out for that high, inside fast ball coming up. . . " But that was baseball, and this was fishing. The contemplative, quiet past-time.

At first it was amusing, but after a few hours of Vern's chatter, it was annoying. No wonder Vern fished with a different partner in his party each day; they probably couldn't take him for more than one.

There was a long lull of several hours without a strike. Or a "follow." Or anything.

"Are you sure there are fish here, Big Story?" Vern asked.

"Of course there are! Why, last week we had some of the best smallmouth bass fishing right here." I wasn't exaggerating.

Vern was not convinced. Then came his challenge. He handed me his rod, "Go ahead. Take some casts . . . show us that there are fish here!"

Yikes!

So I took a cast with his spinning outfit and No. 2 Mepps, and sure enough, a big bass comes barreling out of nowhere, grabs the lure, is hooked and jumps all over the place until I land it. About three pounds, we estimate. Okay, it was probably closer to two pounds.

Vern and his partner were impressed. Very impressed. I was stunned. I was shocked.

"Do that again!" Vern directed.

My mistake was that catching this wonderful bass went to my head. It was obviously a lucky cast. Right then and there, I should have insisted that Vern continue with his fishing.

Guide's Rule #11: *If a client insists you take a cast during a lull, and you happen to hook and land a fish, do not, repeat, DO NOT make another cast. Hand the rod back to the client immediately and insist that he fishes while you pick up the paddle without hesitation."*

After about a couple of dozen casts, we all knew I was just lucky, and Vern took his spinning outfit back.

Spending a full day in the boat fishing with Vern and his chatter was tiresome. I tried to make myself scarce on the island so I wouldn't have to take him out fishing after dinner. No matter where I hid—and there were some good hiding places on the island—he would find me.

"This evening I want Tom Hunter to fish with us," Vern said.

I shook hands with Tom at the dock, helped him into the boat, cranked the Johnson 25 hp and headed for Boiling Point.

They started talking business. Big money. How their businesses could attain a bigger market share if they could find fresh capital. Clearly, these guys were wealthy. Very wealthy. But they needed more money. Many millions, it appeared.

"What do you think of all this, Big Story?" one of them asked me.

"Huh?" I didn't know market share from a marketplace.

They went on and on, the numbers becoming bigger, and suddenly I realized that Vern wasn't interested in fishing this evening. This was some kind of a setup.

That evening I told Ernie and he said he had a similar experience the other day when he was guiding Tom Hunter. "He was talking big business, all the time."

Hmmmm!

After Vern's party left, Ernie and I mentioned this to Jerry, the camp owner.

He burst out laughing. "You mean they fell for it?"

"Fell for what?"

"Hey, when I told them his party would be guided by two Greeks from Chicago, in addition to the Indians guides, they balked. They wanted to know why you Greeks were up here in the first place, guiding instead of running a restaurant, and what did you know about fishing. I needed this party badly. So I told them a little lie."

"What lie?" Ernie demanded.

"I told them that your fathers are brothers and extremely wealthy

Greeks in not only the shipping business, but also in many other global businesses, including in the United States. But you guys didn't want anyone to know about it, for security reasons." Jerry was still laughing.

"I asked them if they heard of Onassis? Of course, they had. I said your dads were wealthier!" Jerry continued. "They probably were hoping that you guys might be good investors."

"We'll get you for this, Tricomi!"

I know we got even with Jerry, but I don't remember how.

PART FOUR

Lifelong commitment?

The Safari Outfitters days;
starting the first international fishing travel agency;
Costa Rica's fantastic angling and the tarpon scales episode;
Norway's sometimes great salmon fishing
(but oh, the frustrations);
the perfect put down; and the eventual "break up."

The Safari Outfitters days:

the golden years of international fishing

I WAS ALWAYS INTRIGUED by the little where-to-go ads in *Field and Stream, Sports Afield* and *Outdoor Life.* The Safari Outfitters' ad especially grabbed my attention. The company was located at 8 S. Michigan Avenue, Chicago, just around the corner from Cahners Publishing Company, where I now worked as an associate editor for *Brick and Clay Record* and *Ceramic Industry.* Working on these magazines was fun—well, I made it fun—but, again, I wanted to get back into fishing. So one day, I went to Safari Outfitters on my lunch break.

He was sitting behind a desk, his tie pulled up tightly against the heavily starched shirt collar. He was wearing a suit coat, very formal. I expected him to be wearing a safari jacket or something more casual. He was a man in his late 50s or early 60s, but seemed older, and peered suspiciously at me through horn-rimmed glasses.

He did not look like an outdoorsman, certainly not like a big-game hunter. I guess I anticipated a professional hunter type, like Clark Gable in *Mogambo* or a Stewart Granger in other safari-based movies.

The office seemed small, because the walls were literally covered with exotic animal mounts, presumably collected from his various hunts throughout the world. No matter where you stood or sat, it appeared that all 40 or 50 animal heads were staring at you at once. Weird. The office was church quiet except for the *clickety-clack-click* of typewriters as two or three women worked diligently at their desks.

"Are you the owner of Safari Outfitters?" I inquired.

"I am Roman H. Hupalowski. I am president of Safari Outfitters, ***Incorporated*** and also president of Safari-Shikar Tours and Travel," he proclaimed very stiffly but with obvious pride. The emphasis was certainly on the ***Incorporated***. He spoke with an accent, continued to look at me warily as though I was a spy for someone, and only after I extended my hand did he seem to relax. Not much, but a little.

I told him that I was interested in fishing in Yugoslavia and had noticed his ads featuring exotic hunts all over the world.

"Perhaps you have some fishing arrangements in Yugoslavia?"

"We don't offer fishing. I am a hunter. But last week someone from the Yugoslavian Tourist Office came to our office. A Mr. Stojan Pudar, I think that was his name. He wants to attract fishermen to his country. He left some material with me," Roman explained and then he buzzed Mrs. Stollenwork, to bring the information to us.

I told him that Bob Kukulski, a good fishing friend, would be going with me, and that we were also interested in fishing in Ireland for salmon and trout on the same trip. I provided him with our vacation dates, and Roman said he would have all details the following week.

True to his word, we met for lunch at the Pittsfield Building a week later. He was very officious. He had a neatly typed itinerary, and even an invoice and passport information plus general fishing brochures on Yugoslavia and Ireland. Heck, I was just making a casual inquiry and he had me already booked.

106

"I have good news!" He said. "I spoke to Mr. Stojan Pudar at the Yugoslavian Tourist Office and they agreed to host you! The fishing arrangements, hotel, meals and transfers will be free!"

Hey, this Roman guy is all right, I thought.

The Irish fishing package would cost us some money but it was also a bargain. Our biggest expense was the air fare.

Bob and I found Yugoslavia to be a fascinating country. We were headquartered in picturesque Mostar, an enchanting city with its minarets reflecting the Muslim influence during the time Turkey occupied Yugoslavia and other countries during its 400-year rule. We fished a half-dozen rivers and in addition to browns and some rainbows we caught five other species of salmonids that we simply could not identify; our hosts called them *zubatec* and *mekousna* trout and other unusual names. We landed some fish that looked like char, and another species that resembled a combination of grayling, char and trout. The Yugoslavian landscape was incredible, among the most beautiful I have ever seen anywhere in the world. That was in the early '60s; unfortunately, the recent wars that have ripped this country apart.

We then flew to the west coast of Ireland and stayed at the marvelous Dromoland Castle, the Breaffy House and several inns in County Kerry. We enjoyed the trout fishing but didn't have any success with salmon. It was not the best time for this species. Although we discovered many rolling salmon in a stream near Dromoland, we simply couldn't interest them.

When we returned to Chicago I called Roman and we had lunch again, and I gave him the trip results. He listened carefully and nodded often, but clearly he had something on his mind.

"I've been thinking, Jim. Perhaps you would like to join Safari Outfitters **Incorporated** as a fishing consultant? If you are interested, you could work part-time . . . and you could develop fishing programs all over the world. Of course, you would have travel privileges."

Wow! What an opportunity. I accepted.

Safari Outfitters, Inc. was really a travel agency that concentrated 100 percent on international hunting arrangements. Safari-Shikar Tours and Travel was involved in handling the air travel and hotel arrangements. Roman was proud that he had not one, but two companies.

I asked him how he got started in the business. Roman had always been interested in hunting in his native Poland. He became a federal judge and ruled heavily against the communists before and during the beginning of World War II.

"The Russians were after me because I was tough on communists. I escaped and decided to go to our family hunting hut in the south, because I thought I would be safe there. I walked for days to reach our lodge in southern Poland, and I remember I was sucking on a wooden spoon for mental nourishment. I was hungry but just kept walking. All I could think about was reaching the lodge where we had food in tins hidden under the floor. That's all I could think about. The food at the lodge. I hadn't eaten a good meal for days.

"I was within a few hundred yards of the camp when the Russians caught me. I was sent to a Siberian labor camp near the Pechora River. I was very sick most of the time. Many prisoners didn't survive and died at the camp. I was a prisoner until the end of the war, when I was finally released. I returned to Poland, which was under Russia's control, left there and escaped to America!" His voice cracked with emotion.

"And you went into the safari travel business?"

"Oh, no! No!" He chuckled nervously, as he allowed himself to think of the past. I could see moisture in his eyes. "I had no money. I didn't know the language," he responded. "I worked as a valet at the Sherman House hotel, studied English and then went into business with a travel agent. It didn't work out with him. We parted. We are enemies."

Later, I found out that he was in business with Ernest Prossnitz, Special Tours and Travel, who had an office across the street but later moved into Roman's building. They never spoke to each other. They remained bitter enemies until the end. There was at least $60,000 held in escrow for years, pending a court ruling. I believe the judge decided that it should be split equally. Both parties lost great sums of money due to substantial attorney fees, but each claimed a "fantastic victory."

I DIDN'T GIVE UP my day job at Cahners; I worked at Safari Outfitters in the evenings and on weekends. I had a key to the office, my own desk and typewriter. Roman was helpful in explaining the travel business basics and office procedures, but left the rest up to me. We decided that the future was in international fishing—outside of the contiguous United States—because most fishermen could make their own arrangements at U.S. fishing lodges. Where to start?

There was no such thing as a fishing travel agency in those days. E. L. "Buck" Rogers attempted to start one in the early 1950s, but was not successful. He was well ahead of his time. Few anglers were interested in traveling to other countries, and, of course, jet-plane service was not offered until the end of the decade. It took some time after that for some countries to build airports that could handle jets. I went into the fishing travel business at the right time, just as jet travel was flourishing in many parts of the world.

Still, there were problems. A major one was that, except for Canada, there weren't many fishing camps outside of the United States. There were the resort hotels along Baja California that offered fishing and a few "pure" fishing lodges such as Panama's Club de Pesca (later renamed Tropic Star Lodge), Andy Growich's El Tarpon Tropical in Mexico, Barothy's new setup in Belize and four or five camps in Alaska.

The anglers who fished exotic places such as New Zealand, Peru, Chile and elsewhere were generally extremely wealthy. Some of the billfishermen sent their cruisers and crews in advance to such places as Cabo Blanco, Peru (where 1,000-pound marlin were being caught), Iquique, Chile (for world record swordfish) and other far-off places.

The angling press seldom printed articles on foreign places so it would also be necessary to create the demand.

Prepayment of fishing trips was also a problem. Whereas the hunters had accepted the general business policy of a substantial deposit at the time of booking, and the balance of the trip paid before the trip commenced, fishermen balked at this idea.

"Hey, when I go to Canada we pay a $50 to $100 deposit per man and pay the balance at the camp at the completion of the trip. Why should I pay you 25 percent deposit and pay for the trip before I go? What if the lodge burns down? " These were typical, logical complaints.

The general travel industry had embraced prepayment. If you bought a cruise or an American Express package trip, or an airline's tour to Europe, you prepaid the trip well in advance.

One of the main reasons why many of the foreign fishing camps adopted the prepaid policy was that the customers' checks took weeks to clear. Another reason was that occasionally, a client who may have been dissatisfied with an international fishing trip would stop payment on his check when he returned to the United States.

Another barrier for booking international fishing trips was the perceived language problem, not in Belize (because it is an English-speaking country), but certainly in Mexico, Panama and other Latin American places.

I quickly found out that selling international fishing trips was not without obstacles.

First customer!

I WAS IN CONTACT with Emmett Gowen, an outdoor writer, who decided to offer fishing arrangements in Belize (then called British Honduras) and was looking for customers. I had not been to Belize at that time and knew very little about Emmett, although I had read some of his articles in fishing magazines. I knew he had a modest live-aboard boat and camped out much of the time. I placed small ads in *Salt Water Sportsman* and other publications, and very shortly I received an inquiry from an E. K. Bohner from New York. He explained that he was "up in years but wanted to experience a tropical fishing trip."

My first customer!

After the trip, I received a message from Gowen, the outfitter.

"I think E. K. enjoyed the trip, but I have to warn you we had some problems. While I was preparing camp on shore, he fell off the boat head first into the muck. Good thing I happened to return to the boat and saw his legs flopping in the water. I was able to pull him out but he nearly drowned. Then I took him on land, and told him to sit down and relax under the shade of a tree while I attended to cleaning fish and preparing lunch, but he saw a big snake and was so alarmed that he took off and got lost. Good thing I was able to follow his footsteps. A few other things like that happened. Anyway, he was a good sport, very nice man, he caught some fish and I think he was happy he made the trip."

Welcome to the fishing travel biz, Chrapalis! Life in the trenches!

"You must call Mr. Bohner right away," Roman said after I showed him the cable, "and get a recommendation. See if you can use him for a reference."

Recommendation? Reference? Good grief! I was hoping that we wouldn't be sued! (Later, I learned that one of Roman's potent selling techniques was to obtain written references. When he responded to potential clients, he would include copies of several reference letters. He had developed a superb collection of reference letters.)

So I called Mr. Bohner (we always referred to our clients as "Mister," "Miss" or "Missus," never, never by their first names) and he told me that he enjoyed the trip, but that perhaps he was a little too old for this type of adventure. I think he was 80 years old. Maybe older.

" I saw a new lodge built on the Belize River. Very comfortable. Deluxe, really. It's called Barothy's. You ought to investigate this for customers who need more conveniences," Mr. Bohner offered.

In the meantime, I don't know what happened to Emmett Gowen. I think he left Belize soon thereafter, so I contacted Vic Barothy in Belize and soon we had a solid fishing resort to offer future prospects.

"Come on down," Vic suggested. "We've got something special to show you."

Vic Barothy was famous for his houseboat fishing trips out of Isle of Pines, Cuba. When Fidel Castro took over Cuba in 1959, Vic and Betty, his wife, loaded two of the cruisers with whatever valuable possessions they could and sailed at night for British Honduras (Belize).

I flew TAN airlines to Belize City. One of the things that I found puzzling in those days was the fact that a stewardess ("flight attendant" today) would walk up the aisle spraying the cabin with some kind of a disinfectant from an aerosol can. I only saw this done on flights between the United States and Latin America. *Hmmm!*

When I arrived in Belize, Vic showed me his marvelous, modern main lodge on the Belize River. It was very impressive. I was transferred to one of his houseboats.

"I want you to see Turneffe Island Lodge! It's brand new and I think you'll like it. You can fish the main lodge when you return."

On our way to TIL, the cook baked bread and prepared lunch over a very modest stove in a tiny galley. Man, that was some lunch! The homemade bread was delicious! I tried to imagine what that cook could do with a proper stove, modern cooking utensils and a complete supply of food ingredients.

Turneffe Island Lodge was a very attractive, remote lodge, strategically located to take advantage of the nearby bonefish flats, but convenient to the cuts and deeper flats that harbored tarpon mostly in the 15- to 60-pound class.

It was a wonderful trip: lots of action. I hooked and caught many tarpon, bones and snapper, and I felt honored in being among the first guests at Turneffe Island Lodge. More importantly, I had a solid fishing camp to offer future clients.

A few months later, friend Bob Kukulski and I fished Andy Growich's El Tarpon Tropical, located in the province of Campeche, Mexico. By the time we left, Andy and I had struck up a solid friendship and a very good business agreement. The Fishing Division now had exclusive booking arrangements with El Tarpon Tropical. All reservations, whether from individuals or through other travel agencies, would have to be funneled through Safari Outfitters (we'd retain a commission, and remit the balance to the camps). I thought Roman would like this negotiated arrangement and he did.

I was booking some camps in Canada including Camp Manitou in Ontario (where I had guided one season), and business was picking up in Belize and Mexico, but by no means did we need a Brinks armored truck to bank our deposits.

Roman came into my office. "Jim, you must make your own decision, of course, but I think for the Fishing Division and you to succeed you need to work here full time. It will be tough at first, financially, but you are a hard worker."

I enjoyed my work at Safari Outfitters, because, in effect, I was exploring and popularizing new fishing places for future guests. Because of the "free" fishing trips and often complimentary airline tickets, I was able to fish places that previously I could only afford in my dreams.

"Risks are always necessary for success," Roman explained.

To illustrate his point, he told me that when he and Ernest Prossnitz split, Roman started Safari Outfitters with only enough money for about two months' rent, Mrs. Stollenwork's salary, some ads and incidentals. Hedwig, his wife, worked elsewhere but her salary was minimal.

"Weren't you afraid that Safari Outfitters would fail?" I asked Roman.

"Of course not! I knew hunting and how to serve customers. There was never any doubt in my mind!" He was confident, all right.

The Hunting Division was growing quickly and Roman was booking very expensive hunting safaris on a regular basis. If Roman could do it, why couldn't I?

I agreed to work full time. Roman's attorney drew up a contract. It seemed fair and was really a continuation of our original agreement. Profits from the Fishing Division, less some expenses, such as secretarial, ads, phone and other items, would be divided 50-50.

I gave my notice at Cahners Publishing Company and soon I worked full time at Safari Outfitters. At first, I thought I would go crazy with the office silence. Everyone worked and spoke to others in low, almost whispered, tones. No noise except when the phone rang and the *clickety-clack-click* of typewriters. At Cahners there had always been some action. There were a couple of hundred employees including some very good-looking talent, and I was single at the time. Furthermore, there was the fabulous, creative art department. Toe Nojiri and Francis

Kaihatsu, Claude Zajakowski, Al Trungale and others. There was always something going on. Bets on the football games. Contests as to who had the better legs among the males (I tied with Claude). Whatever. I was never bored. Despite all the "activities," our publications won design and editorial awards.

Eventually I became accustomed to the strictly work atmosphere at Safari Outfitters, and, besides, I had a Herculean task ahead of me. Clearly, I was not going to make much money for the first couple of years, so I would have to dig into my savings. I made only $2,450 during the first year and $3,500 the next year, and my reserves were melting away.

Luckily, some good breaks fell my way. I maintained very good relations with Cahners Publishing Company. One of the publishers was interested in running a ceramic trip to Japan and a brick-building trip to Russia. Would I be interested in handling these types of trips? Of course I would! Never mind that I knew nothing about group trips. I had to submit bids and I won.

I went to Percival Tours, a very professional wholesaler, experts in general group trips, and entrusted all the hotels, transfers and meal arrangements to them. I would give them part of my commission, which was fine with me. My responsibility was the airlines and all arrangements for visits to Japanese and European factories.

The problem was that some of the Japanese factories would not respond to my urgent cables as to whether they would accept the *Ceramic Industry* magazine group (which totaled close to 50 people). Not much time was left. Anxiety and panic were my constant companions now. I went to the Art Department and spoke to Francis Kaihatsu, who was very familiar with the Japanese customs.

"Here's what I advise. They have a lot of pride over there. I know the culture. Send a cable to the ones who haven't answered and thank them for their reply, even though they never did, and inform them that the group will arrive on such and such a date. Send your groups anyway. They won't be turned down. I think it will work." He seemed confident.

I had my doubts, but I was desperate. I tried it. It worked. The *Ce-*

ramic Industry magazine tour was a huge success, and our group was well received everywhere. Thank you, Francis! The publisher was pleased, and the Fishing Division made a very good profit.

The other tour, a brick-building trip through Europe and Russia, was to be deluxe all the way. Nothing was spared. For Paris, I asked Percival Tours to obtain the Ritz Hotel for the group of 60. In my tour brochure, I praised the Ritz as the world's best hotel. But our request was turned down. The Ritz Hotel did not accept groups. Buses pulling up, lots of luggage, confusion and a lobby full of people was not the Ritz style. Bernard Gordon, president of Cahners in Chicago, was upset with me. Rightfully so.

"Here you promise the Ritz, and you can't deliver!" He was angry.

"I will get the Ritz!" I answered, but I'm sure the tone of my voice was not very confident.

I cabled Charles Ritz, whom I knew from my Army days in France via casting tournaments and other fishing programs. I begged for the favor.

He came through. He instructed his people to accept the group. However, the buses would have to park a couple of blocks away and two-by-two the group would check in at the front desk. The Ritz Hotel would arrange for cabs. It worked.

The group enjoyed the trip, except for one disaster: One of the older members died of a heart attack in Germany. I quickly informed his family, and worked with Pan Am Airways to have the body and casket shipped to his home town near Atlanta. However, in the process Pan Am "lost" the casket. Well, not really; it was sent to South America by mistake. I'm sure my ensuing phone calls with Pan Am sounded like one of Bob Newhart's hilarious, imaginary phone conversations that he did on TV.

I don't think the body arrived in time for the scheduled wake, so the family used an empty closed casket instead.

The Costa Rican breakthrough

THESE TWO nonfishing trips bolstered the Fishing Division's bottom line. It helped line Roman's pockets, too. We moved to bigger, somewhat more luxurious offices. While I was delighted with making more money, it was mostly from the Cahners' tour business, not the fishing programs, although they were growing slowly. But I wanted to be in fishing exclusively, not in the general tour business.

How could I generate more fishing business? I got another break.

The man was tall, stately, distinguished and obviously well educated. He looked like Walter Pidgeon, the actor. He came to our office with his wife, Ruth. His name was Donald Dobbins and he was a partner in a prestigious law firm downstate. He insisted from the outset that I call them by their first names.

"Ruth and I would like to go to Parismina," Don said.

"Certainly. When would you like to go?"

I had absolutely no idea where Parismina was.

"I think March . . . that's a good month, I hear. What do you think?"

"Oh, March is an excellent month. One of the best."

Again, I had no idea if this was true. I told the Dobbins that I would find out the details and get back to them.

Today, one could go on the Internet, type **"Parismina"** in Yahoo or any other search engine and in minutes you could retrieve more information than you need.

Not in those days. Lots of research and library time were required. I finally found a reference to Parismina in one of the exotic travel books. I discovered that Parismina was in Costa Rica! I felt very accomplished. Now what?

In another travel book, maybe it was *Fodor's,* there was a cable address for Carlos Barrantes, the owner of Parismina Tarpon Rancho.

I cabled Carlos with my questions. He replied quickly.

"The weekly rate is $420 per person. We fly the guests to camp in and out early in the morning because that's when the weather is better. Yes, March is our best month. Perhaps avoid the full moon. The best lures are the Deep Diver and Sea Hawk for tarpon, and yellow Darters for snook. Can accommodate them any time . . . warn them that accommodations are not luxurious. Deposit $100 . . . Ten percent commission . . . Carlos."

I called Don and gave him the information.

He booked immediately. Ruth and Don went to Parismina and had a fantastic time. Don called when he returned.

"Parismina Tarpon Rancho is a converted school house. There are cows running around the front yard, so you have to be careful where you step. It's not a very comfortable camp. The guides don't know how to change a spark plug, but Costa Rica is going to be *the* place for tarpon and snook fishing. Lots of fish. By the way, you had no idea where Parismina was when we first came in. Right?"

I confessed.

I trusted what Don said. I decided to vigorously promote Costa Rica. Carlos Barrantes, who was very knowledgeable, invited many of the topnotch writers and communicators to fish Parismina. Erwin Bauer, Tom McNally, Dick Kotis, Hal Lyman, Frank Woolner, Stu Apte, Tom Paugh, Al McClane, Bill Cullerton and Lamar Underwood. Lots of guys.

He also invited me.

In those days I traveled in a suit and tie, because the travel world was more formal than it is today. "We must always look neat and prosperous," the always formally attired Roman used to say. Having a little extra money, I purchased a suit from Capper and Capper.

Carlos met me at the San Jose airport and transferred me to Parismina in a small Cessna. During the next couple of days I hooked fish just about everywhere. Big tarpon. Snook. Mackerel. Lots of action. With fly. Spinning. Plug casting. Trolling. I wasn't landing many tarpon, but I was certainly hooking them.

Carlos flew into camp, unannounced.

"Pack up immediately! You're leaving Parismina!" he ordered.

"Huh?"

"We're going elsewhere, but we must hurry!"

So I packed as fast as I could and merely took my Capper and Capper suit as it was, on a hanger.

"We'll take two boats in case of a breakdown," Carlos said. His guides gassed up the engines and were all set to go.

The skiffs were Costa Rican copies of the famous 14-foot Boston Whalers. While they looked identical, they were very heavy and sluggish.

"Where are we going?" I thought it was okay for me to ask at this point.

"We're going to Colorado, but we gotta leave quickly before it gets too dark. It will probably be rough. Hang on. I'll explain when we get there."

Colorado? We were in Costa Rica and Colorado was in the United States. I didn't understand.

First Carlos' boat headed out into the Caribbean to test the waters, so to speak, and when Carlos gave the "thumbs up" sign, my guide headed our skiff through the precarious river mouth, slowly and very cautiously at first. There were huge rollers and Carlos' boat would disappear for a long time, when it was at the trough of the big waves, but then it would emerge again. I looked for a life preserver, but the guide told me not to bother.

"*Grande tiburon aqui*," I interpret this as "don't worry about the life preservers if we go overboard," because the huge sharks would get us anyway. I understood perfectly. Just the day before, I had hooked a big tarpon and as it came down from one of its spectacular leaps, a monstrous shark was waiting for it on the surface with its menacing, teeth-lined jaws wide open. *Crunch!*

These were huge waves, I'll tell you. But once we traveled a few hundred yards beyond the river mouth, we didn't have the huge rollers, just short choppers, you know, the kind that sends repeated shock waves through one's spine. At first, I was trying to keep my Capper and Capper suit dry as the guide did his best to dodge the big waves, but this was hopeless, and besides I had to use both hands at times to hold on to the boat seat. I placed my suit on a duffle bag, but soon it fell off, and there it was on the bottom of the boat, soaking up salt water, fuel and fish slime. I wish I had packed it in my duffle bag instead of holding it on a hanger, so that it wouldn't wrinkle.

It was a long trip, maybe three hours, because of the choppy sea. I was soaking wet. My bags were wet. Everything was soaking wet with salt water. Now, my spirits were getting wet. Why did we leave Parismina, where the fishing was so heavenly, so incredible, and where were we going?

The skiff was taking such a pounding that my wooden seat broke. So much for these Boston Whalers knockouts. I sat on my duffle.

But eventually we arrived at the mouth of a big river.

"*Rio Colorado aqui*," the guide pointed to the mouth. Now it dawned on me. There was a river called "Colorado" in Costa Rica.

We pulled up to a village. Probably to get fuel, I concluded. Barefooted kids of various sizes and ages, all with big, bright eyes and huge smiles, ran to our boats to greet us. Carlos ordered the bigger kids to take our luggage up to the village.

Okay, the rooms were dingy and small, but they were dry. So what if there was no glass in the windows? We had survived an angry Caribbean. There were two small beds, not at all designed to accommodate my 6'2" frame. An older boy brought in some mosquito netting, placed it on the small table, and said something to Carlos about the "gringo." I thanked him by nodding. This was the village's best place, according to Carlos.

"Actually, there are few or no mosquitoes here, but there are spiders and scorpions and tarantulas, so use the netting," he said, laughing. I didn't know if he was kidding or not. I didn't ask. I'd use the net.

Our dinner of boiled fish, rice and refried beans was actually quite tasty. Now dry and relaxed, Carlos told me that Don Dobbins had been in touch with him and the two of them were going to build a new, modern lodge on Rio Colorado. Don and Carlos wanted me to see the area, test the fishing, and check out the piece of jungle that was being cleared for the lodge.

"We will move very fast on this, and you might be the exclusive agent," Carlos told me.

Wow!

"I'll drink to that!" And we did. I think it was beer. At least, it tasted like beer.

The fishing was superb. Tarpon were all over at Samay Lagoon. Fishing from two different boats, Carlos and I hooked dozens of tarpon and after a jump or two or three, we were thankful if the tarpon threw the lure rather than fight the fish for a long, long time. It was that kind of fishing. You could see long, silver flashes, even in the discolored waters, as hordes of 50- to 80-pound tarpon migrated through the river mouth from the Caribbean. There were lots of snook, too. Big snook. Giant snook.

On the final morning, Carlos told me to pack up everything because after fishing we would not return to the village. Instead we would go to an air strip where he had arranged for a Cessna to take us back to San

Jose. I had soaked my precious Capper and Capper suit in a tub of fresh water in the village and brought it into the boat so that it would dry in the sun. Carlos shook his head when I brought the suit on a hanger into the boat, while the guide found this so amusing that he allowed his wide smile to transform into downright laughter.

I hooked a very feisty tarpon and when we finally hoisted him onboard to take a picture, it thrashed violently, slipped off the lip gaff, landed on my suit, and promptly deposited about a gallon of milt. I gave the suit to the guide, who wasn't exactly sure of what to do with it. Anyway, the suit had shrunk a couple of sizes from all the water anyway.

Maybe I could return it to Capper and Capper for a refund? Naw.

When I returned to the office, I described the entire trip to Roman and his eyes lit up.

"Ahh, Costa Rica is the place you must promote in a big way. The future is there. Mexico and British Honduras [Belize], too. But Costa Rica is the main place for you."

And promote it we did.

The fish scale episode

CARLOS BARRANTES was overseeing the construction of the new lodge, which consisted of four modern duplex cottages with showers, modern plumbing and other conveniences. The main lodge hosted the dining room, sitting room, kitchen and tackle room.

Don Dobbins christened it Casa Mar Fishing Lodge. Now, "Casa Mar" or "sea house" wasn't an accurate name, because first of all it wasn't built on the sea; it was built "inside," next to a freshwater lagoon in the midst of a jungle. But Don had a houseboat named *Casa Mar.* He and his wife, Ruth, had planned on sailing it to Texas and then along the Latin American coast, fishing whenever and wherever they pleased. Unfortunately the new houseboat had taken in water and sank en route; they made it to shore, but the boat was a total loss.

"It seemed like such a good name that we decided to call the new camp Casa Mar," Don explained later. Incidentally, he financed Casa Mar without first seeing it.

Meanwhile, I was to book Casa Mar for the coming season. The camp would be ready in January. I ran some ads in *Salt Water Sportsman,* and I printed an inexpensive folder. Good friend Al Trungale designed a wonderful logo for Casa Mar. But how could I quickly attract attention to the lodge?

The proverbial light bulb flashed above my head. I asked Carlos to have one of his guides at the Parismina village pull out the scales from several big tarpon and send me several thousand scales as soon as possible. The locals often caught tarpon for food, so nothing would be wasted.

The plan was to send one big scale with a pitch letter praising Casa Mar to everyone on our prospect list. Our message was, *"This marvelous, brand new, modern fishing lodge, amidst the best tarpon fishing, will be available to a few lucky anglers who book immediately . . . blah, blah, blah. . ."*

Well, the scales came and they were impressive, two to three inches in diameter, but they were dirty, sandy and muddy. They smelled, too. I wanted bright, white, shiny clean scales. What to do? Janice, my secretary, suggested that I put them through a washing machine. I was a bachelor then, and I had no idea how to operate a washing machine. I used a laundry service for my clothes.

But there was a laundromat in my neighborhood. Janice told me how to operate the machines.

"And then you put the scales in a dryer . . . " she continued. "Oh, another thing. Go late at night when the place should be deserted. There aren't many people who wash fish scales at laundromats."

I went to the laundromat very late at night with my huge box of scales. There was no one else there. Good. I placed the scales in the washer, followed Janice's explicit instructions and watched the scales tumble, rumble and grumble inside while the cascading, frothy suds did their thing. Kinda fascinating stuff, I thought.

The washing machine went through whatever cycles Janice predicted and finally came to a stop. I reached inside for the soggy scales and began to place them in the big box to transfer them over to the dryer machine. It was almost midnight.

Just then an older woman entered with a big bundle of laundry. She greeted me only with a nod, and then watched me warily as I placed the wet, soggy scales in the box.

She seemed startled. No, alarmed! "Why are you washing *potato chips*?"

"These are **not** potato chips," I was indignant. Why would anyone on earth wash potato chips? "Lady, these are fish scales!" I said proudly as I transferred another handful of the giant, soggy scales. Hmm. They did look like wet white potato chips, I thought.

"You're washing fish scales? What for?" she demanded. "Aren't they very big for fish scales? And what happened to the fish?"

She certainly was inquisitive.

Before I could explain, she picked up her bundle of laundry, turned around and huffed and puffed out of the laundromat. Hey, I can't really blame her. There are lots of nutty people in Chicago. Then and now.

Fearing that she might call the police, I skipped the drying machine cycle, and hurriedly took the soggy fish scales home. I spread them all over my apartment to dry, and just about every square inch of my floors was covered with a tarpon fish scale. They dried to some extent, but not totally.

I brought them to the office and Janice and I agreed that they were dry enough to begin mailing. The scales were still moist but were quite flat.

"Let's put a scale, the Costa Rican brochure, and the pitch letter into each envelope and mail them," I suggested to Janice. Roman seemed amused by this promotion. We stuffed, addressed and stamped two thousand envelopes, which I took to the main post office on Van Buren street.

Two days later a post-office inspector came to our office, flashed an official-looking badge and gave me a warning letter that stated I had violated a post office rule and then sternly told me that this must never happen again. Apparently the main office began distributing our envelopes to other post offices around the country, but when the scales continued to dry further, they began to pop and hop in their envelopes like Mexican jumping beans, according to the inspector, and post offices around the country complained. I wanted to laugh, but he did not look amused. He took his job seriously. Very seriously.

I know that the mail was delivered, because soon we received phone calls from around the country. Now I had to convert these calls into bookings.

"Say, I received your mailing with the tarpon scale. You know, this sounds like a good place, but I don't know if our party wants to go to Costa Rica, wherever that is . . . " was a typical call.

My response?

"Wait a second . . . before we go much further. Are you talking about *this* coming season, or the following year?"

"Why this season, of course!"

"Okay, let me see what I can do. How many people are in your party and when do you want to go?" I would ask.

"Usually we have four to six."

"Can you keep it to four and maybe I can book you the third week of February? We can waitlist the other two in your group. There seems to be an opening then because a party hasn't confirmed. We don't have much room left."

Of course, we had plenty of room left; February, and some other months, probably didn't have a single booking.

The caller was astounded, "But I just received your letter! How can you be booked so fast!"

"I know, I know, but some people received letters yesterday and the day before and our phones have been ringing all morning."

"Okay, pencil us in that space, and I'll let you know next week."

"Can you let us know *by Friday*? I can only keep the space for three days."

"Okay, okay!"

And that's how I started selling Casa Mar. The camp was sold out almost completely during the first season. If I was *strong sell* in those days, which I guess I was, I became very soft sell in later years. I had all the confidence in the world that Casa Mar was an outstanding place, and I didn't feel guilty about using this and other similar ploys. Well, maybe a little guilty, but I did it anyway.

When Casa Mar was fully booked, I starting selling the open weeks at Parismina. Soon I was booking both camps and our reputation as a fishing travel agency soared. *The American Sportsman* television series and many national outdoor magazines featured Costa Rican fishing.

The tarpon were mostly cooperative. In those days, hooked Costa Rican tarpon had a bad habit of jumping into the boat early in the fight, much to the astonishment of the anglers and consternation of the guides. It's a chaotic event when a fresh, 80-pound tarpon jumps into the boat and thrashes wildly. Rods, cameras, tackle boxes—just about anything— may go overboard. There's not much you can do about it but stay out of the tarpon's way until it has thrashed itself into submission. During a season, 20 to 30 tarpon would leap into the boats.

Sports Afield editors Lamar Underwood and Tom Paugh were skeptical of these reports when they arrived at Parismina Tarpon Rancho. Naturally, I was anxious to hear of their results at the completion of the trip, so I contacted Carlos Barrantes.

"Well, they had an accident. They were fishing in two boats and Tom hooked a powerful tarpon and it leaped into Lamar's boat. It broke Lamar's leg and bruised his ribs, but he is okay. His leg was placed in a cast and his ribs were bandaged in San Jose, and we got him a pair of crutches. He'll be all right. I think they liked the trip."

They wrote a humorous editorial about that flying-tarpon incident in *Sports Afield*. Carlos' camps were receiving more publicity than any other fishing lodges in the world! We were building a solid future for the Costa Rican fishing camps.

And for Safari Outfitters' Fishing Division.

I continued fishing more and more places around the world, and for years I visited a new place every month or so: I went to Argentina for trout (before the "crowds" started going there), New Zealand, Norway, Panama, Paraguay, Angola, Mozambique, just about every place where there was a hint of good fishing and a promise that our future clients would enjoy it and be well treated.

We were able to negotiate exclusive agreements with just about any fishing outfitters we wanted. Roman was encouraging all the way. I learned a lot from him. His hunting business was also booming, and he had a number of exclusive contracts with topnotch outfitters and professional hunters.

We attracted a lot of attention. Even the *Wall Street Journal* featured us on its front page. Pan American Airways, a giant at the time, was willing to sponsor expensive travel brochures for us, one for hunting and one for our fishing destinations.

I developed a fairly attractive 24-page brochure on fishing. There was one empty page: What to put on it? I thought about it for a while, before the light bulb flashed above my head.

The idea? I would create the most deluxe, most expensive fishing trip for that page. I assembled a 20-week international fishing trip that encompassed all the great places . . . fishing from castles in Ireland, the Alta River in Norway, Takaro Lodge in New Zealand, trout fishing in Yugoslavia, marlin fishing in Mozambique. On and on. I think the trip was priced at $33,000 (probably it would cost well over $100,000 today). In those days, you had to include the air fare in various classes in airline-sponsored brochures. For snob-appeal, I only offered this trip in *first class only*. After all, it was the world's most deluxe fishing trip, wasn't it?

I didn't have time to figure out the exact costs and whether it was humanly possible to do this trip as the completed brochure was long due to the printers.

Roman liked the idea of the world's most exclusive fishing trip. "Did you price it out?"

"Naw . . . I think it will be okay but it would take weeks to get all the new rates, transfer costs, etc. Look, Roman, no one is going to buy this trip, but we will get a lot of publicity from this."

He agreed and we laughed and laughed. Laughing in the hallowed halls of Safari Outfitters was not common. Like drinking a special wine to celebrate a special occasion, it was done very sparingly. This was a very special occasion.

The brochure came out. I sent it out with a news release to many publications. A few writers announced our fishing brochure in their columns, and then the fun began. *Playboy* magazine wrote about our deluxe trip. Red Smith—probably the most famous syndicated sports columnist at the time—devoted an entire column to our deluxe fishing trip. His column appeared in hundreds of newspapers. *Sports Illustrated* also described the trip.

One day, I received a call for the deluxe trip. I gulped.

"When do you want to go?" I said. Nervously.

"As soon as you can arrange it!" That voice sounded disguised. Someone was putting me on. It must be Frank Zachary. Or Jim Richardson. Two friends who would pull a prank. Or Elmer Bergendahl!

Assuming it was one of my friends, I said that the trip was "pretty much sold out."

"I can see that it would be!" The disappointed voice at the other end said.

"Are you on the level?" I asked. "This isn't Frank? Jim? Or Bergendahl pulling my leg?"

"Of course not! Look if you want . . . what's your bank and I'll have a deposit transferred to your account!"

Yikes! He was legitimate. He gave me his name, address and phone number. I said I would call him back as soon as I could arrange it.

I walked out of the office, went in the alley, and I lost my lunch out of excitement.

I never expected anyone to buy the deluxe trip.

Unfortunately, we weren't able to provide this tour because Norway's Alta River and several other fishing places were fully booked during the specific weeks we requested. However, I arranged a "miniature deluxe trip" that took him fishing through Central America, the Bahamas and Argentina.

The client told me that his wife had died recently, and he thought that an extended fishing trip would ease his depression.

One thing was obvious: the Fishing Division of Safari Outfitters was growing and was like a powerful train increasing its speed.

And many passengers were climbing on board!

Angola's outdoor beer parlor

NOT ALL EXPLORATORY FISHING TRIPS are successful. Many are disasters. Complete disasters. This is especially true when one prospects new fishing grounds where there is little, if any, background or angling history. What attracted me to Angola, Africa, in the first place was a photo of a man standing next to an enormous tarpon. The fish weighed 267 pounds and it dwarfed the angler.

I had to go there!

It was difficult to find accurate information about the best fishing areas and seasons. The Angola's Government Tourist Department wanted to attract anglers to bolster the country's economy and provided me with whatever data it could obtain and even handled all my reservations for me. Since I had planned to fish Mozambique, Africa for its huge black marlin, we just added the Angola portion to my trip.

I flew to Lisbon, Portugal and then to Luanda, the capital of Angola. It was a peaceful, quiet town in those days (October, 1970), and no one would have ever suspected the turmoil and civil war that would eventually rip this country apart.

A car and driver, arranged by the Angola's tourist department, brought me to a tiny village near the Cuanza river. Immediately, kids flocked to the car. They all took turns looking at themselves in the car side mirror. It was obvious that not many cars visited this area; probably only a few supply trucks negotiated the dusty, rocky road.

The accommodations were quite Spartan but livable. What was disconcerting was the huge number of fish fillets that were placed on the roof to dry in the hot sun. The rancid smell was so strong that I decided to close the two windows in my room to escape the odor. This would have been fine except that I'm sure the temperature inside my room was more than 100 degrees.

Joae, a wiry man in his late 20s, was my guide. He lived in a very primitive village up a river, and he knew more about tarpon than anyone else. So I was told. Supplied with a skiff and an old Johnson outboard motor, he was assigned to find tarpon for me and to help develop a long-term sportfishing resource.

He spoke Portuguese, Angola's official language, and a regional dialect, but not one word of English. Somehow we overcame our communication problems, and almost immediately he conveyed to me that this was not the best time for tarpon.

So what else is new!

Tarpon usually show themselves on the surface. We tried many places but saw none rolling or finning about. The big thrill was when we fished a wide turn of the river, that was like a big lagoon, and out of nowhere a hippopotamus surfaced right next to our skiff. We were very concerned because the animal was immense and very angry, so we decided to look elsewhere for tarpon.

Although Joae was convinced that there were a few tarpon in this river—I had shown him a photo of one to make sure we were talking about the same species—we couldn't find any. Joae shrugged his shoulders and shook his head after every place we tried with no success and he appeared very discouraged.

I wasn't. I learned long ago that you roll the dice and hope for the best. It was only a short trip—three days' fishing—and by now I was used to the smell of dried mackerel on the roof next to my window. Traveling up and down the rivers provided an endless series of changing backgrounds, with lots of wildlife on land, water and in the air available to the keen observer.

On the last day, we traveled about an hour down a river to look for tarpon in a lagoon. No sign of them. We trolled. We cast. It looked like ideal tarpon waters, but no fish. It was a hot, sweltering day. Even Joae, who lived there, felt the heat. The tarpon fishing was a bust. I was there at the wrong season. It would be impossible to market this trip.

Joae said something about visiting a place downstream. He used the word *cerveja* which I assumed was Portuguese for beer, quite similar to *cerveza,* the Spanish word for beer.

An ice-cold Budweiser or local beer would be refreshing. I agreed.

We traveled perhaps five miles, and now we began to see a few signs of habitation: huts, made from natural materials, dotted the river banks in increasing numbers. Families were busy washing clothes, cooking and cutting wood, but a few men and boys were fishing for supper with handlines from dugouts. We waved, they waved back and they went on with their chores. Periodically, Joae would ask the fishermen if they had seen any tarpon. They had not. I searched the banks for a store where cold beer might be sold, but I didn't see any. Perhaps down the river there would be a town or a store where we could buy a couple of cold, frosty beers.

Joae mentioned *familia;* perhaps his family ran the store. He pulled in next to a small hut. Suddenly, I realized that this was where his family lived. He greeted them warmly and in his dialect introduced me. They smiled and nodded. I smiled and nodded and waved my hand.

"*Cerveja?*" Joae handed me a gourd with some liquid that vaguely smelled and looked like beer without the foam.

There at the side of the hut was an elderly woman who probably was Joae's grandmother and she appeared to be chewing on some sort of fruit and nuts.

And spitting into a large gourd.

It finally dawned on me. That is how they made "beer." They chewed on some fruits and nuts, spit into a large bucket of water and apparently allowed the mixture to ferment.

Joae's drank some of the "beer." He rubbed his stomach to indicate that it was good. I diplomatically declined his *cerveja* but took a piece of bread to acknowledge his family's hospitality.

Oh well, they used to stomp on grapes with bare feet to make wine, didn't they?

The great drinking bout

VIRGILIO MAGRI, who operated Apipe Safaris on the banks of mammoth Parana River in Argentina, didn't have much formal education, but he knew how to communicate. Dr. Rudolph Koucky and I spent a delightful five days' dorado fishing with Virgilio, and we became very fond of Argentina's answer to *Zorba the Greek*. He reminded us so much of Anthony Quinn's *Zorba*.

He spoke about 30 words of English, and Dr. Koucky and I spoke a total of 25 words of Spanish. Magri was an excellent story teller. Through gesticulations and teaching us a few words he was able to convey complicated stories to us.

Like the time he had a drinking contest with a German hunter.

Virgilio was a super drinker. He was so good that he established a standing bet that he could out-drink anyone. He had many comers at first and according to Virgilio he never lost. With his growing reputation as the region's champion beer drinker, he had few challengers.

Hans W., a dedicated bird shooter from Germany, came to the Parana for a hunt. He heard of Virgilio and his great drinking talent and about his standing bet. Hans considered himself a champion drinker, too, and won many bets through the years, so Hans sought and found Virgilio.

They decided that the bout would take place at a small local tavern, not far from Virgilio's camp. The rules were simple. They would drink beer and they could only leave the table to go to the washroom. The one who outlasted the other was the winner.

Hans suggested a $500 cash bet and the loser pays the tab.

Virgilio gulped.

"I didn't have the money, of course, but everyone heard about it and my pride was at stake," he explained to the doctor and me. "There's no way I could lose the bet, because I did not have the money. I didn't have $100! I could not afford to lose. If I backed down, well, I would lose the respect of fellow villagers. So I accepted the bet!"

The great championship was set for next day and would commence in the afternoon.

They shook hands, smiled at each other and started drinking. Pitcher after pitcher. More and more beer was ordered to the delight of the inn-keeper.

"I started feeling it," Virgilio explained. "The German looked almost as refreshed as he came in. We ordered more beer. If this continued I would lose the bet and I didn't have the money. What a disgrace that would be!"

Virgilio realized that, at this pace, he would lose. He excused himself, went to the bathroom. Through the window he saw a young boy who was a neighbor and summoned the lad to the window.

"Find my brother and tell him to come to the washroom in exactly twenty minutes, but to come through the back door so no one sees him in the front. Don't fail. I will give you some money. Be quick!"

Virgilio returned to the table.

The German, sensing victory, asked for another pitcher of beer. Virgilio lit a cigarette. They started drinking again.

In about 20 minutes, Virgilio excused himself and went back to the washroom. He found his brother, Juan, in the washroom.

"*Que pasa?*"

"Quick! Change clothes with me. The German is beating me. Go drink with him, and beat him!" Virgilio left through a back entrance.

Juan, now dressed in Virgilio's clothes, went to the German's table and began drinking.

More and more beer was ordered. Juan felt his head spinning. He didn't know how much longer he could continue to drink.

But alas, the German, could drink no more. He gave up. "This is the first time in my life that someone beat me. Here's the money."

The small audience clapped. They knew that the winner was not Virgilio, but, Juan, his identical twin brother. The resemblance was so close that they often had trouble distinguishing between the two.

"What did you do with the money you won?" I asked Virgilio.

He affectionately patted the late model motor, and pulled the cord. And we resumed chasing the fabulous dorado.

Chicks & fishing

THE PIMP (a.k.a. Donald Gustafson) was sitting over by the Philco radio. Horseface (a.k.a. Martin Johnson) was staring out the window. I was lying on the floor while Leroy Gauss was nervously pacing the room. Leroy always was in motion. He had lots of energy. We were all 11 to 12 years old, and mostly we argued sports: The Chicago Bears. The Green Bay Packers (the Pimp's favorite team). Who was the greatest hitter of all time? Sports topics, ad nauseam. But on this day the conversation switched to girls, or "broads," as Leroy preferred to call them.

A girl by the name of Janine wanted to join our baseball team–the River Park Gremlins. This was in the days when girls didn't do sports. Oh, they swam or ice skated in their cute little skirts, or twirled a baton, or played croquet or badminton or, if they were very athletic, they played tennis, but not our kind of sports.

Manly games, like baseball and football.

The fact is that Janine, who was quite attractive (although we didn't dare to admit this; after all, we were the River Park Gremlins), was also very athletic. Didn't she beat Horseface in a foot race (he claimed he had sprained his ankle)? Didn't she hit one of the Pimp's curve balls a helluva distance ("It slipped," he said, "and besides I'm a third baseman")? And fielding? She could shag flies and throw almost as well as Dale Archer, and no one had a better arm than Dale. Yeah, she could play, and she certainly would be a better right fielder than Larry "The Bullet" Gaines who could run as swift as a gazelle but often he misjudged the flight of the ball.

Leroy—whose hormones were more advanced than ours—started the talk about "broads." We all joined in, timidly. It was the first significant, serious conversation I can remember about girls. Ahh, the days of innocence! No sex education courses in those days! Fathers would hem and haw and bring up sex when their sons were in their 20s.

"It would be very sad," Donald, the Pimp, announced, "to live to be 80 or die of old age without having felt a girl's tit."

We laughed at his seriousness, and then we each privately thought about it and then considered the dire possibilities. We were very pensive—each with his personal thoughts—until Horseface broke the spell by mentioning something about next week's game. This was the extent of our first serious girl conversation. We were not comfortable in recognizing or addressing confusing sexual issues. That was in the 1940s. My, how things have changed!

Don and I were the co-captains of the team, but really it was Lee Pedersen's team. He was a couple of years older than us, strong, powerful, and he thought Janine should be on the team. I heard about some sort of initiation, but I think only Leroy got the details, and I think Pedersen swore him to secrecy, or else.

"Guess what?" Pedersen announced one day, "Janine is our right fielder, and if you guys don't start playing better she may be our third baseman [Don's position] or catcher [my position]."

She was now our right fielder, which aggravated Larry the Bullet so much that he quit our team and joined the hated Welles Park Eagles, our archrivals.

Janine was a good player. She was very quiet. She wanted to play baseball, but when the game or practice was over, she left for home and was a loner. She was very serious, a good student, but didn't seem to have many friends. Her real love was baseball. I'm sure we all allowed ourselves to think about Janine in private moments.

We disbanded our baseball team when we went to high school, and eventually the River Park Gremlins drifted apart, so I don't know what happened to each friend, but I assumed that they married and no one will die or has died without at least experiencing the intimacy we discussed on that first day when we talked about "broads."

The life of a serious, dedicated fishermen often follows a set pattern. Usually, another sport (baseball, football, soccer, etc.) captures a youngster's initial attention. A bit later fishing might become important, and then all interests are "on hold" while the maturing guys discover girls and become totally confused. They walk around in a stupor bumping into things, constantly look for facial zits, practice dancing in the privacy of their room, study kissing techniques from movies, check for bulging biceps in mirrors and dab their face with an overabundance of Old Spice or Mennen Skin Bracer.

A strong conflict develops between feelings for the opposite sex and fishing. In the earlier years, the girls win easily, no matter how strong the latent fishing addiction may be. This often results in bashful conversations, casual dating, serious courtship, marriage and eventually a child or two (well, at least, that's the *preferred* order).

But alas, eventually fishing takes over. It happens slowly at first, and our angling interest becomes stronger as the years pass by, while our hormones—the inexplicable ones that totally ruled us earlier—seem to weaken. True, as we get older, we may even cheer for those hormones to regain that special trait, but sadly their best days are gone, for most of us anyway, and so our fishing interest continues to grow.

We do equally insane things for the love of fishing that we once did for the love of the opposite sex. Well, almost. Now we trade a comfortable room for a tent next to a remote stream to take advantage of the late evening hatch or early morning rise. We fish in the rain, often ignoring lightning as we wave our 9-foot graphite fly rods for just a few more casts. We endure peanut butter sandwiches or we watch our guide prepare shorelunch when we know darn well he never washed his hands, but heck, we're too busy shooing away mosquitoes and deer flies or inhaling no-see-ums to meekly protest. We may forsake our daily hot shower, perhaps bathing quickly in a cold lake or river, sometimes accidentally. Without hesitating we hop into an ancient Norseman float plane, which should have been retired decades ago. The amazing thing is that we may pay $300, $500, or a $1,000 a day for the "privilege," yet we think this is fun, and, you know, it probably is.

I didn't exactly follow the usual pattern. By the time I was 37½, I was still "playing the field." I would like to think that this was the reason why I delayed marriage, but in reality I was working out of the financial mess from the Sportackle International days, and then I started the fishing division for Safari Outfitters, Inc. I dated, yes, but I also fished in dozens of countries and helped build up fishing camps at Safari Outfitters, so I wasn't exactly suffering.

I feel compelled to digress for a moment: Becky Bisioulis, the tall, lean, stunning friend who first modeled in Paris and later became a famous fashion designer in the States, invited me to a special party at the Playboy Mansion in Chicago. I had always wanted to visit the Playboy Mansion. Could it be as appealing as it was depicted in Hef's magazine? Did gorgeous, busty, long-legged damsels unabashedly flit about in flimsy baby-doll outfits? I was very curious and very tempted to go. But no, I had planned a trip to the Shack, our Wisconsin trout fishing camp. I told Becky that I would be delighted to accept a rain check *after* the trout season. Strange, I never heard from her again.

Today, I sort of regret that decision. After all, I could have gone to the Shack at another time, as this was the only invitation I ever had to visit the Mansion. On the other hand, it was late June when the *Hexagenia limbata* hatches take place, and even the big brown trout lose their wariness. Hank Looyer, the Wisconsin trout-fishing guru, called and told me to hurry on up. "This is a good opportunity to get a big fish and the *Hexi* hatch won't last forever."

I did hit it right and landed a beautiful 17-inch brown that mistook a Disco Fly pattern for a delectable *Hexi* insect. At the time, this was my largest trout from the Shack waters. It was caught at night, of course, on the Dead Deer Stretch. When I landed this fish, I held it up high, to admire it in the light of a fading moon.

"You made the right decision," I convinced myself, and it was a great thrill.

Today—after having landed many big trout from the Shack waters—I still wonder if gorgeous, busty, long-legged damsels unabashedly flitted about in flimsy baby-doll outfits at the old Playboy Mansion.

A T THE TIME, I worked at Cahners Publishing as an associate editor on–get this–*Brick and Clay Record* and *Ceramic Industry* magazines. I still had some hefty bills from the Sportackle International fiasco as I didn't want to file for corporate or personal bankruptcy. Besides, working at Cahners was a fun job.

Although Cahners had a splendid personnel department, I somehow convinced Peg Miller, who was in charge of hiring, that I should do some of the interviewing. I interviewed mostly women for secretarial or editorial assistant jobs. I didn't bother asking them more than a few questions after briefly studying the application form. Instead I expounded on business philosophies: why it's necessary to give 110 percent on a job; how we can learn from even menial tasks; on and on. Sometimes, I wouldn't even bother discussing the job, but wandered off on some philosophical back road, such as trying to prove the existence of life after death based on Charlie Parker's jazz chord progressions. Junk like that.

Hey, I thought I was cool.

One of the interviewees, Sally Ross, was about ten years younger than I was. She was very good looking, resembling Mary Tyler Moore in those days. She had an easy, frequent smile and superb legs. She seemed amused by my interview ("you didn't ask many questions," she said later). I highly recommended her for editorial assistant on the two magazines I worked on. Peg Miller made the final decision and she hired her. Sally did a helluva job, too.

I knew Sally for a few years but I didn't date her until after I left Cahners and went to work full time for Safari Outfitters to start its new Fishing Division. We dated on and off for several years, and it was obvious that love, attraction and compatibility had grown and blossomed, but there were some compelling family problems that I felt I had to monitor, so I was indecisive on getting married.

What to do? Others were showing substantial interest in Sally.

Furthermore, my Safari Outfitters' salary was based on commissions derived from the sale of international fishing trips, and in those days, fishing out of the country wasn't as popular as it is today.

How could I get married?

I was promoting sportfishing in Costa Rica along with Carlos Barrantes (Costa Rican sportsman who owned Parismina Tarpon Rancho). Good friend and mentor Don Dobbins had financed the Casa Mar Fishing Club, built 30 miles north of Parismina, and it was becoming a popular light-tackle destination. Several other camps sprouted up and were beginning to attract attention, too, so while the present was bleak, the future showed promise, especially through the rose-colored glasses I chose to wear for my unrealistic view of the international angling world.

Don and I had planned a trip to Costa Rica's Casa Mar, and our group included *Salt Water Sportsman* magazine publisher Hal Lyman and editor Frank Woolner. I told Don that I was contemplating marriage and had recently thought of a "logical" way to decide whether I should get married.

"Which is?" Don inquired.

"If I land a tarpon on a fly rod at Casa Mar, it means I should *not* get married, but if I don't land one, it means that I should get married to Sally," I replied. "Of course, I expect to catch several on a fly."

He laughed. He thought I was kidding. I wasn't. Heck, a lot of people make important decisions with a flip of a coin, don't they?

Certainly there shouldn't be any problem in hooking many tarpon on a fly at Casa Mar, I reasoned. In those days, you could go to Samay Lagoon and see dozens if not hundreds of tarpon rolling on the surface, sometimes simultaneously. What a sight! And didn't Bill Leef land more than 20 tarpon in one day, on a conventional tackle? *Duck soup!*

I assumed I would remain a bachelor, for the time being anyway.

Fishing was slow. In fact, terrible. I was worried that Hal Lyman and Frank Woolner wouldn't get any material or photos for an article in their legendary, influential magazine.

Three days went by and there were almost no tarpon landed by the dozen guests in camp.

"You know what I think?" Don asked, but didn't wait for an answer. "You, my friend, are snake-bitten, which means the heavens are telling you to marry Sally."

But there were still a few days left. As Yogi Berra philosophizes: "It ain't over, til it's over!"

Mr. L. A., a client of ours who was booked at Casa Mar at the same time, approached me one morning.

"Jim, I have two customers on this trip and they aren't hooking any tarpon. There's a big business deal pending, and the decision-maker takes his fishing seriously. Very seriously! You've gotta to do something to get them some tarpon!"

"Do something? You're talking about business! I'm talking about my freedom!" I quickly related how I was going to decide whether I was going to marry or not based on catching a tarpon on a fly. He thought I was joking and he assured me that this was not a time for levity.

Although we all fished very hard, success eluded us. Hal and Frank fished for guapoté and machaca, two indigenous bass-like species that are fun to catch on light tackle. Mr. L. A. and his party, Don and I didn't catch any tarpon. The week was over. We were packed and waiting for the charter planes to take us back to San Jose.

"Here comes the bride, all dressed in white . . ." Don was humming.

I wasn't laughing.

Meanwhile, Mr. L. A. was very grim. "I don't think the deal will be consummated," he told me privately. "This is a huge package and he seems hesitant."

I realized now how important these clients were. After all, Mr. L. A. used a private jet to fly them from their home town to Costa Rica.

Lloyd Boyes, Casa Mar's laconic camp manager at the time, found out that the charter planes that would take us back to San Jose, would be late for at least a couple of hours. Weather conditions in the mountains.

"Why don't you guys fish for a while. No sense sitting around the camp."

Reluctantly we did. Don and I put some tackle together and decided to fish the Big Hole behind camp. By now I had given up on fly fishing and changed my decision—whether to marry—to *any kind of tackle*.

"It won't matter. You could use live bait and you are not going to hook a tarpon," Don chortled.

We even trolled, for gosh sakes! No fish.

We noticed another boat behind us. It contained L. A.'s Number One Customer. *N.O.C.*, as Don and I referred to him. The decision maker. The head huncho.

Don motioned to Winston, our guide, to change our trolling course, so that the other boat would have a chance at these prime waters.

"What are you doing, Don? Remember me? My freedom!" I asked.

But Winston and Don paid no attention to what I was saying and veered off for unproductive waters. The other boat was now in prime waters.

There was the rod bend. . . the hook setting. . . the screeching reel. . . the exhilarating scream. . . the big majestic silver torpedo up in the air . . . gills rattling. . . the crashing crescendo into the water.

The Number One Customer did a magnificent job of fighting the tarpon. It was huge. After a long fight N.O.C. landed it. That tarpon was 140 pounds. N.O.C. was smiling.

He was king, not only of our group, but of all fishing trips to Costa Rica, for according to Lloyd Boyes and the guides, his was the largest tarpon ever landed in Costa Rica!

The Aftermath:

• The Number One Customer became deliriously happy and the deal was consummated, which, of course, pleased Mr. L. A. tremendously.

• During the week, Frank Woolner and Hal Lyman decided to fish for other species that are indigenous to Central America (such as guapoté, machaca, mojarra). They wrote a fine article for *Salt Water Sportsman* and featured a Casa Mar fishing photo on the magazine cover (*December, 1970*)

• Me? I got married and (knock on wood) it has been one of the happiest marriages I know of.

And that's how I made the most important decision of my life!

Marta's special bread recipe

DON DOBBINS, a PanAngling founder and one of my mentors, loved to investigate new, exotic fishing places. One year, after studying large scale maps, he and his wife, Ruth, decided to explore Rio Blanco, a river in Guatemala near the Mexican border. Don felt that there could be some big tarpon and snook in this river.

They found an outfitter in Guatemala who could provide the necessary tents, dugouts, staff and cook and made all necessary reservations. Although Ruth and Don enjoyed the experience—the lush flora and fleeting glimpses of fauna—the fishing quality didn't match their reasonable expectations.

At the outset, they were concerned with the quality of meals, because Marta, the cook, had so few ingredients to work with due to lack of refrigeration and sufficient ice, but after a few days, they considered the meals among the highlights of the trip. Marta's dinners included several species of small fish that were freshly caught from the nearby river and creatively prepared.

Miguel, the outfitter, who took charge of the fishing and explorations, provided a suitable camp, quite comfortable when one considered the jungle location. In addition to food staples, Miguel thoughtfully had bought some live chickens from a nearby village which, from time to time, were transformed into delicious dinners. The breakfasts were ample and nourishing: eggs, juice, coffee, bread and jam. The bread was particularly delicious; in fact, it was so tasty that the Dobbins usually had several additional slices with each meal.

"This is probably the best bread I've ever tasted," proclaimed Don practically every day. Ruth agreed.

"Do you think you could get the recipe?" he asked.

"Well, first of all, there is a language problem, and secondly, Marta is very shy, although she nods if spoken to. And she bakes the bread very early in the morning," Ruth explained.

"Yeah, but you could go early in the morning, pretend you are on a walk, give her a *'Buenos Dias'* and observe how she makes the bread. Hey, this bread is the very best I've ever tasted. She probably has some unique baking methods or secret ingredients, I'm sure."

After much persuasion, Ruth agreed to find out. She was curious herself.

Ruth approached the outdoor cooking "shack" and noticed that Marta was busy preparing breakfast. The coffee was brewing over an open fire, the eggs were neatly set, ready for the pan, and Marta was busy kneading the dough to make the daily bread. There were several ingredients on the table, in various shakers, and perhaps they contained the secret to Marta's delicious bread.

Ruth's strategy was to saunter slowly in the area and after saying good morning and a few Spanish phrases she would casually look at the ingredients. She would "play it cool." After all, many cooks don't like to give out their recipes, and if they do, they often change the ingredients or quantities. "This probably applies even in Guatemalan jungles," Ruth had concluded.

One of the live chickens running helter-skelter kept pestering Marta, and when she tried to shoo it away, the chicken jumped on a chair and finally on the other side of the kitchen table, leaving frantic little imprints in the flour dust.

Marta was very upset with the chicken, and tried to chase it off the table. The chicken responded by pooping right on the table. This infuriated Marta!

Before Ruth could announce her presence with a "hello," Marta said something very nasty to the chicken in Spanish, but the chicken was oblivious to her threats and seemed to taunt her even more, so Marta, in a fit of anger, reached across the table, grabbed the chicken's "poo-poo" on the table and threw it at the chicken along with some dough. The chicken, now sensing Marta's anger, quickly jumped off the table. Marta brushed off the rest of the poo-poo from the kitchen table with her hands. Now satisfied that the pesty chicken would not bother her again, she sunk her hands into the dough and continued kneading.

Without washing her hands.

Ruth, horrified at the lack of sanitary conditions, returned to her tent.

"Did you find the secret ingredients?" Don asked.

"Yeah, it's very special," she lied, "but we can't get it at home. I'll tell you another time." The subject was temporarily put to rest when José, a guide with a wonderful Pepsodent smile, summoned them to breakfast.

"You know, Ruth, this bread is even better today than what we had the other mornings," Don said as they ate.

Ruth said something about her diet and reached instead for a stale saltine cracker.

150

Scalped in Panama

EXCEPT FOR THE FACT that our freshwater supply tasted "rubbery," because of the new rubber hoses, living on the brand-new 31-foot Prowler for four days wasn't bad despite the fact that there were six of us sleeping onboard. In addition to the Prowler, we had a 23-foot SeaCraft, which was ideal for light-tackle fishing, but it wasn't suitable for providing sleeping arrangements. There was Stu Apte, Bob Griffin, Capt. Don McGuinness, ChiChi, the mate, Danny, the guide, and me. McGuinness, easily one of the top captains of Central America, was an American who had lived in Costa Rica all of his life. ChiChi and Danny were locals, who were being trained to be guides. Danny's English was quite fluent because he had lived in Gary, Indiana with some relatives for a few months and also worked at the Panama Canal.

Bob Griffin had established a very modest fishing camp on Panama's Pacific coast, 60 miles south of David. The problem was that this temporary camp was too distant from the incredible fishing grounds, so Bob invited Stu and me to help explore some of the waters near Coiba Island, where he was considering constructing a deluxe fishing camp.

What a splendid opportunity to fish practically virgin waters! We were not disappointed. We fished Coiba, Contreras, Montuosa and Jicaron islands and several other places. Our fishing hours were very long, since we lived aboard; thus we explored many places and experienced some of the best variety fishing in Central America. I remember that fishing the Montuosa was so spectacular that by 11 A.M. I didn't want to hook another fish that day. But, although I was exhausted, I continued to fish and learned a ton from Stu, Don and Bob.

One day, Bob, Danny and I decided to try for roosterfish near the big Island of Coiba. We used the Prowler while Stu, ChiChi and Don fished from the SeaCraft, about a mile or so away from us.

Fishing for roosterfish was excellent. Roosters are a fun fish, especially when they can be enticed to the surface to bang topwater plugs. It was one of those glorious fishing days, and we had the whole place— ocean, islands, bays, reefs and, of course, fish—to ourselves!

Until a cutter suddenly appeared!

One of the men on that boat was waving two small flags, obviously signaling us in marine code. The cutter came closer and closer. The flag signals were more frantic.

"I think we better go there," Bob said as he fired up the engine. "Let's see what they are up to. Maybe they need our help."

Yeah, right.

As we got closer to the cutter, we realized that one of the guys had a machine gun aimed at our boat while about ten other uniformed men had guns pointed at each of us. *Yikes!*

"I think this must be the Panamanian National Guard," Bob said casually.

"Don't make any sudden movements," Danny said nervously. "I've heard these guys can be trigger-happy." He had served briefly in the National Guard.

I looked at Danny. There was a very concerned look on his face.

As we approached, I noticed that there was a handgun on our live-bait well. It belonged to Bob Griffin, who used it to scare off sharks when they attacked the fish we fought.

I looked for a towel or something else to cover up the gun. Maybe it wasn't registered, I thought. Since there was no towel handy, I took off my wide-brimmed hat and placed it casually over the gun.

"What's the matter?" Bob inquired when we got within shouting distance.

"You're under arrest! You're in restricted waters," the guy behind the machine gun said.

We were relieved that he spoke English, but we were still uneasy because he continued to point the machine gun at us.

"What to do you mean, *restricted*?"

"You're not allowed to be near Coiba Island. It's off limits!"

The man in charge seemed to lose patience but suddenly came out from behind the machine gun.

"Why are ya here? Don't ya know there is a prison around the corner!" And then he added, "You're all under arrest!"

Danny was distressed. "Be polite," he urged Griffin in low tones.

Bob Griffin looked puzzled. "I know there is a prison here, but I got permission to fish these waters from General Omar Torrijos."

General Torrijos was the most powerful man in Panama at the time, and in essence ran the country. I was relieved to hear that Bob had permission. Danny exhaled.

"Let's see it," he ordered.

"I don't have anything on paper. General Torrijos told me that I can go anywhere. It was at a party at Rancheria . . ."

Now I was getting nervous again. Danny was frantic. "They're gonna shoot us. Or throw us in prison to rot. Or overboard for the sharks and take the boat!" Danny certainly covered most of the negatives.

Bob was getting a little impatient. "Look, I got permission to build a fishing camp on this island. *'Bring lots of American tourists'* Torrijos told me. That's all I know. No one told me I can't be here."

"I'm telling ya! Don't move."

Then he said something to one of his people in Spanish.

"I think he told the guy to call headquarters and see if they can contact General Torrijos," Danny said, doing his best to read their lips.

Now Bob was worried. "They'll never find him. He has many places. Some without phones. A villa in the mountains . . . he's probably at the villa in the mountains."

"Who's in the other boat?"

"Stu Apte . . . world-famous fisherman. He's helping us explore the waters."

"What's your name?"

"Griffin. Bob Griffin. *Roberto* Griffin."

The commander relaxed a bit. My head was broiling under the hot Panamanian sun. And my hat was covering the gun. I could feel my brain turning to jelly in the heat.

"Better tell the *'bald one'* to put his hat on," the commander told Danny in Spanish.

"Thanks, sir, but I like hot sun on my head. They tell me that you can grow hair back in the hot sun. It's good for you," I said, expecting him to laugh. He muttered something about gringos and shook his head.

Hey, at least he was concerned about my health.

Of course, I wanted to put my hat on. But I could visualize disaster. If I reach for my hat, the Panamanians see the gun under it, think that I'm reaching for the gun, and *Bam! Bam! Bam! BAM!* I could picture the headlines in the *Chicago Tribune*: "Crazed American killed in shoot-out with Panamanian Coast Guard."

So I did nothing but take the hot rays on my bald pate. I would have given anything to put on that hat.

A guy rushed from the wheelhouse to the commander and whispered a message. The commander nodded that he understood and dismissed the messenger.

"Okay. Ya guys can go. We reached General Torrijos and he sez you can fish here. He said to tell you, 'Good luck'."

He commanded the other guys in Spanish. They reluctantly, if not sadly, put down the guns and started to file away as their powerful engines began to roar.

I caught another roosterfish while the cutter was still within our sight.

When we saw Stu Apte, ChiChi and Don McGuinness later, we asked if they had noticed that we were detained by the cutter.

"Yeah, we thought of coming over to see what was happening, but we were hooking cubera snapper on surface plugs . . . and you know how it is when fishing is good."

We laughed. Danny was still a little nervous. "I think those guys would've shot us if they hadn't reached Torrijos. Then throw us overboard for the sharks. Man, this place is loaded with sharks. But then we'd be dead so it wouldn't matter."

We had plenty of beer at supper while munching on snapper. That's when Griffin, Apte and I named Bob's soon-to-be-built lodge, Club Pacifico de Panama.

P.S.: I had to have numerous, expensive treatments for my sunburned scalp when I returned to Chicago.

©mitchell

156

The perfect put down

I FELT VERY GOOD about my fishing results. First, I fished at Pez Maya (Yucatán, Mexico) and during 1½ days of fishing, I landed probably 40 bonefish. I only missed a half-dozen, had a couple of shots at semi-interested permit and caught some small tarpon on poppers. In the evening under the bright moonlight, I went over to the channel behind my cottage and hooked four or five big cubera on fly rod poppers. There was no stopping them, and after losing several fly lines and lots of backing, I called it a night. A magnificent night.

After Pez Maya, I went to Club Pacifico de Panama where I landed sails on a fly rod almost at will. To add a little excitement Bob Griffin, the camp owner who fished with me, suggested I try for a sail on a fly rod using a 6-pound tippet. We came close. Boy, did we come close! If there were a longer gaff on board, Bob Griffin assured me that we would have landed that fish. At the time, no one had landed a sail on 6-pound tippet.

So I felt very good about myself as an angler, and I unabashedly placed myself in the above-average category.

On my way back from Panama I stopped off in Miami for a South American Travel Organization meeting. There was a half day at leisure. What to do?

Years ago, I saw a wonderful, hilarious Lee Wulff film about party-boat fishing. That's it! I would go to the docks and fish off a party boat. I would be on water and I would be fishing. I had never fished from a party boat before.

The boat was big, well organized, and there were about 20 fishermen and four or five couples on board. The captain said that we would be fishing for several varieties of snapper, grouper, amberjack and other species. Grab-bag fishing. At each place or position, there was a heavy rod and reel, and a mate attended to a half-dozen places and fishermen.

The captain shifted the engine into neutral and, after chumming the waters with ample tidbits, we baited up and started to fish.

Almost immediately people started to hook fish. They roared with excitement. They laughed. Hollered for the gaffer. "Hey, you with the gaff—I got a big one. Hurry. Hurry!" Some of the snappers and amberjacks were big—more than 30 pounds—and everyone caught at least a few fish.

Except me.

I changed positions. I changed tackle. I changed bait. I didn't lose any fish fighting them, because I never hooked one. The whistle blew. Time to reel in. Back to the docks.

The fishermen were jubilant as they snapped pictures of each other with their fish, and they were justifiably proud of their catch. For many, this was their first time fishing.

I enjoyed being out in the fresh air, and the few dollars it cost me for the party boat was well spent, I thought. The excitement and exultation of the other anglers were refreshing to see, because sometimes we who have been able to fish some of the world's best waters become jaded and do not realize how fortunate we are. It had been a good afternoon, yeah, a very good afternoon, I concluded.

There were cabs available at the dock to take the patrons to the various hotels. I shared a taxi with a young, good-looking, exuberant couple, Jonathan and Carol. They were on their honeymoon. They had very good fishing, especially Carol, who had landed an amberjack of more than 30 pounds. They were enjoying their ride back to the hotel, but they noticed I was rather quiet.

"I'm sorry you didn't do so well," Jonathan offered sympathy.

"This is your first time fishing, isn't it?" Carol said, but she didn't wait for my reply. "Yeah, we could tell. Don't let it get you down. You'll get the hang of it."

I was almost ready to defend myself. I wanted to tell them that I had fished in more than 30 countries at the time, and frankly did quite well, and for much more difficult species, and with light tackle. *Blah . . . blah . . . blah.* But I said nothing.

Carol continued.

"Look. This was our fourth trip on the party boat. The first time we didn't do so well. Right Jonathan? We caught a couple of small fish, but we kept at it, and now that we have the hang of it, we just love fishing! Can we go tomorrow, Jonathan? Please, please." Her blue eyes sparkled with joy.

"Don't give up! Fishing is fun! Try it a few more times and I'm sure you'll do well," Jonathan added.

When the cab pulled up at my hotel, I thanked them for their advice.

"Yeah, you're right. This was the first time I fished . . . "

"We thought so," Carol said. "But don't give up."

"I probably won't," I replied.

And I haven't.

160

"Screw the Duke of Roxborough" and other Norwegian fishing stories

THERE WAS NO WAY I could afford to fish Norway's Alta River. I was developing the Fishing Division for Safari Outffiters, Inc. at the time (late 1960s), and I was barely making a living. The Alta was among the most expensive fishing trips offered: $3,500 per person, not including air transportation, hotel, tips and other expenses. We were talking $5,000! That's probably like $20,000 today! I heard about the Alta from Charlie Ritz, who had painted glowing images of big Atlantic salmon, giant salmon that would rise frequently to the fly. He described the beauty and the potential of the Alta as only Charles could. "Most of the salmon will weigh more than 18 pounds," he added.

Few rivers in the world are more steeped in tradition than the Alta. The English aristocracy began to fish the Alta in the late 1800s and established all the ground rules that are followed religiously today. The English discovered that Alta salmon "feed" better at night, so you sleep during the day and fish at night. Breakfast is served at 6 P.M., lunch at midnight and supper at about 5 or 6 A.M. Talk about confusing your biological clock! Thankfully, the midnight sun furnishes sufficient light for all the angling essentials. You may not be able to read the classified ads at midnight (who'd want to?), but there is sufficient light to change flies and to pick out the productive stretches.

So when the Higgins brothers—Bardon, Bob and Ray—booked a trip to the Alta and asked me to join them, I was more than tempted. The demand for Alta reservations far exceeded the number of rods allocated for each beat, so there was no chance to obtain a travel agent's discount, but I found out that for a mere $1,000 I could stay at the Alta as a nonfishing companion. I seized the opportunity. Although I wouldn't be allowed to fish, just seeing the Alta, being there, would be a privilege. That's the kind of a brainwashing job Monsieur Ritz did on me.

On the first night, just before the Higgins' fishing time was to begin, we all wandered to a pool where we watched Mead Johnson finish up his week. Mead hooked a salmon, fought it brilliantly, captured it, released it. It was a 25 pounder.

I could feel the excitement grow within me. It's great to watch another angler land a fish—no doubt about it—but it's a greater thrill if you are doing the reeling, the fighting, the releasing.

During our flight to Norway, I read some of Hemingway's philosophy about living life to its fullest, no matter what the cost, so I decided that I should fish one day, and I convinced the powers of the Alta Lodge to sell me a single day's fishing. After all, prorated at only $500, how could I resist?

Fishing on the Alta is from long river boats, seldom by wading, with two ghillies (guides) at the oars, fore and aft. The Alta is a swift, sometimes angry river; hence, two oarsmen are required to hold the boat at a pool so that the "sport," who is standing in the center, can cover the water with ease.

We learned that fishing on the Alta had been poor and that some of the previous anglers left at midweek because they weren't going to waste their time. For them, there would be other years, and the thousands of dollars they forfeited didn't matter. For decades I had fantasized fishing the renowned Alta, only to discover now that we had picked a lousy year. Damn!

Unfortunately, on the night I decided to fish, I landed one grilse and an 18-pound salmon. It was "unfortunate" because I was now hooked on the Alta salmon fishing, and I knew that I was going to fish the next night. And the night after that. And the entire week. Hang the cost! Live life to its fullest! Right, Mr. Hemingway?

The Higgins brothers fared much better that first night. They each caught a salmon in the low 20s, and Ray hooked but lost a very big fish.

Fishing may have been considered lousy by some of the Alta regulars who often land 30-pound salmon, but this was our first taste of the Alta so no one in our quartet complained. Even when fishing is poor, Norway's jaw-dropping scenery and pristine waters are worth the high price of admission. That is, if you can afford it.

I must tell you about those midnight lunches. First of all, we each had our own beats so we were separated. Secondly, our Norwegian guides spoke no English, so any communication was done with Ole Mosessen, the camp manager, either prior to or after fishing.

Every midnight lunch was the same. Two hot dogs, a can of sardines and one apple. At exactly midnight, the guides would row to a shorelunch spot, prepare a fire, and hand you a couple of sticks for the weenie roast. Having fished in Canada dozens of times, I'm a shorelunch person. I look forward to them. But not on the Alta. Hot dogs? Every lunch?

The menu never changed!

Visualize this: You are sitting on a rock, holding a stick and a hot dog over the campfire. A ghillie sits on each side of you, jabbering in Norwegian. Invariably, one ghillie tells what apparently is a helluva funny Norwegian joke. The other guide breaks out in a crescendo of guffaws and laughter. Both are shaking uproariously, their bellies wiggling, their eyes tearing from laughter, and there you are, poker-faced, holding a wiener on a stick over a fire. Laughter is quite contagious, so eventually you laugh, and they laugh harder until they realize you couldn't possibly understand the joke, so they stop laughing and look at you strangely. Serious conversation resumes for a while, but minutes later, the second ghillie thinks of a joke, and the whole episode repeats itself.

They have a strong guides' union so the midnight lunch lasts for a full hour, which under these circumstances seems much longer.

One night, it was my turn to fish home beat, close to the lodge. At midnight, wishing to avoid the usual shorelunch ritual, I suggested that the guides drop me off at the lodge and pick me up after lunch. I was fantasizing eating lox, sliced ham, homemade bread, desserts and other goodies that were always available at the camp. But no! They couldn't permit this. Something about the Duke of Roxborough. For decades, the Duke's predecessors had subleased beats on the Alta and apparently established all the ground rules for this river.

The Duke. His name came up each day, every night. The Duke this, the Duke that. He had set the pace, the rules, the guidelines.

After our third night of fishing, we came to the conclusion that two beats were extremely good, and two were apparently void of fish. To our logical minds, our party of four could share the two good beats. Surely there was plenty of potent water. Miles of it! Furthermore, the two anglers sharing a beat could have lunch together at midnight. You know, some chatter at the wiener roast?

We suggested this to Ole, the Alta manager. No way, he said. The Duke of Roxborough would object. Hey, the Duke wouldn't have to know about this; he wasn't on the Alta. We finally convinced Ole to broach the subject to the guides. He did. Reluctantly.

You wouldn't believe it. Suddenly, eight guides were talking at once. They were furious.

"They won't do it. The Duke of Roxborough would never approve!" Ole said.

"Screw the Duke of Roxborough!" One of the Higgins brothers shouted in disgust.

There was silence. The Norwegian guides understood this blasphemy. They decided not to guide us for the rest of the trip!

They were going on strike!

Now what?

Only through persistent apologies, via Ole, did the guides finally agree to take us fishing. So for the remainder of our week, we did it their way, the way it was done for decades. We had our little individual midnight lunches, with the weenie sticks, our sardines, and our apples for dessert. And the Norwegian jokes and the wiggling bellies of laughter.

I think that my two guides thought that the sharing-the-beats idea was mine. For the rest of the trip, they kept the boat a considerable distance from the holding waters while they rowed in placid waters. This required vigorous double-haul casting on my part, in order to pump out a 4/0 Green Highlander great distances. This was very tiresome, but at those prices, you forget about the aches and pains. You cast one more time.

It was my turn to fish Broadway Pool. It was aptly named "Broadway Pool" by some New Yorkers because this was the only place where the townspeople could watch the Americans or English clients fish. Because of the very high rates, it was assumed everyone who fished the Alta was extremely wealthy. Apparently, there's not much happening in the village of Alta. On most nights, several dozen people came to this observation spot. As my boat turned the bend, we were greeted with some car honking, applause and cheers from the gallery. The Higgins brothers, who had already experienced "Broadway," told me that good manners dictate that you take off your hat and bow to the audience before beginning to fish these "sacred" waters.

So I did just that. I heard the buzz-buzz of the Norwegian spectators, but I couldn't tell from the guides' expressions whether the bowing was

SOP or whether it was a Higgins' put on. With my arms and back still in great pain, there was much teeth-gritting with each cast, but because there is also sufficient ham in me, somehow I unfolded some good, long, lucky casts with the single-handed Orvis bamboo rod I was using. I heard a few *oohs* and some *ahhs* from the grandstand.

I hooked a fine salmon that tore up and down the pool. There was cheering from the gallery but some critical comments, too. Now my arms felt numb, as though they had been punctured with a dozen no-vocaine shots. But I continued to reel, parry, fight the fish and finally I landed a 26-pound Atlantic salmon. Cheers from the audience. Then they got in their cars and left. Some honked their approval. I felt good about this episode even though my tortured arms didn't. I can see why the Europeans, and now Americans, favor the two-handed fly rods, especially when throwing big flies.

We fished another pool where I lost a very big salmon: 35 pounds, at least that's what one of the ghillies estimated.

Upstream I noticed a small object, almost metallic, splashing periodically. At first I thought it was a bird or a small fish but concluded it was neither. I was curious. I pointed it out to the ghillies. They observed the same splash, spoke hurriedly in whispered tones to each other, then rowed furiously and in unison to that spot.

When we finally arrived there, we surprised a young man winding some heavy monofilament around a tin can. The silver object that we noticed was a fishing spoon. He spotted us, wound the last few feet of line on the big can hurriedly and scurried through the woods, while the ghillies cursed him and threatened his life. You didn't need to understand Norwegian to comprehend their anger. You could read it in their eyes. Hear it their voices.

The man was a poacher. He had not noticed our boat downstream and was flinging out the lure with the hope of hooking or snagging an Atlantic salmon. Even in those days, a salmon could bring $40 or more.

What was peculiar about the whole episode was that the man from a distance appeared to be black. At camp, Ole explained that some poachers apply lampblack or charcoal on their faces and hands and wear dark clothes so that they wouldn't be spotted or recognized easily.

It's hard to poach on the Alta because of the rugged terrain and the great distances from the roads, but there are a few places where it can be done. The Norwegians guard heavily against poaching, even using patrols and dogs to discourage these "get-rich-quick" schemers.

For the most part, the Alta has been kind to anglers. Sure, this river can be stingy at times, giving up very few fish during a week of poor water/weather conditions, but usually the Alta is in a very generous mood and each year it yields salmon of over 40 pounds.

The trip was over. Oddvar Kjelsrud, who oversaw the Alta Lodge, met me at the airport. It was time to pay the fiddler! I was able to reduce the price to $1800, and although this was more than I could afford, I felt good about my negotiations.

After all, I had fished the mighty Alta!

THIS WAS NOT THE FIRST TIME I fished Norway. I had fished a number of rivers a few years prior to my Alta experience. The earlier experiences were very frustrating.

First on my itinerary was the Namsen River, and to get there I had to take a night train that made lots of scheduled stops.

"Don't worry. The conductor calls out the stops and you'll be there a little after midnight, if all goes well," Oddvar Kjelsrud told me. "The lodge people will meet you at the little railroad station. No problem."

There's nothing more disconcerting than traveling on a train at night in a foreign country if you don't understand the language and you are not sure of the destination. The conductor bellowed out the stops periodically. The trouble was, I couldn't understand him. I wasn't exactly panic stricken but I worried that I would miss my station.

Luckily I sat across from several young Norwegian students. They perceived my anxiety, and I showed them my itinerary. The students spoke very little English but told me not to worry, they would alert me prior to my stop. They did.

I managed to drag all my bags from the train. I had a camera case, a large, heavy duffel bag, a long rod case and a small bag for my waders.

I never learned the art of traveling light, so I struggled off the train with all my belongings. So far, so good.

Except that it was raining. Raining very hard. Here I was in my suit and tie, a standard practice at Safari Outfitters ("We must always look neat and prosperous when we are traveling," Roman Hupalowski used to say. "Remember we are representing Safari Outfitters, *Incorporated,*" he always stressed the "incorporated").

There was no overhead shelter or cover to protect me and my luggage from the pounding rain.

There were about a dozen cars waiting. The arriving passengers hurried to the various autos, and the cars drove off, one by one. I was looking for my car, telling myself that soon I would be at the lodge, perhaps enjoying a hot meal and beverage before retiring in a warm, cozy room.

The last auto left and I came to the realization that there was no one at the station to meet me. What to do? The rain was coming down harder, and now I was soaking wet.

It was 12:30 A.M. on my Timex. I transferred my luggage to the dark highway and assumed that perhaps the driver was delayed.

1 A.M. No car. No driver. No phone. No contact. Lots of rain.

I was mad at myself, because I didn't insist on obtaining a phone number when I was in Oslo. "The lodge will meet you. And besides there are no phones at the station," Oddvar said, and he was right about the phones.

Now I noticed a car approaching. Would it be the lodge's? I was not going to take any chances, so I stood on the highway, with my thumb out, in a hitchhiker's pose. After all, there wasn't much traffic on this highway, especially at this hour, so I could not allow this car to escape.

Luckily, it came to a halt, but the driver was not from the lodge. I spoke quickly in English, but when he didn't understand me, I *e-nun-ci-a-ted* every syllable. Because that didn't help, I tried a combination between pantomime and charades, pointing to my fishing rods, pretending I'm casting. He understood that I was a fisherman. Although he didn't know what to do, he felt sorry for me and motioned me to put my gear in his car and to get in.

168

It was almost 1:30 A.M. and I assumed he was asking where I want to go, but I couldn't tell him except that I was scheduled to fish the Namsen River. The Namsen is a huge, long watershed, with many inns, hotels and resorts. My itinerary was of no help since it didn't list the lodge. The driver looked weary and tired.

He drove slowly for a few minutes, obviously considering various possibilities (or perhaps he was cursing his bad luck), when suddenly he seemed to have an idea, turned the car around and headed in the opposite direction. About 15 minutes later he came to a stop in front of big, dark building and honked his horn lightly.

A light on the second floor appeared, then a woman in a robe opened a window. She stuck her head out, and asked something in hushed tones. He replied and she gasped, said something in Norwegian, and I saw

lights turn on one by one as they marked her progress downstairs. Then the woman in the robe rushed out of the door, clutching a huge umbrella.

"Oh, I'm sorry, Mr. Chapralis," she said. "I thought you were coming tomorrow. Oohh, I'm terribly sorry no one met you. And it's such a terrible night."

I thanked the driver profusely, tried to give him a nice tip, but he refused, smiled and was relieved to be on his way.

"Do you mind sleeping in the living room and tomorrow we will get your room ready?" she asked, and then provided me with two sheets.

I was glad to get out of the wet clothes and in a warm lodge. So much for the warm meal and hot beverage.

I slept very well. Then early in the morning, guests, mostly British women, filtered into the living room for their breakfast. They were quite surprised to see a stranger sleeping on the sofa. One of them said she heard a horn last night and some voices.

I pretended to be asleep, which I had been until they came into the living room. This would have been alright except that I had to use the bathroom, but I didn't dare get up, as I was wearing only a tee shirt and boxer shorts.

Yappity, yappity yap! They talked on and on. Their fishing husbands were already on their way to the waters and these women were planning their sightseeing for the day. Finally, they left the living room and it was safe for me to get up and go to the washroom.

I was introduced to my guide, who was very pleasant and knowledgeable, and although he tried very hard, we didn't hook or see a salmon on the Namsen. It was a beautiful day, but I really wasn't into it. First of all, I don't like trolling (harling) for salmon. Second, I was exhausted from the previous night's ordeal. So much for my Namsen experience.

THE NEXT DAY I left for the Malangsfoss Pool. Ahh, the beautiful Malangsfoss! The fabulous Malangsfoss. Home of big salmon. The previous party was headed by Elliott Donnelley and family members and friends.

I found out that they had superb fishing. In fact, the camp manager told me, "they were so delighted with their fishing that they rewarded their guides with huge tips; about four or five times more than a good tip."

According to the manager, I was the only guest there for the next three days because a group had to postpone its trip.

"You will have the whole camp, guiding staff and the famous pool to yourself," he said. Finally, I was going to cash in on great salmon fishing. What a stroke of great luck.

Wrong!

The guides didn't show up the next day. Or the day after. Having "earned" a huge tip, they apparently celebrated the next couple of days. They were informed that the big group cancelled, and that I was the only fishing guest. They probably concluded that I, a travel agent, would probably tip a very modest sum, so why bother?

The manager, who had little control over the guides, was very apologetic. He obtained a daily fishing license for me on a different stretch of the Malselv river, but he admitted that there weren't many salmon resting there and it would be useless. I proved him right.

To fish the Malangsfoss Pool you needed a guide and a skiff. The guides, who apparently had a union of sorts, prohibited anyone else from guiding on the Malangsfoss except members of the union. They owned the boats, too.

On the third day one of the guides arrived but he said he was too sick to guide. He looked as if he celebrated for several days, and he probably did. He sat in a chair, drank coffee, chain smoked and read his newspaper. I waited patiently, hoping that he

would recover from his "illness" and take me fishing. No such luck. He picked up his belongings and paycheck and left. Obviously this experience left a terrible impression on me. To be so close to the Malangsfoss, with tons of salmon presumably milling below the falls, and not being able to make a single cast, well, it was disheartening. I cussed the guides under my breath when I left the lodge.

Norway is a stunningly beautiful country, and the fjord regions are among the most incredible sights I've seen anywhere in the world. Yes, I was upset with some of the guides' attitudes, but most of the people I met were very helpful, friendly and conscientious. Undoubtedly dealing with mostly wealthy American and British anglers may have spoiled some of the guides.

The Winchester storm

ROMAN HUPALOWSKI was paranoid about competition in the hunting travel business, and he considered any competitor as the enemy. His most hated enemy, of course, was his former partner Ernest Prossnitz, who operated Special Tours and Travel located across the street. He almost never referred to him by name but merely pointed in the direction of Ernie's office. We were absolutely not allowed to have any contact with Special Tours and Travel. This was a little awkward for Irene, Roman's secretary, and Julie, Ernie's secretary, because they had become very good friends when they all worked together before the schism and the law suit. When Julie and Irene wanted to get together for lunch, they would wave in the windows to each other, across Madison Street, because both offices faced each other and were on the 11th floors. One would write the name of a restaurant and time in huge letters on big paper while the other confirmed.

I thought Roman's paranoia was counterproductive. I strongly felt that it was important to get along with my competitors that I knew would eventually emerge in the fishing travel field.

I received a call from Mike Fitzgerald, a dentist who lived in Pennsylvania and was attracted to the outdoor travel field. He came to Chicago and we met for dinner.

"You're a dentist and you want to go into this fishing travel business?" I asked Mike. He nodded. "Geez, If I were you, I'd pull a few teeth and go on fishing trips, then complain if things weren't exactly right. This is not an easy business."

But Mike had a dream, and he pursued it. Despite some serious blips in his road map, he succeeded more than any travel company serving the outdoors. He and his family operate Frontiers, Inc., Wexford, Pennsylvania, and it is by far the most successful outdoor travel agency in the world. We've enjoyed mutual cooperation through several decades.

Other travel agencies appeared on the scene. World Wide Sportsman, Fishing International and Sportsman's Travel Service were among the first.

Bob Nauheim and Frank Bertania were customers of mine at Safari Outfitters, and they later decided to go into the fishing travel business. I wrote a very long report for them giving them advice, and even suggested a name for their agency (Fishing International), which they used. Jerry Samuels of Sportsman's Travel Service and I became good friends, and 35 years later we still remain in constant contact. I've chatted with George Hommell and Billy Pate (World Wide Sportsman) on several occasions, and we've cooperated nicely through the years. Later, I enjoyed a fine, cordial relationship with Mike Michalak's The Fly Shop and other fishing travel agencies.

By setting up this friendly spirit I believe that we, the pioneers of modern international fishing, were able to promote the outdoor travel business more efficiently and successfully than if we were back stabbing each other.

174

When Club Pacifico, Panama's fabulous light-tackle fishing camp, was gaining tremendous popularity, I suggested to owner Bob Griffin that he ought to invite Bob Nauheim and Frank Bertania as his guests.

"Why do that? You are the exclusive booking agent for the club and we're well booked. Why would you want a competitor of yours to go to Club Pacifico?" Griffin was puzzled.

"Because if they can provide a couple dozen additional clients each year, that's almost total profit for Club Pacifico, which means you would have some extra cash to improve the camp, buy an additional boat, whatever. Everybody wins: you, the customers, the outdoor travel agencies and the airlines."

And that's exactly what happened.

In return, Fishing International, Frontiers and other agencies similarly cooperated and we were and are basically one happy family. Sure, we would compete for customers and try to find new, exciting fishing places, but at the same time we pulled on the oars together so that international fishing would continue to progress in a relatively calm albeit tricky sea.

Business was picking up nicely for each of us and our little industry was gaining momentum. The mass circulation outdoor magazines (*Field & Stream*, *Outdoor Life* and *Sports Afield*) were printing more and more articles on these distant out-of-the-country places. ABC's *The American Sportsman*—featuring Curt Gowdy and such luminaries as Bing Crosby, Stu Apte and Lee Wulff—also drew attention to international fishing and hunting opportunities. Many close-to-home fishermen became interested in exotic places and began to book these trips.

Bookings were improving and new fishing lodges and outfitters were sprouting up annually. It's hard to believe, but in the 1960s there were only three or four pure fishing lodges in Alaska. Today there are hundreds of fishing lodges in the state.

While Roman was paranoid about competition he also had tremendous confidence in his ability, knowledge and business procedures. International hunting in the late 1960s and early 1970s was at its apex and many new hunting travel agencies entered the field, but most of the newcomers were followers rather than leaders. They would offer the same programs that Safari Outfitters, Klineburger Brothers and other established agencies were promoting and selling, when they should have concentrated on finding and publicizing new hunting places. Each year many failures occurred, including some bankruptcies in which clients lost considerable money. While in other industries established companies might pop the champagne corks at the news of failing competitors, this was not at all true for our small fraternity. It reflected negatively even on the established companies.

Winchester, the giant arms company, decided to go into the outdoor travel business and conceived Winchester World-Wide Adventures. While Safari Outfitters could compete with any medium-sized travel agency, we now faced a huge corporation with unlimited funds, marketing and PR resources, and, I'm quite sure, cozy arrangements with publishers of the various outdoor media. After all, they were a giant advertiser, weren't they?

What was even more threatening for the existing outdoor travel agencies is that Winchester struck up a very important arrangement with TWA, one of the three largest domestic and international airlines in the world at the time. TWA, in conjunction with Winchester, created and sponsored a magnificent spiral-bound, full-color hunting and fishing brochure. The rumor was that TWA invested $500,000 in Winchester World-Wide Adventures in the late 1960s. The strategy was to interest general travel agencies to book their clients on outdoor fishing and hunting trips through Winchester, and this beautiful brochure would help. TWA, of course, had all the contacts with the more than 25,000 travel agencies. If they were successful in getting the general travel agents to book the fishing and hunting tours, these destinations would be filled quickly due to the limited capacity of fishing and hunting lodges. Then the outdoor travel agencies, Safari Outfitters, Frontiers, etc., would have no place to send clients and eventually would have serious financial problems.

Clever. Very clever, indeed.

"We will survive this," is all Roman told me when I informed him of the Winchester/TWA partnership. He wasn't entirely confident.

Next we heard that a relatively new conservation organization, called GameCoin was starting up in Texas and that it would hold its first annual international big-game hunting and fishing conference in San Antonio, Texas. GameCoin invited many of the world's best hunters and outfitters to the conclave and most of them planned to attend.

I perceived this to be a major threat to our hunting division because the hunting organizations would have a chance to meet face-to-face with many of our clients and the possibility for direct bookings was imminent.

"Jim, we will survive this, but we need to go to San Antonio," Roman was a little worried. So we went.

THE FIRST THING that alarmed us in San Antonio, was the cozy arrangement between GameCoin and Winchester. Winchester World-Wide Adventures had bought nearly all the exhibition space at the convention.

The convention was loaded with the big names in hunting. Although it had been advertised as a hunting and fishing convention, there was almost no talk about fishing. Billy Pate—one of our most accomplished fly rodders of all time—attended, and I'm sure there were a few other anglers present, but clearly it was a hunter's convention.

It was quite a bash, and there was even a black tie/formal night.

Winchester's brochure was beyond spectacular. With its sophisticated layout and design, unique spiral binding, overlays, lavish photography and other expensive printing devices, this brochure would be incredible even today, more than 30 years later. Originally, I thought that Winchester was going to concentrate entirely on hunting, but I was wrong. Dead wrong. Its brochure featured fishing places all over the world.

There was more bad news. Winchester World-Wide Adventures unveiled a huge, magnificent office on New York's Park Avenue; furthermore, it was staffed with hunting and fishing experts, including some of Africa's best known professional hunters. They even had a "toll free" number, which was very rare in those days. This meant that people could call from anywhere in the United States and speak with an expert and not be charged for the phone call. Unheard of then! José Simoes, the famous professional hunter in Mozambique, paid them a visit and reported to us that they had about 30 people working in the office. Winchester World-Wide Adventures ordered full-page ads in the outdoor magazines, while we bought three-inch, column ads.

Yikes!

As we flew back to Chicago from the convention, I could see that Roman was shaken by all these events and revelations. We spoke very little during the flight as we were each in deep thought about the future.

"We will survive this," he said, when we parted for our homes that night, but his voice lacked the usual confidence and he had to force a smile.

A CCORDING TO A THIRD PARTY, someone suggested to Winchester that they should buy us out, which made sense because of the valuable exclusive hunting and fishing booking contracts we held.

"Buy Safari Outfitters? Huh! In a few months they will be kneeling in front of us begging for mercy, and their camps and outfitters will be kneeling right next to them," one of the Winchester's marketers quipped. I didn't tell this to Roman.

Winchester made a run for many of the fishing places, some of which were under exclusive contracts with my Fishing Division.

Client and movie producer Ned Payne reported a conversation that he heard between a Winchester executive and Carlos Barrantes, who operated the highly popular and successful Parismina Tarpon Rancho and Casa Mar fishing lodges in Costa Rica.

"Why should I change? Jim is doing a very good job for us," Carlos said.

"Yes, but you don't understand. We will also get you a brand-new U.S. car," the Winchester executive allegedly said.

"Have you seen my car? I have a brand new Mercedes Benz," Carlos countered.

Winchester World-Wide Adventures also visited Andy Growich at El

Tarpon Tropical, Campeche, Mexico, and he too said he was fully satisfied with Safari Outfitters and wasn't impressed with Winchester's promises and boasting. Not one of our popular fishing camps changed to Winchester, which I found very satisfying. And flattering.

I received a call from a prospect who said he was planning a trip to Argentina for trout and wanted to ask some specific questions.

I had recently returned from a very successful Argentine fishing trip and answered his questions to the best of my ability. Most of the questions had to do with tackle suggestions. What type of fly rods? Leaders? What fly patterns? Would the trout take dry flies? I seemed to satisfy the caller that I knew what Argentine fishing was all about.

"I'm embarrassed! I'm going to level with you," he said. "I had phoned Winchester World-Wide Adventures to book a trout trip in Argentina and spoke to someone who had not been there. I asked about tackle and was told that their Argentine expert was out of the country for a month, but that I should call you, pose as a prospect, get the tackle information and then call Winchester back to book the trip with them."

I was flattered that Winchester had such a high opinion of our knowledge, but I was also very alarmed with the devious tactics. If Winchester had called me directly, I would have answered their questions.

"You know I'm a businessman myself," he continued, "and you've been so nice and patient to answer all my questions that now I feel ashamed and I want to make it up to you. Why don't I book this trip with you instead of Winchester?" And he did.

Bingo! Chalk one up for Safari Outfitters' Fishing Division.

Despite the big hoopla, sparklers, flairs and firecrackers that marked Winchester's spectacular entrance into the outdoor travel field, the giant company apparently overestimated the market at the time. There were cutbacks. The TWA executive who authorized the alleged $500,000 commitment in Winchester's brochure was uneasy about his future. Winchester World-Wide Adventures closed its travel division. Safari Outfitters and all the other travel agencies that mainly offered hunting and fishing trips could exhale and breath normally again.

"We will survive it," Roman had said all along, and he was right.

El Tarpon Tropical

Bill & Andy

BILL EGAIN was on the phone and said he needed to get away on a fishing trip sometime in July because, as he put it, his nerves were jangled.

"Instead of the usual Canadian fishing trip, I'm looking for some place that is not crowded and fishing is good: where I can fish from a boat, but cast from shore, too. Some soothing, restful place. I want about five days, maybe six."

"I have just the place for you. El Tarpon Tropical, near Ciudad del Carmen, Mexico. In the Yucatán Peninsula region," I suggested. "It's not crowded at all, because everyone goes there in the winter and spring. You may be the only guest there. It's owned by Andy Growich, an American, so there's no language problem. Super guy. And the fishing for tarpon and snook is usually better at this time, because the weather is stable. "

It was an "easy sell." Reservations were made, tickets issued, and Bill was on his way.

As soon as he saw the camp and met Andy, he knew he'd love El Tarpon Tropical, especially since he was the only guest there. By the end of the second day he had hooked and fought several tarpon and snook and even had some success casting from shore.

The third day was even better. Bill now was totally relaxed, and he felt better than at any time in the past decade. Annoying problems that appeared mountainous in the big city, suddenly vanished.

Good fishing trips can do that to a person.

"You know, Andy, this trip is exactly what I needed. This is the perfect fishing trip for me," Bill said, as the two of them sat outside enjoying the star-bright sky on a warm summer night, fanned by soft, soothing breezes from the Gulf.

The next morning after breakfast, Bill and Tomás, his guide, placed all the gear in the boat and headed for "Tarpon Alley."

"Wait, Tomás! I want to go back to the camp. I forgot to buy some more Sea Hawks and a few other lures," Bill explained.

Tomás, who spoke only a dozen or so words of English, spun the boat around and headed back to the beach.

Bill hurried to the lodge and looked for Andy. He noticed that the door leading to Andy's room was not closed and walked in.

He was horrified.

Andy had a pistol next to his head, his finger on the trigger.

"Andy! What are you doing?" he shouted and startled Andy. "PUT DOWN THAT GUN!"

Andy obeyed. He put it down.

Bill emptied the cartridge, put the bullets in his pocket, and placed the gun on the table. He spoke quietly to Andy and tried to settle him down. Andy was embarrassed, but suddenly snapped back to reality.

"Maybe it was the new medicine I'm taking," Andy offered sheepishly. Or perhaps it was because he was growing old, when he didn't want to grow old. Maybe it was a lot of things that produced a temporary despondency.

"Andy, you're so lucky. You are the owner of a famous fishing lodge. You live in this beautiful region. My God, people dream of your lifestyle," Bill was searching for the right words and he found them.

Bill didn't fish that day. He and Andy had long conversations about how he discovered this fabulous fishing spot, how he got started in the business, and about his wife who lived in the village but came to the camp periodically. Andy promised that whatever made him feel so depressed—a feeling that he could not explain, identify or isolate—had evaporated.

"Go fishing!" he told Bill the next morning, "I feel great. I promise that I won't do anything crazy!"

Andy certainly appeared relaxed, as he sprawled his legs and arms over several chairs as he drank his morning coffee on the patio.

Bill went fishing, but to this day can't remember if he caught any tarpon. He was concerned about Andy. How could Bill relax or fish? What if he had not returned to camp to buy some lures from Andy? What if he had arrived a couple of minutes later?

As was my custom in those days, I called Bill Egain upon his return to hear of his results.

"Find me another place," Bill said, "one with a lot of other fishermen around, maybe in Canada. My nerves are jangled worse now than before."

He related the story to me.

I was stunned.

Andy?

He lived a full life and died of old age. Unfortunately, the fishing at El Tarpon Tropical deteriorated because of pollution and overharvesting by locals. It was truly a magnificent fishing area in its day and many anglers caught their first tarpon at El Tarpon Tropical.

White water canoeing

BERT HAMEL had established a neat little canvas camp on Quebec's Kaniapiskau River, noted for its brook trout, ouananiche (landlocked salmon) and lake trout. In 1967, Bus Duhamel, U.S. district manager for Air Canada, developed a party of four which consisted of Bill Wanke, a prominent Chicago taxidermist, Harry Ruther, an engineer for Sears, Harvey Duck, a newspaper columnist, and me.

"Your mission is to fish this camp and report on the quality of fishing, meals and guides, because this lodge is a candidate for the airline's *Fin-Fur-Feather Club.*"

He handed us complimentary Air Canada tickets and off we went. Ahh, the good old days.

Club Chambeaux on the Kaniapiskau River could only be reached by float plane. The outpost camp included several cabins made from plywood floors and canvas sides and tops. Since Bert only booked one party at a time we had the entire camp to ourselves. Two French-Canadian Indian guides, Henri and Gilbert, were assigned to us. Although they spoke only French, amazingly we had no major communication problems despite my limited French vocabulary of a couple of hundred words.

We immediately realized that Henri and Gilbert were topnotch guides. Not only did they put us over heavy brook trout, ouananiche and some river lakers, but they were also expert canoeists and superb cooks. Many of the brook trout were more than three pounds and a few topped five. We had the whole river to ourselves!

It was one of the most enjoyable Canadian trips I've ever had.

After a few days of incredible fishing, the guides asked us if we wanted to try another downstream section that was about a dozen miles away. We could stay at another outpost camp that was unoccupied, and Bert could pick us up with his float plane there. From what I understood, there were some white water stretches but they were fairly easy except for one tricky, angry stretch of a couple hundred yards.

The guides explained that if we were concerned about the rapids, we could walk along the bank and they would negotiate the canoes down the stretch by themselves. We were content with the present camp and overwhelmed by the beauty and quality of fishing, but why not try another area?

While Harry, Bill and Harvey opted to walk the shoreline to avoid a rock-infested stretch, I decided to stay in the canoe. I learned that my guide was a Quebec champion in white water canoeing. Why walk, when you can ride? After all, I was with the champ.

My three companions made their way along the bank to a point beyond the raging rapids. Henri, their guide, expertly maneuvered his loaded canoe through the white water and avoided all the rocks. Well done!

A piece of cake.

My guide pushed us off, said something in French—probably "don't worry"—and off we went. We progressed nicely until we hit a rock which lodged us against some other boulders. We were stuck. Gilbert didn't want to scrape the bottom of the canoe, so he gracefully stepped out on a big rock and finally dislodged the canoe. We were on our way again. As the canoe progressed downstream we picked up speed. Faster and faster. The sound of the rushing waters was deafening.

At the point downstream, I saw Bill, Harvey and Harry waving their arms, undoubtedly cheering us on. I waved and yelled back. What an exhilarating experience! At one time I owned an Old Town canoe and could well appreciate Gilbert's superb paddling skill. These were not easy rapids.

Bill, Harvey and Harry continued to wave their arms fiercely and appeared to be shouting.

It was when the canoe finally whizzed by them at the point that I heard them scream, "No guide! NO GUIDE!"

I turned my head around. Gilbert was not in the canoe; he was still on the rocks way upstream. When he dislodged the canoe, it escaped from him and he was not able to jump back in. I was traveling solo.

"Oh my God!"

There was nothing I could do, and there was no way I could reach for a paddle. Fortunately, the worst stretch was behind me.

Amazingly I missed all the rocks except for the last one that jarred me. I made it to calmer waters, and Henri, the other guide, towed me in with his canoe.

Gilbert made it to shore by wading carefully and then walked along the bank. He was wet and probably cold. Worse, his pride was damaged.

We caught lots of big brook trout at the new camp, ate well, and that night we toasted the Kaniapiskau and our fine experience.

"You won't tell this to Bert, *ne c'est pas?*" Gilbert asked. It was a pride thing. The white water canoe champ of northern Quebec.

"No, I won't," I promised. And I didn't.

185

The chair

THEIR NAMES were Bob and Tony, young guys just starting out in business, and they were interested in taking a reasonably priced fishing trip to Latin America. I suggested a number of destinations, and when I described Club Pacifico de Panama, they booked it.

As they left, they noticed an old "executive chair" in my office: you know, the kind that has a high back that's adjustable and is on rollers? This chair had served first Roman Hupalowski and then me, and was in such disrepair that even I—who hate to throw anything away—was now convinced that a replacement was in order. So the old chair was in a corner of my office, waiting to be thrown out.

As they were leaving, one of them, I think it was Bob, studied the chair, turned to me and inquired about it. "Excuse me, but if you are throwing out this chair, do you mind if we take it? We're just starting out in business, and we're trying to control our expenses. We're adding another person and I think we can fix that chair."

"By all means, if you can use it, take it, but it's in terrible shape and ripped."

They wheeled it from our office to the freight elevator (despite the one roller that kept falling off), out of our building, down Madison Street, and then over to La Salle Street, where their office was located.

Later, they told me that they were able to repair it and put it to use.

B OB AND TONY had an excellent trip to Club Pacifico. They caught most of the important species, including some of the biggest cubera snapper ever to come out of the Club Pacifico's waters. Their guide was Don McGuinness, one of Central America's all-time best (unfortunately, he lost his life a few years later in a private plane accident in Costa Rica).

Bob and Tony were ecstatic about their fishing. "Don took us to a carefully selected place near Hannibal Bank and he said it was impossible to drop a big heavy bucktail jig over the side of the boat, allow it to go all the way to the bottom and then retrieve it to the surface," Tony related.

"Well, we made some friendly bets, and you know what? He was right. No matter how we retrieved the jig, fast or slow, something would grab it. You could feel the tremendous power of the fish. We never once got the lure back to the boat. We lost some money, because we tried it a number of times, but we're going to return to Club Pacifico next season to win our money back from McGuinness. We have some ideas!"

So the next year Bob and Tony returned to Club Pacifico with the provision that Don McGuinness would guide them again.

This time they arrived with a very heavy rod and reel that was wrapped with thick paper to "camouflage" it. Coyly, they told Don that they would like to fish that same spot again at Hannibal Bank. Don agreed.

"I got an idea," Tony said. "Why don't we bet like we did last year. You know, to make it more interesting?"

"Yeah, and why don't we increase the bet. We can afford to lose a little more this year," Bob added.

The "hustle" was on.

"No problem," Don said. "I had a good year in tips, so I don't mind losing some money to you fellas."

When they arrived at the chosen spot, Bob and Tony unwrapped their special gear. They had purchased a 130-pound outfit—like the type of gear used for 1,000-pound marlin. They even had a big-game fishing harness. They were going to win their bets this time. They grinned devilishly as they put their tackle together.

Don grinned, too.

Bob dropped the jig overboard, waited patiently for it to sink to the bottom and then began to retrieve. A big fish hit the lure and, at first, he was able to pump-and-reel and recover a few yards of line. Bob smiled sensing that victory was close at hand, but then the fish had enough of this little seesaw game, and began to demand more and more line. Using all his strength, Bob fought the fish as best as he could. Now it was a standstill. The fish swam slowly about, but there was no way that Bob could bring the fish closer to the surface. After about 20 minutes, an exhausted Bob told Don to cut the line. They lost the bet again.

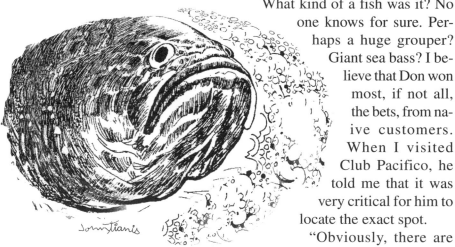

What kind of a fish was it? No one knows for sure. Perhaps a huge grouper? Giant sea bass? I believe that Don won most, if not all, the bets, from naive customers. When I visited Club Pacifico, he told me that it was very critical for him to locate the exact spot.

"Obviously, there are

some huge fish, but I don't know what they are. If there are also small fish, and they hit the lure, I think the big boys grab them," Don explained and that makes sense. "There are probably some cave-like formations down there, too, and the fish know how to use them!"

Oh, the discarded chair at the beginning of this story?

From their very modest office and meager start, Bob Van Kampen and Tony Wauterlek prospered and grew and grew into a giant investment company. About a dozen years later, Van Kampen Fund was sold for $200 million to Xerox. That's two-hundred million dollars!

You don't suppose my broken down chair was listed as an asset when the firm was sold, do you?

The break up

JOHN PROKOP, our accountant at Safari Outfitters came into my office. He was carrying some papers and a worried, puzzled look. I found this disturbing. I felt both the hunting and fishing divisions were doing very well.

"I better alert you. Roman said you are no longer to get the 50-50 split after expenses in the Fishing Division. He instructed me to give you only 25 percent and 75 percent goes to him."

"What?" I was stunned. The fast growing Fishing Division was gaining prestige and publicity for Safari Outfitters. Articles about our fishing destinations appeared in *Field & Stream, Sports Afield, Outdoor Life* and *Salt Water Sportsman.* The immensely popular *The American Sportsman* TV series featured several of our lodges.

Furthermore, the fishing clients had bolstered air ticket sales to a point where airlines not only noticed us, they were also proposing lucrative co-op programs. Our month-to-month progress was satisfying.

I stormed into Roman's office. "John said that you are reducing my share of the Fishing Division. Is that right?" I demanded.

"Yes, that's right. You are making too much money. Money can spoil people. People don't work as hard," he was visibly shaken, if not scared.

"Then why won't more money spoil you?" was my logical question.

"I am an old man. I lived many years. I know the value of the money, and besides I won't live long, and this company will belong to you some day," he forced a weak smile.

"Roman. I don't believe this! When you were in the hospital for two months, I handled your division and mine. Then, when you go to Africa for a month several times a year, who handles the hunting? Who booked Fred Bear to Angola on a bow-hunting trip? When I do these things, it takes time away from my division, but I never complained."

"Jim, I gave you a wonderful opportunity," is all he could muster. His voice now was weak and he seemed pathetic.

"Yes, and I worked very hard. You drew up the original contract up. I didn't. I signed it and I lived up to it. Look, during the first few years, I made less than $3,500 a year." I was furious.

Again he mumbled something about my inheriting the company.

"I quit!"

Roman was stunned and tried to calm me. My mind was made up. Even if he gave me all of the profits from the Fishing Division, I still would have walked out, because once that fabric of trust in an important relationship is ripped apart, it's impossible to mend it to its original condition.

I stalked out of his office and headed for the University Club where I had an appointment with Tim Clark and Bill Cullerton Sr. They were clients and friends interested in putting together a big group for a Costa Rican fishing trip.

"What's wrong?" Tim asked, when I sat down.

"No sense in talking about the Costa Rican trip. I just quit my job at

Safari Outfitters," I related the events. They shook their heads is disbelief.

"No problem! We'll start our own company. People know you now, and you will succeed. The camps respect you," Bill Cullerton spoke calmly. During the next half hour we informally formed a new company and then talked about Costa Rica and other fishing destinations.

I SOON FOUND OUT that Roman was hoping to sell the company to Harry "Skip" Cody, a young, local sportsman. So much for Roman's leaving the company to me after he died! I never found out why Roman suddenly changed the agreement.

Skip and I got along famously and I stayed on for the completion of the fiscal year, which primarily meant working a couple of months for free since most of the future sales wouldn't be credited to me because we were on the accrual accounting system. No problem. Business as usual. I trained Skip as best as I could, to operate the Fishing Division.

In the meantime, I drove to Champaign, Illinois to seek counsel from Don Dobbins, a partner in the Dobbins, Fraker and Tennant law firm. Don and I had become very close. Basically, he told me that Roman broke the contract, that he owed me 50 percent and I could go into business for myself, provided that I followed certain guidelines that he would outline.

"As a matter of fact, I'd like to be an investor in the new company along with Tim and Bill."

Don's decision to participate in the new company was a fantastic event. In addition to being a superb attorney and a very important mentor in my life, he was very knowledgeable about fishing camps.

L AST DAY at Safari Outfitters. I am a very emotional person. I cried when I saw *Brian's Song* and similar movies. For many years it was very difficult for me to attend funerals, even when I hardly knew the deceased.

When I said goodbye to Army buddies in France, tears rolled down my face. For heaven's sake, I was *leaving* the Army!

I worked at Safari Outfitters for more than a dozen years. Sure, I was furious at Roman, but the experience of starting the first international fishing division, the explorations, the exhilaration of new angling discoveries, yeah, and the disappointments, too, were fond memories. Great, wonderful memories that can never be duplicated.

Would I be able to control my emotions on my final day, at least until I left the building?

Roman and I went to lunch on that last day. He hinted that we could go back to the original agreement, but I was not interested. The trust was broken; it could not be repaired. When we returned to the office I placed my fish trophies and other belongings on a cart, shook hands with Roman, wished him luck, wheeled my stuff down the hall into the elevator and finally to a waiting truck.

Just like that. No tears. No regrets. No special feelings.

I was amazed at the lack of my emotion on my last day at Safari Outfitters, Incorporated.

A new chapter was about to begin.

UNTIL THE LAST DAY, I never told any of the clients or prospects that I was leaving Safari Outfitters. As long as I was in the office, I would perform my job to the best of my ability.

I had planned a fishing trip to Club Pacifico with Stu Apte. We would meet in Panama the day after my last day at Safari Outfitters.

I received a call from Francis Pandolfi. I had booked Francis and Joyce, his wife, to Club Pacifico, but I had never met Francis.

"Jim, I can't find any Rapala CD 18 lures here in New York, and according to your equipment recommendations I definitely should have them. A tackle store promised to get them in time, but here we are two days prior to our departure and I don't have them," he said.

"Don't worry, Mr. Pandolfi, you will have them in time," I said casually.

"But how? We're leaving tomorrow!" He was puzzled.

"Trust me, you will have them," I finally convinced him.

I had lots of Rapala CD 18s and took an extra supply for Francis.

I met Stu Apte in Panama City, Panama at the hotel, which was headquarters for Club Pacifico. The next morning, in the hotel restaurant I looked for Mr. and Mrs. Pandolfi. I saw a young couple, walked near them, and the man sounded like Francis.

"Mr. and Mrs. Pandolfi?"

"Yes?"

"Welcome to Panama. Here are the Rapala CD 18s for Club Pacifico."

Francis was floored. He couldn't acquire them in New York City and here they are, delivered to his table in Panama. He was dumbfounded.

"Who are you?"

"Jim Chapralis. I said I would get them to you and I did. I believe in great customer service."

He was surprised until I told him that I was going into Club Pacifico also. We all had a wonderful trip.

Stu, Francis and I became friends and continue to stay in touch more than 25 years later.

PS.: Roman eventually sold Safari Outfitters, Inc. and died at the age of 91.

PART FIVE

Feelings, emotions, &
relationships

PanAngling is born;
crazy, weird episodes in Colombia;
a camp owner's shocking adventure;
strange encounter in the Pacific
(what are the odds of this happening?);
fishing with four of the greatest anglers of all time!

The birth of PanAngling

THE NEWS SOON GOT OUT that I had left Safari Outfitters and that Harry "Skip" Cody, a prospective buyer had replaced me. Tim Clark, Don Dobbins, Bill Cullerton Sr. and I were in the process of forming a new company, but we kept our plan confidential. I received many flattering phone calls at home from camp owners, friends and clients wishing me well. Several offered financial help if I were interested in starting a new fishing travel agency.

I told Hank Looyer, a good friend and sometimes fishing partner, that I left Safari Outfitters. Without blinking, Hank offered to loan me money to start a new company. I thanked him but told him that I was already in the process of starting a new corporation.

Ned Payne, a hunter/fisherman whom I hardly knew at the time, phoned me at home. "Look, Jim, life's been kind to me financially. I'd be happy to loan you up to a couple of hundred thousand dollars to get started. When you get it going, you can pay it back."

Bob Nauheim, of competing Fishing International, offered me a job with his company. "Perhaps you could start a Midwest office for us," he suggested.

Then Alfonso Alvarez, one of the most brilliant young business people I have ever met, called from El Salvador and offered to go into partnership with me. "We'll start a new outdoor travel company. I'll put up $400,000 so we can do it right."

I was stunned. That was serious money in the mid-'70s. Alfonso was very successful in a dozen different businesses, but he had one failure that always troubled him: he started a general travel agency and it lost a lot of money. Remembering this, I asked him, "Why on earth would you want the headaches of a travel agency?"

"Because I failed at it, and I want to redeem myself."

The most flattering of all calls was from A. J. McClane, my angling hero/writer. He called me at home early one morning.

"I heard you left Safari Outfitters and I have some wealthy friends here in Palm Beach. We would like to back you financially to start a fishing travel agency. You would have to move to Palm Beach. . . I think this can be a superb opportunity for you and you can get away from those senseless winters in Chicago. I don't know how you live up there in the winters without any local fishing. . . some days I hitch a plane ride into Deep Water Cay Club, fish for bones for a day and come out the next morning. Everything is so convenient here."

No one knew more about fishing than A. J. In my opinion, there was never a better angling writer than McClane. No one had more international fishing experience than he did. He fished in what? More than a 100 countries? He did not disclose who would finance the corporation, but I knew that Al traveled in some wealthy, influential circles in Palm Beach.

"Think about it and let me know," he said.

I told my new prospective partners about Al's phone call.

"Look, Jim, you have to decide what you want to do," Tim Clark said. "As you know, Bill, Don and I do not expect to profit financially from the corporation. We were going to go into this business to help you and because it would be fun. But if you want to move to Florida and work with Al and his friends, that's fine. Your decision."

I called Al and told him that I appreciated his flattering offer but I would have to pass it up as my wife and I would have to remain in the Chicago area. That was one of the hardest decisions I ever made because of my great admiration for Al.

TIM CLARK, BILL CULLERTON, SR., DON DOBBINS and I held our first official meeting of the new company at the University Club. Not only did I feel very lucky to be involved with these friends, but their individual backgrounds would be very helpful to our new corporation.

Tim Clark was manager of Dean Witter's downtown office, so he was our treasurer. The money man. Tim was an avid hunter and fisherman, but his special joy was flying his Bonanza airplane to various hunting and fishing places, including Costa Rica, Bahamas and Canada. Tim knew many movers and shakers.

Bill Cullerton, Sr. was one of the most respected leaders in the tackle industry, a co-founder of *Fly Fisherman* magazine and a WW II ace. His reputation was so lofty, that many years ago the political powers in Illinois considered naming the new airport in Chicago after Bill. However, it was named O'Hare Field, after another WW II hero, deceased Butch O'Hare. As one politician coldly explained, "We named it after Butch because he's dead and there is no way he could embarrass us in the future. Bill? Nice young man, a hero, but you never know what anyone is going to do in the future." As I write this, the mammoth Illinois State Park and Winthrop Harbor have been renamed Bill Cullerton Complex.

Don Dobbins? He was not only an astute lawyer, he was a superb human being who had fished many international places and even financed Casa Mar Fishing Club in Costa Rica without seeing it. He was,

199

in fact, a very important mentor.

We needed a company name.

"How about PanAngling Travel Service?" Don suggested. "It has a nice ring to it. And it says what we do."

Pan of course means "all," and since we would offer angling trips all over the world, the name made sense.

We toasted to PanAngling.

I found suitable office space at 180 North Michigan Avenue. We hired Bill Cullerton's son, also named Bill. "Young Bill" as we referred to him, had just finished college with a degree in communications and was extremely knowledgeable in fishing. He and his dad were among the first to fish in Colombia for peacock bass. Young Bill and his brother Mark spent a summer guiding in Canada at Camp Manitou and then guided and worked at Parismina Tarpon Rancho in Costa Rica; consequently, they knew fishing from various perspectives and, most importantly, they knew the importance of customer service from their dad.

In our strategic planning stages, we decided that what was needed was a monthly newsletter on international fishing. This was back in 1975 when publications and other angling media weren't featuring many international fishing places. We called our newsletter, *The PanAngler.*

"Since people pay for a subscription," Don Dobbins instructed, "you are not to ever mention PanAngling Travel Service in the newsletter. If the newsletter is to succeed, you must present unbiased information. Provide reports from clients, news from camps even from those that we don't represent and we must print conservation articles and try to steer international fishing on the right path."

And that's what we did—or tried to—for many years.

We advertised *The PanAngler* in various outdoor magazines and mailed sample copies of the newsletter to prospective subscribers. The response was terrific. On some days, we would receive several hundred subscriptions! Soon *The PanAngler* was the most important selling tool for our travel business; it probably accounted for 70 percent of our direct and indirect business. I once told the directors that *The PanAngler*, despite its limited circulation, was the most quoted fishing periodical in other publications. I said this in jest, but I think it turned out to be true.

Many of the camps that had signed exclusive agreements with Safari Outfitters' Fishing Division did not renew and switched to PanAngling Travel Service.

Within a few months, PanAngling was booking about the same amount of fishing travel business as Safari Outfitters had when I was there.

Skip Cody and Roman could not agree on the sale price for Safari Outfitters so Skip left. The Fishing Division at Safari Outfitters crumbled and Roman went back to concentrating entirely on hunting trips.

PanAngling's future was bright. We were off to a great start.

YOUNG BILL CULLERTON did a spectacular job for PanAngling. Raised in the Cullerton household, he heard fishing talk just about every day and participated in numerous family fishing trips to Canada, South America and elsewhere. His experiences at Parismina, Costa Rica, and Camp Manitou, Canada, also proved invaluable.

We sent him to several fishing lodges so that he could become familiar with more camps and different types of fishing.

We increased our stockholders/directors to include Cameron Dobbins, Don's son. Cam was practicing law at his dad's law firm and was just as enthusiastic about fishing as we were.

We sent Cam and young Bill to Tropic Star Lodge, the glorious lodge in Panama known for its fantastic marlin and sailfish.

Booked during the same week was Henry Norton, who started Isla de Pesca, a very fine lodge on Costa Rica's Rio Colorado. Henry was very successful in many business ventures but knew little about the fish-

ing camp business. Although I had not met him at the time, I was angry with Henry because he built Isla de Pesca resort near Casa Mar Fishing Club. He was furious at me because I was boycotting his camp.

I strongly felt, and always will feel, that it is wrong to build a fishing camp next to an existing one, because anglers go to exotic areas not only for the quality fishing, but also for the solitude and remote setting.

Henry, his fishing partner Tom Gowenlock, Bill Cullerton and Cam Dobbins made the best out of an awkward situation. By the time they left Tropic Star they were all friends. Good friends.

At the same time, PanAngling's relationship with Casa Mar was deteriorating. Since we represented Casa Mar on the Rio Colorado and Parismina Tarpon Rancho on the Parismina River, each camp thought we were favoring the other (Carlos Barrantes had sold both camps to different owners).

At the next board of directors' meeting young Bill and Cam recommended that we represent Isla de Pesca because of the negative circum-stances developing with Casa Mar. I was stunned. So was Don Dobbins, who had a particular fondness for Casa Mar, since he had originally financed and named it.

"For the sake of PanAngling," Don said, "I think we should promote Isla." We all agreed. It turned out to be a wise decision.

THE FOLLOWING YEAR, we represented Isla de Pesca and ac-tively promoted its many fine features. As a result, Isla had more bookings than any other tarpon fishing camp in Costa Rica.

Henry and I became good friends. As it turned out, he was one of the easiest, fairest and most generous camp owners we represented.

Henry Norton brought new, creative approaches and ideas to the rela-tively staid fishing camp business. Many camps were "ma and pa," un-imaginative operations—not all, but many. However, in the 1970s a dif-ferent, younger breed was beginning to penetrate the fishing resort busi-ness. People who were very successful in other businesses became in-terested in owning, managing and developing fishing camps. Henry Norton was a good example. He was among the first to introduce "mod-ern technology" into the fishing resort business. Among the innovations was a computer that cost him more than $150,000. Never mind that a few years later one could purchase a more powerful computer for a frac-tion of that price. Henry believed in having a day-to-day knowledge of every financial aspect of the businesses he operated.

Sometimes he would operate on hunches without sufficient back-ground data. One day we had lunch at his Shuckers restaurant and he told me that he and his partners were constructing a new lodge on the Pacific coast of Costa Rica, in the province of Guanacoste.

"It's called Bahia Pez Vella. You know, Bay of Sailfish? Want to know how we came up with the name? There is actually a sailfish that jumps periodically in a small bay in front of the lodge!" Henry explained. He had hired Rick Wallace, a young, talented American, to oversee the con-struction and management of the lodge. "Fishing for sails, roosters, marlin, cubera and dozen of other species I'm told is terrific."

"But when is the best time?" I asked.

"Well, the best sailfishing is definitely from May until late September."

When I heard that the best time for the main species was during the summer months, I thought that there was little chance that the resort would succeed.

"Henry, American fishermen don't want to go to Costa Rica in the summer! They want to go Alaska, Canada or where it's cool. They don't want to fish closer to the equator," I said.

But there was no turning back now, and the lodge was built and we promoted Isla and Bahia. We offered a unique split trip during the spring and fall months between both coasts. Anglers could fish for tarpon and snook in a jungle setting at Isla de Pesca on the Caribbean and then fly to the Pacific side and fish for sails, marlin, roosterfish and other gamefish at Bahia. The trips proved very popular for a number of years and even the summer months for sails were well booked.

The sailfish that Henry said jumped periodically in the bay? It was true! I saw the sail leaping not far from the shore on two different trips to Bahia Pez Vela. In fact, a good caster with a two-handed spinning rod and a heavy plug probably could have reached the sail from shore! At first I wondered if Henry had built some sort of a mechanical sailfish that would pop up periodically. I wouldn't have been surprised.

Unfortunately, Henry had an argument with a partner later and both camps were sold for a fraction of their worth.

204

Rick Wallace, who was the manager of Bahia Pez Vela, went on to construct his world class El Ocotal resort.

B ILL SR. CAME TO MY OFFICE ONE EVENING. "Jim, I understand that things are going well at PanAngling and I know this is going to be a problem, but I need to have young Bill in my tackle business. We're expanding and I'm not getting any younger and, besides, I want to do a lot of things," he said.

Ouch! I had known this day was coming. It didn't make sense for Bill Jr. to work for PanAngling when his dad had built a very successful and lucrative tackle representation business that was expanding in many directions. Bill Sr. still had plenty of energy and an endless string of creative ideas. Now he wanted to fish and travel and do the many other things we all plan to do, but never quite get around to doing before it's too late. Mark, his other son, was already working for The Cullerton Company but the firm would also need young Bill. I understood perfectly. We thanked Bill Jr. for all his contributions and we started our search for a replacement.

One of the persons interviewing for the job—we'll call him Jack S.— had just finished Northwestern University with a degree in marketing. The interview was classic, especially when you consider it took place in the late 1970s.

Jack S. told me that he liked to fish and that he was very good at it. He preferred spinning but one day he would take up fly fishing. I told him that our agency focused on international fishing and we were hoping to find someone who had at least some experience in fishing in other countries.

"No problem," Jack S. seemed confident. He was about 22 years old. "I just broke up with my fiancee and I'm willing to fish all these countries you represent. I could be gone for a year or so, you know, fish at two or three places a month. I would have to be back home for the important holidays and for my vacations, of course."

"Well, who would pay for all this travel, and what sort of salary arrangements would you want?" I was curious. Very curious.

"Well, naturally PanAngling would pay for the trips and I would expect to receive a salary of about $50,000 a year to start with," Jack S. said in a matter-of-fact manner. Remember, we're talking about $50,000 in the late 1970s! A 22-year-old kid. No job experience! Man, where can I apply for a job like that, I thought to myself, and I had experience.

"Let me get this straight. PanAngling pays you $50,000 a year, and I assume, medical benefits and paid vacations. You go on a year-long trip, to all the great fishing places to gain experience at PanAngling's expense. Right?"

He nodded.

"I have another question. Let's say that after eight months into this fishing trip, or on-the-job training, you decide that you didn't want to work for PanAngling . . . let's say, you meet a girl in Argentina and you decide to get married and live there. Then what?" I asked.

"Well, that's the chance PanAngling's has to take. You know, in business today, there are risks that one must take. Sometimes they work out and sometimes they don't," Jack S., the 22-year-old applicant, explained.

Well, at least he didn't ask about stock options, though I'm sure that probably would have come up had the interview continued.

TWO WEEKS LATER, Bill Cullerton Sr. noticed a margarine container with a plastic lid on my desk. There were a dozen, beautifully tied, revolutionary trout flies inside the container. They were imitations of the *Hexagenia limbata* hatch that is so prevalent in Michigan and Wisconsin. This nocturnal hatch takes place in June and early July and the trout cannot resist these big flies. They come out from their hiding places and slurp these delicacies from the surface with such gluttony that even the wise old browns can be hooked at this time.

Bill inspected these flies carefully: "Wow! Where did you get these?"

"There's a young guy who joined the Lincoln Park Casting Club. Paul Melchior. Very good fly caster. Chuck Mitchell told me that Paul's a superb fly tier, among the best in the Midwest. So I hired him to tie up a dozen *Hexis*. Pretty good, huh?"

"Pretty good? Darn good! These will be terrific for Rainy Lake smallmouths in Ontario." He took the container of flies, put it in his pocket, but then decided to give me about half of the flies.

"What does this Paul guy do for a living? Tie flies?"

"I don't know. I see him at the club, casting away. I think he went to the University of Chicago, but I don't know much about him."

"Get in touch with him. Tell him to cut his hair, put on some shoes and report Monday to PanAngling."

Bill Sr. guessed right about one assumption: Paul's hair was long in those days, but he wasn't shoeless (he wore sandals).

I told Paul that we would meet with Tim Clark at the University Club. "It's a little formal there," I hinted. I didn't go into any detail.

Paul was hired. In fact, as I write this he is starting his 24th year at PanAngling. He has fished in many countries and was and is responsible for a large share of PanAngling's success.

All because of the *Hexi* flies he tied!

©mitchell

Colombian episodes

COLOMBIA IS ONE of South America's most verdant, beautiful countries. It's a pity that she is held hostage by the drug lords who have an unrelenting stranglehold on her people. Colombia, of course, was also the source of many incredible fishing adventures for visiting sportsmen.

I first heard about Colombia's fishing potential through Kjell (pronounced "shell") von Sneidern. He emigrated to Colombia from Sweden back in the 1920s, and became the country's leading ecologist and ornithologist. Kjell offered mostly fishing trips. He particularly loved the La Raya region: pure, clean waters, exotic fishing, even some tarpon. It was, in fact, environmentally perfect.

"We waded the waters of La Raya, and it was really a sensual experience to be in these transparent waters," said John W. "The fishing was a little disappointing, but the beauty of the area made up for it."

Unfortunately, Sam, a member of his party, slipped on a rock while wading and smashed his knee cap. He was in intolerable pain and was immediately taken to camp where Kjell administered a medicine to relieve the tremendous pain.

The charter plane that had brought the party into La Raya was not scheduled to return for several days, so Kjell initiated a "May Day" call on the two-way radio that he kept at camp for emergencies but never had to use before. He called for assistance over and over again, citing the location of the camp. He begged for help. A doctor. A plane. Anything. Did anyone hear his plea? Did the radio work?

Everyone gathered around Sam to comfort him, but his agony persisted and Kjell administered an even stronger medicine that he saved for such emergencies. He sat at bedside and held Sam's hand throughout the entire night.

The next day two men paddling frantically in a big cayuga, or dugout, approached the camp. Would one of them be a doctor? As they paddled closer and closer, everyone was confident that the men in the cayuga were answering the emergency call. Surely the man in the bow, who was less skillful as a paddler, must be a doctor.

And he was.

A witch doctor.

He explained that they had traveled a long distance. The doctor was old, not colorfully painted, and asked to see the patient immediately.

The doctor removed a small doll-like item from his bag, mumbled a few phrases, and kept passing it over the smashed knee cap. He obviously was trying to obliterate the bad spirits. It was jungle exorcism.

When the doctor finished his "medical treatment," he and Kjell argued briefly in hushed tones before Kjell pulled out some money from his pocket, crumbled it up angrily and gave it to the witch doctor.

"What was that all about?" John asked.

"The doctor said that he removed the evil spirits that caused the pain and that Sam would be fine in a few days. Then he wanted the equivalent of 30 U.S. dollars," Kjell explained. "I told him that it was too much money, and he said that normally his fee is $10 if you go to him, but since this was a 'house call' he was charging $30!" Kjell had no confidence in the witch doctor's treatment, but since he was the only one to respond and had traveled a long distance he paid him and even waved to him as he and the other man paddled away.

"If it weren't for Sam's agony, we would have all burst out laughing," John W. confessed later. "Even Sam smiled when he heard about the house call fee. Even in the jungles, they're learning."

Thankfully, a light plane landed a couple of hours later and taxied up the crude airstrip. Somehow the message had been transmitted to the pilot and he made an emergency landing. Sam and the rest of the party were flown to Bogota, Colombia where substantially better medical procedures could be administered.

"The plane was old and more suited for cargo," John W. recalls. "No seats. They were removed for the cargo. We were sitting on big bags of what we thought was flour, or some other pulverized food product, and then it dawned on me! We were sitting on 100-pound bags of cocaine and other drugs! And here I was on the President's antidrug committee! But what can you do? You are up in the air . . . our buddy was in pain . . . but it was so embarrassing."

After some medical attention in Bogota, Colombia, Sam was flown back to New York, where his knee cap was surgically repaired. Come to think of it, the witch doctor was right when he predicted that Sam's leg would be fine in a few days!

The La Raya camp was soon closed because locals, upon hearing of this great fishery, began to fish it with nets.

"They destroyed one of Colombia's most beautiful places," Kjell lamented. "At times it's difficult to explain to locals the importance of fish conservation and the irreparable damage done by overharvesting. Many places are destroyed because locals feel that the supply of fish in a river, lake or ocean is endless. It is not!"

E RLAND, ONE OF KJELL'S TWO SONS, was very interested in hunting and fishing. He had read about the fabulous peacock bass in neighboring Venezuela in *The PanAngler*. At that time, it was very difficult to get permission to fish the interior waters of Venezuela and only A. J. McClane and a few others were able to do so. A. J. described his great peacock bass fishing adventures in *Field & Stream* and in some of his books. Here's what he wrote me:

"The trip to Amazon Territory was fantastic! Caught 1,000 fish (honest estimate) with an average seven to nine pounds and top 18 pounds. All fly fishing with bugs and streamers. Nothing like it . . . I leave tomorrow for Europe. Be back in July. Still planning on Mozambique—Regards, Al."

The only peacock bass camp in Colombia at the time was E. L. "Buck" Rogers' El Dorado Lodge near Miraflores, Colombia. It was attracting a fair number of American fishermen, as reports of the fabulous peacock bass filtered back to the United States. Buck vigorously promoted South American fishing, but his tremendous efforts were never sufficiently recognized.

Erland was searching for something spectacular in Colombia; he was looking for an incredible fishing place, removed from any traces of civilization. His dad suggested the Rio Inirida and Matavani watersheds.

"That's where Colombia's largest peacock bass are to be found," Kjell told him.

Erland found out that his dad was right. The logistics were very difficult (close to impossible), but Erland inherited his dad's adventurous spirit and soon announced his Orinoco Ark's fishing trips in 1981.

The Orinoco Ark, which would house clients and staff, was built on a big barge and was actually fairly comfortable. It had six "cabins," a shower-and-toilet bathroom, dining area, and some sort of water filtering unit. The boat was moored against a rocky island on the Matavani near the Orinoco. While the Ark listed to one side, occupants adjusted to the slant after a couple of days and it never bothered anyone.

Getting to the "Ark" was not easy. Guests would fly to Bogota, overnight there, and the next morning they would be transferred to an airport for the four-hour flight to Puerto Inirida, on the Venezuelan side of the Orinoco. Then there was the five-hour boat trip to the Ark, that is, if there were no breakdowns en route.

Puerto Inirida was similar to the "Old West" frontier town: the bars, the honky-tonk places, the shootings, the characters with fuzzy pasts. Erland arranged it so that clients would be transferred quickly between the plane and the dock where the boats and guides would be waiting.

The flights between Bogota and Puerto Inirida were usually white-knuckle adventures. The Satena planes carried bicycles, chickens, fruits, vegetables, and, oh yes, passengers. Today, Dennis Wolters, a former American Airlines pilot and a fishing client, just shakes his head. Here's his report on his experience:

My flights between Bogota and Puerto Inirida proved to be very "interesting." As you may recall, the crews on those Satena flights were Colombian military officers and the flight attendants were sergeants. Before takeoff, I asked the captain about our route and told him that I was an American Airlines captain. We were in the air for about an hour, when one of the sergeants told me that the captain wanted to see me and escorted me to the cockpit.

The captain asked me if I had ever flown a DC-4 before. The plane was ancient, and I told him that I had never even been in one before. At this point, he got out of his seat, pointed to it and invited me to sit there. I did so, noticing that there was no autopilot but that the copilot in the right seat was flying the plane. The captain told me to fly the plane. I was reluctant to do so, but the copilot removed his hands from the controls, pointed to me, and said, "You've got it."

I grabbed the yoke and started flying. The captain watched me for about five minutes, then pointed to a large river, winding through the jungle, on the left side of the airplane.

"Fly this heading and make sure you keep the river in sight," he instructed and left the cockpit. The copilot followed him. I turned around and saw that a large lunch, complete with wine, had been set up on a table in the radio operator's compartment, which was right behind the cockpit. The two pilots and crew sat down and dined in style.

I was not comfortable with the situation but there was nothing I could do, as I had to concentrate to fly this ancient machine. The navigation instruments were so primitive I didn't even recognize most of them.

I flew about two hours, but every 20 minutes or so the captain checked the compass and made sure that the river was on the left.

"Bueno!" He'd say, patting me on the shoulder, and then return to his companions. Later he pointed out a runway a few miles ahead, carved out of the jungle, and told me to start letting down for a straight in approach. At about 1500 feet he motioned for me to get out of his seat, he climbed in and landed the plane. I guess having me for their autopilot was a real treat.

We had a week of wonderful fishing while living aboard the Orinoco Ark. Several times we were playing small peacocks of a few pounds, when all of a sudden a huge peacock would appear, attack and try to gobble up the hooked fish. These experiences indicated to us the necessity for using much larger lures.

At the end of our week, our guide brought us back to the airstrip by boat, and said he had to return to the Ark at once so that he could make it before dark. It's a long boat ride with huge boulders in the river.

We waited for the plane at the airstrip. And waited some more.

No plane. No flight.

Dick Winders, my fishing partner, and I seemed to be the only concerned people. Everyone else was getting drunk. Finally, I found an official-looking person in a brown uniform. Between his poor English and my few Spanish words, we learned that the flight was not coming in that day. He said the weather between Bogota and Puerto Inirida was bad, because this was the beginning of the rainy season, and it might be one day or ten days before the plane could come in.

There was no hotel in Puerto Inirida.

Dick and I had no idea of what to do since our guide had left. Finally we found some missionaries from the United States and they made arrangements with some local school teachers to put us up at their homes. We were grateful to all concerned.

After several days we were notified that the Satena flight would be arriving shortly. Soon we were flying out of Puerto Inirida but with the number two engine sputtering and backfiring until power was reduced on it.

About an hour later we landed at a small strip in the middle of the jungle. We were told to get off, and line up alongside the airplane. Several military types with weapons looked us over, grabbed a young couple and hauled them away. No one argued or commented on this event.

We boarded the plane once more. But after 20 minutes we were told to disembark again. Dick, my fishing partner, exited from the plane, while I waited for the others to go by first as I wanted to retrieve my camera from an overhead bin. I headed for the front exit door, but just before I got there, the sergeant told me to wait and closed the door. I told him that I was a pilot. He ushered me to the cockpit and told the captain who I was. The captain told me that the starter for the number two engine wouldn't work and they needed all four engines for take off, so we were going to do a windmill start. I had been flying most of my life and had never heard of this procedure before.

He then proceeded to start the two outboard engines and headed for the dirt runway. Once there, he added full power and started accelerating down the runway. The air passing through the number two propeller made it spin, and when it reached a predetermined RPM, we added fuel and ignition and got it started.

The jungle at the end of the runway rushed to meet us; I was positive we were going to crash into it. Suddenly the captain applied full brakes, and we came to a stop about a hundred feet from the end of the runway. He calmly turned the aircraft around, taxied back to the area where he had left all of the people and luggage. They reboarded, the baggage was reloaded and soon the plane was airborne with all four engines running.

I can't tell you how relieved Dick and I were when we heard that "sweet" screech of the tires and felt the bump as we touched down in Bogota.

Satena airlines definitely did things differently than what I was accustomed to—at least in those years!—*Dennis Wolters.*

More Orinoco Ark stories

GEORGE GREY MISSED a connecting flight in Miami, arrived in Bogota a day late, and was informed that there would not be another flight to Puerto Inirida for a couple of days. The other members of his party were already fishing in camp. He found out that there was a small military Cessna plane going to Puerto Inirida, but it would cost him 300 U.S. dollars. Cash. Did he want to go? Of course, he did!

What he didn't know was that, in addition to the pilot, there would be a guard and his prisoner aboard the small plane. The information concerning the prisoner was very vague, but apparently he was to be delivered to the Venezuelan border authorities.

"Don't worry about the prisoner. He will be handcuffed and the guard has a gun," he was told as he boarded the craft. *Good grief!*

The prisoner and his guard sat in the back while George sat next to the pilot. About halfway there, while George and the guard had dozed off, the prisoner evidently decided to hijack the plane. He reached for the guard's gun, which woke up the guard. There was a struggle. *BANG!!!* The gun discharged. Or more accurately, the guard shot the prisoner in the heart. Blood gushed out from his chest like a water fountain at first but then only in spurts, and finally only in dribbles. The prisoner was dead. There was blood all over the back of the plane.

"No problema! El es morte . . . " And the guard went back to sleep.

When they arrived at the air strip, the Orinoco Ark representative was there to meet the plane.

"How was your flight?" he asked, as George prepared to unsqueeze himself from the tight confines of the Cessna. Then the rep noticed the blood and the dead prisoner in the back. He recovered nicely: "Oh well, the fishing is terrific at the Ark!"

JAMES "BUD" WALTON, one of the Wal-Mart billionaire brothers, was among the Ark's first guests. Bud had a fine trip, except that he lost about a half-days' fishing because of a motor breakdown. Upon his return to the States, he wrote me and requested a refund of about $120.

As per PanAngling's usual procedure, I asked Erland von Sneidern, the outfitter, about this refund. Erland said he couldn't make refunds for minor boat breakdowns. After all, he was operating in a frontier region where there was little or no control over constant problems.

"Just about every week someone could have a complaint. If you make a refund to one, you should make them to all the others who lost fishing times," he said.

Bud was very disappointed when I reported this to him. I must confess, that back then I thought of Wal-Mart as a glorified regional variety chain—which it was at one time. I believe the letter requesting the refund was typed with a cloth-ribbon typewriter. The letterhead was not impressive—it looked like it was produced by a quick print shop.

I wish I'd saved that letter.

Bud Walton never returned to the Ark because he was peeved that PanAngling or Erland did not make a partial refund. After a few years, he resumed booking trips with PanAngling to other destinations. He even perused and recommended a fishing marketing plan that I conceived for Wal-Mart. I was to fly to headquarters at Bentonville, Arkansas to discuss it further, but his brother Sam passed away. Bud, who had severe leg problems, died soon thereafter.

L IVING CONDITIONS on the Ark were not that bad, except for the first week or two of its maiden season when the generator malfunctioned. There's nothing worse than not having ice or refrigeration in the tropics.

The fishing reports filtering back from the Ark were spectacular: many peacocks of more than 18 pounds were landed on a consistent basis. Later, Dr. Rod Neubert caught his 26½-pound world record from these waters. The peacock bass was suddenly becoming a highly-coveted species and the Orinoco Ark a popular place. Popular? It was the only facility at that time where big peacocks could be caught with any regularity.

Meanwhile, Homer Circle, the charismatic *Sports Afield* writer, was publicizing another tropical species available on an Orinoco Ark fishing trip: the payara! This species has the body configuration of a steelhead and is easily recognized by its two long saber teeth that protrude from the bottom jaw and neatly fit into two cavities in the upper jaw.

Caught in slow waters, the payara is a fairly good species. When caught in fast rivers or rapids, the payara is perhaps South America's second best freshwater fighting species, just a notch or two below the golden dorado.

One of the fabulous payara places in Colombia is called "Rapids of Death," and it was here that Papa Kjell von Sneidern set a world record with his 31½-pound payara. Also, it was here where the aging Kjell slipped from the rocks into the fast current which swept him downstream. The strong undertow prevented him from surfacing. Two anglers fishing from a boat downstream noticed a casting rod tip cutting across the surface. One of them quickly grabbed it and was startled to discover a half-drowned Kjell at the other end! Kjell was still fighting the fish underwater.

Because I was involved with some projects, I asked my "lieutenants" Paul Melchior and Al Schaefer, the Legend, as we called him, if either wanted to go to the Ark, as it was necessary for PanAngling personnel to have first-hand experience before we could publicize and market the trip successfully. They had

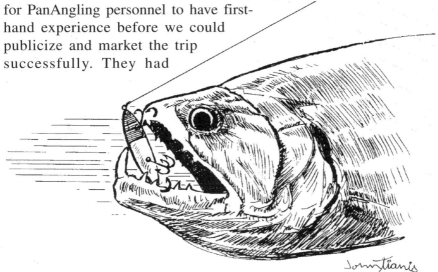

other commitments so I went in 1981 (the Ark's first year of operation).

I had a number of favorable surprises when I arrived at the Ark. First, I was pleasantly surprised that at least the creature comforts were there. I thought the Ark meals were marvelous and the cook was superb. I later found out that she had been the family cook at the von Sneidern home in Cali. She was not a happy camper on the Ark, easily preferring the luxuries and comforts of the Cali residence to the tropics where "savages" such as jaguar, anacondas and alligators lurked and stalked victims. But she cooked up a storm with the few appliances and ingredients that she had at hand.

It was one of the most memorable trips I've ever had. One day, while fishing at a distant lagoon, I hooked a huge peacock bass that made one of the most spectacular leaps I've ever seen from any freshwater species. It just hung up there for an instant, before the violent thrashing of its head got rid of the Mirrolure. The fish won its freedom.

John Renk, Cuenca, our guide, and I got a very good look at this fish, and we thought it would weigh 25 to perhaps 30 pounds. It was a bittersweet experience: I had hooked a magnificent fish, surely among the largest peacocks ever jumped; on the other hand, I had lost a possible world record that would help to establish the Ark's potential and reputation. Landing this fish would certainly increase bookings at the Ark and help PanAngling's bottom line.

"I wish that I had a photo of that fish up there in the air," I lamented.

"You do. It's in your mind and you'll never forget it," John said. He was right. I can still see that gigantic peacock up in the air, shaking, tumbling, thrashing.

We explored lots of waters. You must understand that this is a very desolate area with a maze of lagoons leading into other lagoons. One day, John Renk, Cuenca and I went into one lagoon. Cuenca—the area's most experienced guide—thought there might be another lagoon at the other end so we "macheted" a passageway and indeed found another lagoon. Then we accidently discovered another hidden lake beyond that one.

What a magnificent place. The indescribable beauty of the jungle-lined lakes, the unexpected clarity of these waters and the remoteness of this area would appeal to any freshwater angler, but no doubt would overwhelm the largemouth bass fisherman limited to fishing the crowded lakes back home. Except for the sound of feeding fish, the song of birds, or wildlife rustling in the bush, a total stillness prevailed, reflecting an unexpected gentleness of the jungle. Never mind that the survival of the fittest undoubtedly exists in full force here.

Cuenca was convinced that we were the first people to be in this lagoon. Ever. Certainly not any of the locals would bother going in. There was no reason to, and it was almost entirely lined with mangroves. We felt an eerie, overwhelming feeling, really a special honor, because perhaps we were the first humans in this lagoon. Cuenca convinced us that this was true.

Who would make the first cast in these treasured waters? John and I agreed to do it simultaneously. *One-two-three-cast!*

And the fishing was what one would reasonably expect from a truly virgin lagoon. Double-digit peacocks smacked our lures with explosiveness that jarred the quiet waters and surrounding jungle. We were convinced that we saw peacocks of more than 20 pounds, but the smaller fish (12 to 15 pounders) were faster and more aggressive. It was a special thrill to fish this lagoon.

Back at the Ark, John did some crazy things and I wonder about my judgment for going along with them. For example, one night around midnight he couldn't sleep because of the extreme heat.

"Why don't we go in for a dip?"

"Are you nuts, John? We've caught piranha right from the boat and you want to swim here? At night! And the guides said there is a big anaconda that lives near the boat . . . "

John thought about that, but only for a few seconds.

"I'm going in."

I heard this huge splash as big John cannonballed from the deck into the ominous waters.

I don't know what possessed me, since I seldom swim except when necessary, but I went in, too. Soon Erland and the rest of the guests woke up—Bob Miller, Bert Ellison, Kay Brodney, and Ken Cloaninger—and here we all were swimming in the Orinoco watershed at midnight, under the light of a full moon. Someone thought he heard the growl of a jaguar.

I was particularly concerned about the anaconda. I anticipated that Erland, a powerful swimmer, would dive under water and grab my legs, imitating this powerful snake. He did, and, although I had expected it, I still catapulted out of the water.

The next day John Renk wanted to see an anaconda. Cuenca said that he knew of a place where a huge one lived, but we would have to walk over some shallow, muddy flats for about 400 yards. John insisted we do it. I didn't want to, but John talked me into it.

As we sloshed along the muddy flats we noticed trails on the marl bottom, obviously made by some animal.

"What are those?" I asked Cuenca.

"Alligators. Mucho alligators aqui," he answered. "Grande alligators."

Gulp.

We could not find the anaconda, but we weren't attacked by the alligators, so I considered it a good day.

Despite the fact that Cuenca spoke almost no English, and our Spanish was very limited, our communication was excellent. More and more he was becoming familiar with sport fishing. He understood the practicality of spinning and plug casting but not fly fishing. Before the Ark was born, there were only two fishing methods utilized by the locals: netting and spearing. Cuenca, of course, was puzzled by the clients' catch-and-release philosophy.

One day we all went to Sema Lagoon, about two hours away from the Ark. This place was loaded with huge peacocks, and they were voraciously feeding on the surface. Just about everyone was catching big fish, so this was the perfect time to use the fly rod. While the peacocks were aggressively hitting the lures, I was able to attract only smaller fish on the fly rod. Cuenca could not understand why I insisted on fishing with the fly rod.

"You want big fish, then use this or that," he seemed to say in Spanish and point to the spinning or plug-casting rods. Then he would point to the fly rod, shake his index finger back and forth and insist that it was not good for big fish. It may have been the first time he saw a fly-fishing outfit, and he could not comprehend the sense of it. I tried big surface poppers and huge streamers, and although I had some substantial boils underneath, I didn't hook up with any big fish.

Bob Miller, fishing at another lagoon landed a peacock bass on a fly rod which for many years was the IGFA world record. Bob, an accomplished fly fisherman, caught an 11½-pound peacock on a yellow popper.

The Arbogast Jitterbug became Cuenca's favorite lure, although it wasn't necessarily the preferred lure among the peacocks. The Jitterbug is a topwater lure that, when retrieved steadily, wobbles from side to side. The *ploop-plop-gurgle* noise it makes as it waddles on the surface

is mesmerizing. Periodically Cuenca would insist that I put on the Jitterbug, not because he thought it was the best lure, but he liked the sound of it. I caught a number of fish on it, but they were small.

When it came time to say "goodbye" to Cuenca, we were all emotional. We had spent a wonderful week together. We had become friends. John Renk and I decided that we would tip Cuenca 150 U.S. dollars each—which was much higher than the average or suggested tip—but John insisted. When we gave it to him, he politely thanked us for it, but had absolutely no idea of what a U.S. dollar was worth in local money.

"Something's wrong?" I asked Cuenca.

He looked down and then up, and said something in Spanish.

We didn't understand what he was trying to convey.

He asked if I could open my tackle box, and when I did, he looked at the lures. Then he spotted the Arbogast Jitterbug. He picked it up and handed the money back to us and said something in Spanish.

He wanted to trade the $300 tip for the Jitterbug!

We laughed, insisted that he keep the tip and gave him the only Jitterbug we had with us. What a happy young guy!

"And how much happier he will be when he discovers how much a dollar is worth," John said.

Miller's Second Trip

John Renk, Bert Ellison and Bob Miller returned to the Orinoco Ark the following year (1982). Here's Bob Miller's account of what happened:

> During dinner (I think we had snake as the entree) John Renk bellowed: "Tomorrow we will go to the *Rapido del Morte* for big payara."
>
> So the next morning we traveled by boat for about an hour to the mammoth Orinoco, when suddenly I heard the loudest roar or thundering of water possible. We went around a bend and there before us, about 200 yards downstream, we saw and heard a wall of water crashing down a 10-foot fall against rocks that were as big as a house!
>
> The guide ran the dugout up a small feeder stream and into a quiet little bay. We got out and walked to the *Rapido del Morte* or "Rapids of Death." We cast flies and plugs for payara but fishing was slow, so after about an hour I started back to the dugout to get a soda. I walked about 500 yards over the huge rocks and I stepped over a crack that was about two feet wide. I slipped on the debris, gravel and small rocks—that acted like ball bearings—and fell straight down into the crack which was about six feet. I felt myself stopping after hitting rubble at the bottom and then I felt the most excruciating pain ever. It shot from my right foot up my leg.
>
> Of course, I couldn't see anything as the crack was not wide enough for me to look down. I was surrounded by rock walls. After the shock,

I really got scared as I was concerned about snakes and other critters that may live in the crevice. As you know, Jim, anything and everything strikes or bites in the jungle, especially when they are threatened. What to do?

I knew that John, Bert and others would have to use the same trail, but when? What if they had good fishing now and decided to stay there for a long time? Or worse, what if there were another way back to the dugout?

Although I am six-feet tall, I was unable to get a grip on top of the crack to pull myself up. So I put my hat on top of my fly rod and stuck it above the crack of the rocks as a marker.

It seemed like hours, but shortly thereafter I heard big John's booming voice: "What the hell are you doing down there, Miller!"

John then laid spread eagle at the edge of the crevice. I reached up and grabbed his arms and then he got up and pulled me out of my prison. I couldn't believe what he did—the immense strength it required—and thanks to John, I survived. Bert was also there to assist me. The next three days were the most dreadful in my life.

We went back to the Ark houseboat. My ankle to my knee was swollen like a football; another guest, a urologist, looked at it and said it was a "slight sprain!" The camp manager never came down to check with me.

One of the guides looked at my foot and advised that it was "*mucho malo*"—very bad—as if I didn't know this. But he thought he could help. We later found out that he was also a witch doctor.

I sat on the floor as the "doctor" felt the swelling of the ankle and foot. He thought for a moment and then he dug into a bag and pulled out a jar of some repugnant black and grey salve. Before applying the ointment, he opened the bag again and removed a few feathers which he proceeded to scatter around the floor in a circle around my foot. I think there were nine feathers.

He then set fire to the feathers on the floor and mumbled something in a dialect; it was definitely not Spanish. Then he started to chant as he also rubbed or shook some sort of a small gourd. Very mystic. Then he applied that vile salve on my foot and ankle and placed one hand on the heel of my foot and the other in front of the foot and pulled like hell, apparently trying to force the bones back in place.

I let out a heckuva cry as I've never felt such pain before. I then heard feet thundering down the steps.

"What's going on?" John asked.

I told him.

John wanted to scrap the fishing trip and to leave that night by boat for Puerto Inirida, which is about a five-hour trip, and head back to the States, but because it was dark we held off until dawn.

During the night, the Indian witch doctor thoughtfully made me a crutch. The only problem was that the crutch was made for someone

his size and he was about four feet, ten inches tall. I happen to be six feet tall.

It took us between six and seven hours to reach Puerto Inirida. I sat in the front of the dugout with my bandaged foot on the luggage. Bert found a bandage in his gear and with some duct tape and a shower clog he fashioned a shoe for me.

The trouble was that once we arrived at Puerto Inirida dock there were about 50 stone steps to climb. I sat on the bottom step, and using my hands and one foot, and with help and encouragement from John and Bert I crawled up. One step at a time.

Since we didn't have reservations for the plane service to Bogota and onward to Miami and then home we ran into problems, but we worked them out.

Home at last! When I arrived in Toledo around 1 A.M., my wife, Pat, met me and took me to a local hospital. But the next day, after my foot was X-rayed, the doctor said they couldn't (or wouldn't) handle that kind of a break so he sent me to another hospital. There another doctor insisted on immediate surgery. I told him when I broke my foot, and he couldn't believe that I withstood so much pain for so long.

The surgery lasted about two hours and then I was fitted with a cast and crutches. The accident happened in February but it wasn't until September that I could get rid of the leg cast and crutches.

On this trip, I learned how wonderful it is to have superb friends like John Renk and Bert Ellison—they were with me all the time. Now poor John is gone.

The things we fishermen do and endure, for our passion for fishing! —*Bob Miller.*

Aftermath

The Orinoco Ark and Colombian fishing? Well, Erland von Sneidern built a new, more comfortable Ark and had it moved to the same spot. It was fully booked the following season. Tremendous success was guaranteed.

Except that some local people, with an obvious interest in growing and processing certain plants, objected to the fact that the Ark was in this area. American fishermen traveling up and down rivers might interfere with regional "farming." At least that's the theory advanced and it makes some sense. So the new Ark mysteriously sank one night.

Convinced that this was a very dangerous area, Erland then built a fantastic camp called El Morichal on the Beta river, further north, near Puerto Carreno. There was a military unit at Carreno and police and Army personnel monitored the region, so Erland felt secure.

Erland enjoyed several very successful years at El Morichal, and it appeared that he made a wise decision to establish his camp there, until he was kidnapped and held hostage for about 80 days. Finally, after a wild shoot-out in which several dozen people were killed, Erland and an Italian hostage were rescued by Erland's brother, cousin and a half-dozen hired hands.

But that's another story. Or a book. Or a Harrison Ford movie.

Erland is offering a new fishing/hunting program in Bolivia.

John Renk? He returned to his Wisconsin home/farm where he operated a lucrative agricultural business. He was killed soon thereafter in a tragic, gruesome accident involving farm machinery.

John was a super human being. I feel privileged to have known him, and to have fished a lagoon that perhaps no one else ever fished!

Michael's great
bonefishing adventure

I THINK HIS NAME was Michael. He was thirty-something. I remember that he was decked out in the latest bonefishing threads, including new flats wading shoes, but what really impressed me were his top-of-the-line Sage and Loomis fly rods, the Billy Pate reels and the hundreds of bonefish flies, all neatly perched, according to pattern and size in labeled boxes, like little planes on an aircraft carrier ready for takeoff.

This guy was easily one of the best equipped fishermen that I've ever seen!

I was at Rupert Leadon's Andros Island Bonefishing Club, Bahamas. The camp just opened up and I was there for a firsthand experience for PanAngling Travel Service. Part of my job, you know.

"We have another single, Michael, booked for a few days, and perhaps you can fish with him?" Rupert asked.

No problem.

Michael seemed like a nice guy. A little tense—probably business nerves, I thought. Perhaps he bought a huge house in a toney Connecticut suburb and had staggering payments. Whatever.

"Have you fished bonefish before?"

"No, actually this is my first time for bonefishing," Michael replied. "I just learned to fly cast at a school."

"Well, what type of fishing have you done before?" A logical question, I thought, as we sped to some distant flats.

"Actually, I never fished before. This is my first trip."

He then recounted how he read about fly fishing, watched several TV fishing programs, and decided that he wanted to get into fly fishing. Especially for bonefish. He was obviously a very successful, young businessman. Michael said that his wife owned a business that took up lots of her time and that she was encouraging him to find a hobby.

I was about to give him my "fishing-ain't-a-hobby, it's-a-way-of-life," speech, but I resisted.

Our guide stopped the engine, allowed our skiff to coast before he quietly picked up the push pole and began to propel us to a flat a few hundred yards away. His head moved slowly back and forth, as he searched for tails or fins, or any type of movement.

"Michael, you fish first. I'll help you, if you'd like, but I won't fish until you land your first bonefish," I insisted, and he seemed to like that.

He loosened up and even smiled when I related some of my bumbling bonefishing experiences. We tied on a "Charlie" and I asked Michael to cast so our guide and I could gauge his casting skill and range. He cast very well. He could drop a fly fairly accurately within a 40-foot range. I was relieved. Often people who go to these casting schools learn the essentials but don't practice. Then, too, it's vastly different casting a practice fly on a peaceful school pond than a weighted "Crazy Charlie" under actual fishing conditions (the wind almost always blows on the flats). At first I feared that it might be a long time before I would get a chance to cast to a bone, since I insisted that Michael must *land* a bone-fish before I would pick up a rod, but now I could see that my new fishing companion was a well-coordinated, aggressive, fairly accurate caster. Whoever taught him to fly cast did a very good job.

Our guide pointed to a small pod of bones; maybe there were five or six. He propelled the skiff silently to within casting distance of the bones.

Michael had moved quietly to the casting platform, and after a little pointing he picked up the shadowy movements of the bones. Good eye-sight, I noted. He lengthened his line, false casting away from the fish so as not to spook them, and then he dropped the fly to the fish.

A little short.

He quietly lifted the fly and lengthened his cast, but it was not ex-actly on the target. The bones seemed too busy munching on hors d'oeuvres to worry about our presence. Remember, the camp had just opened so these bones were not very wary.

His next cast was "Lefty Kreh perfect."

"Slow down your retrieve . . . it's interested."

Michael did, and the fish hit the fly. He had it on for an instant, but the bonefish got off. I was excited! Imagine, his very first fishing trip—really his first casts at fish—and he hooks a fine bonefish. He never went through that perch-sunfish-bass-cane pole routine that most of us experienced before we went "big league."

We found another pod, a few hundred yards away. It was a repeat of our previous experience. Again Michael only had the bonefish on for a few seconds. The guide and I were elated, because it was a matter of time before Michael would succeed.

We couldn't find any more bones in the area, but the guide said we would run about 20 minutes and surely we would find more bones there, because of the tide. We did.

Michael was casting better and better. He was a quick learner. He stripped the fly just right, and he nicked a few more bonefish. Michael delivered a nice cast to a fine fish, possibly eight pounds, but the bone, although aggressive at first, changed its mind at the last second when he saw the skiff and us. Although I love to fish, I was now enjoying this. It was a challenge of sorts, helping Michael, who never fished before, hook a bonefish.

"Can we go back to the lodge?"

"Huh?"

"Can we go back to the lodge?" Michael repeated.

"Look, if you have to go the washroom, I'm sure our guide can find a suitable place . . . " I was trying to be delicate. "We'll lose a lot of time going back and forth . . . " I pleaded.

"No, I want to go back to the lodge!" He gave no further explanation. Maybe in his business and back home he didn't offer explanations.

So we went back. After all, he was a *paying* guest.

The guide and I waited in the skiff at the camp's dock. We tried to figure out what the problem was.

"Maybe he's sick?" the guide offered.

"Maybe."

After about a half hour, Rupert came down to the dock.

"You guys can go fishing on your own." He offered no explanation, and we didn't ask.

In a selfish way, I was pleased. Great bonefishing waters. Great guide.

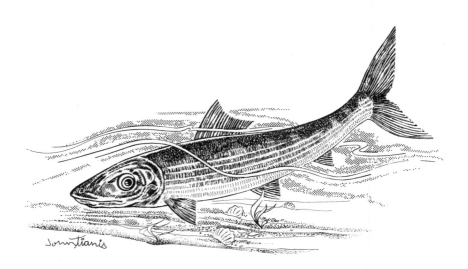

New skiff. Conditions seemed close to perfect. I would have all the chances. Take advantage of the day. Seize the opportunity!

I had a ball. Lots of bonefish landed. Lots of big ones sighted. A couple of giants hooked but lost. Ahhh, what a glorious day. By the time we headed back to camp, I had classified this day as one of my best bonefishing experiences in years. I was bopping around on the return, scatting some jazz riffs, off-key, I'm sure. Hey, it was a great day. Express yourself. The guide was happy, too.

Rupert met us at dock.

"How's Michael?" I asked.

"He's no longer here. He asked me to call for a charter plane and he went back home," Rupert answered. "He said there was nothing wrong . . . you guys were helpful. . . but he found out that he doesn't like fishing. He said he'd rather be home working on some projects, so he left. I told him I couldn't make a refund, but he said he didn't expect one. He didn't care."

I was stunned. Here's a guy who was starting at the top, fly fishing for bones, and surely would have succeeded if he gave it just a little more time.

I wondered about his top-of-the-line Sage and Loomis fly rods, the Billy Pate reels and the hundreds of bonefish flies, all neatly perched, according to pattern and size in labeled boxes, like little planes on an aircraft carrier ready for takeoff.

His perfectly designed, matching equipment just didn't have a chance to do its stuff. Maybe he will give fishing another chance.

Or maybe they will occupy a dark, seldom-opened musty closet.

Next to that drum set or golf bag.

Or perhaps someone will really luck out at a garage sale.

PS: The fishing was even better the next few days!

Sue Ellen and Dave

HER NAME WAS SUE ELLEN. I know that there was a sinister, conniving "Sue Ellen" on the popular *Dallas* TV program, but since I've never watched this long-running series, I wasn't even mildly suspicious at the outset. Besides I bet there are thousands of splendid "Sue Ellens" for every bad one roaming this earth.

The Sue Ellen I met was the type you might want to know casually; heavens, she was never, never boring and almost always very entertaining. At the same time, I would think that Dave, an eligible, somewhat sophisticated bachelor would have immediately picked up on some of the not-so-subtle signals and avoid any type of romantic relationship with her. For, to be involved with Sue Ellen, beyond a casual friendship, would surely result in a substantial emotional or financial loss. Or both.

Sue Ellen, in her late 40s, was an attractive redhead, very bright, had held a number of very responsible jobs, was a quick thinker and wrote fairly good poetry, mostly on unrequited love; in fact, a number of her poems were published in *Cosmopolitan*, although I'm not sure if this is a positive or a negative testament on the quality of her work.

Dave, in his early 50s, was a quiet, soft-spoken man with good looks, accompanied by easy but controlled smiles. He was smart, pleasant and really quite talented in a jack-of-all-trades sense. If Sue Ellen was the temperamental, aggressive type, Dave's seemingly relaxed approach to life served as a calming balm.

They had each been married before. I have since heard that Sue Ellen's first husband, a former pro football jock, allegedly served time in prison, but I don't know why. I don't know anything about Dave's first wife.

Dave and Sue Ellen met. They formed some sort of an alliance or business partnership. With their rich, broad backgrounds, they were consultants to a regional airline, a famous mega hotel chain and several other travel-related corporations. Their résumés were quite impressive. It was perfectly clear from their conversations and actions that they intended to become shakers and movers in the corporate world.

So Gonzalo Moreno, who owned Puedpa, a fine fishing lodge for peacock bass in Venezuela, and I wondered why Dave—her boyfriend who later became her husband—ever got tangled with this redhead in the first place. We considered a number of possibilities: Perhaps Dave was originally a nice guy who just happened to be lulled into a love nest and then became involved in the scam? Or maybe it was Dave who hatched the plan and Sue Ellen went along with it, both intoxicated with the thrill or excitement of the game? Perhaps they were both honest citizens at the outset, but when they sank into a deep financial mess, they resorted to fraud as a solution.

Gonzalo and I debated all these and other possibilities for hours. We rejuvenated past conversations, recreated "suppose" scenarios and reconstructed events in our search for answers. Gonzalo and I never arrived at a conclusion, that we could agree upon, because we constantly altered our opinions as various episodes unfolded.

I sought Gonzalo's opinions and analysis on Sue Ellen and Dave for two reasons: First, Gonzalo had earned a Ph.D. in psychology from Stanford, so he certainly must have a sharp insight into these matters; and second, he is the one who lost several hundred thousand dollars. Me? I, too, could have been a big loser in this caper.

Actually I first "met" Dave and Sue Ellen through phone calls that spanned more than a year's duration. Later I met them in person when they came to Chicago and then I saw them again in Arizona. It seemed that a friend of theirs introduced them to Gonzalo Moreno and Luciana, his wife, who came from very prominent Venezuelan families (Luciana's father was president of the country, and Gonzalo's dad was an ambassador).

The Moreno family owned a huge ranch with thousands of heads of cattle, in addition to other businesses and lucrative investments. They even hosted Jimmy Carter, Indira Gandhi and other prominent and influential people at their ranch house near Guri Lake, an impoundment famous for its mammoth peacock bass.

Gonzalo Moreno, who was probably 42 at the time, loved to fish and realized that if he converted the ranch house to a fishing lodge, he could devote (in the name of research, of course) even more time to fishing than he already was, which was considerable.

Now, Sue Ellen and Dave had little or no experience in fishing or promoting fishing camps, but this did not deter them. They gathered information from PanAngling Travel Service and several other outdoor agencies. They introduced themselves on the phone and proceeded to pick my brain about every aspect of the sport fishing business.

One of my employees pointed out that it was very peculiar that they always called around noon, when I was usually at lunch. I would call them back and the long conversations sometimes lasted more than an hour, on my dime, so to speak.

My interest in this project was that PanAngling was always searching for a new, exciting fishing camp or destination, and it appeared that Puedpa on Guri Lake could be it. I received photos of gigantic peacock bass (some were more than 20 pounds), and the fact that the Morenos had an abundance of political and financial resources was an additional solid reason to invest time and effort in Puedpa. I spent many hours explaining the fishing travel biz and advising this couple, step-by-step, how to proceed. I was confident that this would pay off in the future. Besides, I enjoyed the satisfaction of helping and introducing a new fishing destination to fishermen. Call it ego.

These long phone conversations, as it turned out, were also the basis of their 70-page feasibility report, which I later found out they billed to Gonzalo at more than $60,000! One day, Gonzalo let me read it. Wow! It reiterated exactly what I had said on the phone all those hours. And to think that they didn't even pay for the phone calls!

Before we caught on, Gonzalo Moreno appointed Sue Ellen and Dave his U.S. General Agents, which meant that all reservations, deposits and balances would be funneled through their Phoenix office.

I had no objection. I fished at Puedpa and quickly realized its wonderful potential. I didn't have sensational fishing, but my results were more than satisfactory. Moreover the lodge and Gonzalo's connections were huge pluses. Almost instantly, Gonzalo and I became good friends. The alliance of Gonzalo, Sue Ellen, Dave and PanAngling seemed solid and productive.

We booked a few clients immediately. Upon receiving favorable reports, our reservations soared. There was no question as to the great potential of the lake. Certainly there were huge peacock bass in Guri because of the great amount of readily available food, but it was also this overabundance of food that made fishing difficult. A peacock bass with a full gullet is not likely to attack an angler's artificial lure.

According to the terms of business, clients had two weeks to send in their deposits after reservations were made. We, in turn, would forward these funds to Sue Ellen and Dave in Phoenix. Similarly, the balances were due about 30 days prior to clients' scheduled arrival. The trip was around $2,200 per person plus air fare and incidentals.

PanAngling had adopted a somewhat relaxed policy on deposits and balances because many of the Puedpa clients were our customers for many years and we were never going to press them to adhere to these stringent terms of business. Most people who booked, however, followed the policy very closely, so there was a constant cash flow from customers to PanAngling to Phoenix.

But Sue Ellen or Dave were constantly on the phone. Where is this deposit? What about the balances? Mind you, we were sending them big checks right along, even if some of the payments were a little late.

"What difference does it make? These clients aren't going until next year!" I told Dave or Sue Ellen.

"Gonzalo insists on the money as per the terms of the contract!"

A few months later Gonzalo was on the phone from Caracas, Venezuela. He was pleasant enough, but then he asked about the money.

"I want to make improvements at camp. I want to buy some new boats and build a better pier. I don't want to touch our other assets because other family members are involved."

"Geez, Gonzalo, I'll see what I can do. But I've sent more than $200,000 to Sue Ellen and Dave so far."

"YOU WHAT?"

I repeated my statement. Gonzalo was stunned. There was silence.

"I will call them right away and get back to you. They told me you owed lots of money to them and the little that they have received was used for promotion and expenses."

Later that day Gonzalo called back.

"Can you come to Houston on Wednesday? I have some business to attend to in Houston regarding my cattle. Bring copies of all the cancelled checks you've sent to Sue Ellen and Dave. I'll appreciate it, if you can make it. They'll be there."

"Well, yes, but what makes you think that they will show up?"

"They will show up! They gave me their word, and they will bring their books to show their expenses. They have to come. I can't believe that there is a problem. But something is wrong somewhere, because I called two other agencies and they have sent some money to them also. I think there must be more than a quarter of a million in limbo somewhere . . . I had a very bad connection with Phoenix so I couldn't hear everything Sue Ellen and Dave said."

236

I didn't think they would show up at the hotel in Houston and they didn't. I gave Gonzalo the copies of all the cancelled checks made out to them. Gonzalo was surprised. Very surprised.

We called them at their Phoenix office. "Sue Ellen isn't feeling good and we couldn't make it," Dave said feebly.

Gonzalo then explained that he had seen my cancelled checks, and there was a lot of money somewhere between Phoenix and Puedpa.

"Look, Gonzalo. This is like an accusation. Sue Ellen is not feeling good and she is very upset that we are being accused of some wrongdoing," Dave said. "I think she is going bonkers and I have to hang up and tend to her." He hung up.

Gonzalo was furious at first and then burst out laughing.

"You know in Venezuela we have a thing among the top business men who trust each other. We never ask about money that is due to us. Always, it comes in. To ask for it is an insult. Well, I guess this doesn't apply to Sue Ellen and Dave."

"You asked *me* for the money," I countered.

"You're different. You're family," he replied. I liked his answer.

Gonzalo turned the matter over to an attorney in Houston; I don't know how, but the lawyer persuaded (or threatened?) them to a point that Dave and Sue Ellen showed up in Houston and met with Gonzalo and the attorney a few weeks later.

"It was classic," Gonzalo later told me. "I hired a big, huge private investigator to stand outside of the door of the hotel room where we were going to meet. He had a big moustache and he looked like he could tear anyone apart. I think they were stunned.

"Then when they entered the suite, we sat them in a place where the sun from a window would shine in their eyes. You know, like in the movies when they have a bright light shining on a suspect's face while he's being questioned? Like that."

Say this about Gonzalo. He always maintained a sense of humor.

"What about the money?" I asked.

"They said they had unusual expenses. A wardrobe and lots of shoes for Sue Ellen. Clothes for Dave. When I asked what does this have to do with Puedpa, she said that she needed to look great, have the right clothes to sell and promote Puedpa properly and that I didn't understand PR. Can you believe that?"

"But what about the rest of the money?" I asked in disbelief.

"They charged their wedding in Acapulco, Mexico to Puedpa. They claimed that because of the fishing tournament at Puedpa they had to change their wedding date and site from California and they were charging it to us. They invited and paid for airline tickets for many friends who were disappointed in the postponement of the wedding."

The upshot was that they finally agreed to pay a few thousand dollars each month. They signed the agreement and I think they paid for a couple of months. And that was the end of the payment. It seems that Dave and Sue Ellen had some other business transactions with an English jewelry firm and a French dinnerware company. They owed them huge sums of money; furthermore, they apparently cheated some people in the United States including one major corporation.

Long articles in the *Arizona Republic* newspaper revealed how Dave and Sue Ellen owed lots of money and disappeared when they found out that the authorities were seeking them. They were listed as fugitives.

I've never heard anything about them since they fled. That was about seven years ago. Gonzalo took the big financial hit; past and present clients, who had paid, were hosted at his camp even though Puedpa had not received the money from Sue Ellen and Dave. No one likes to lose hundreds of thousands of dollars, and while Gonzalo took it in stride, he was obviously upset that two people whom he befriended and trusted cheated him. It could have been disastrous for PanAngling, too, if Gonzalo didn't honor the bookings for which he had never been paid. After all, our clients paid PanAngling and we'd be responsible.

Did Sue Ellen lead Dave astray or was it the other way around? Were they simply irresponsible and actually thought they would repay the money? Did their high living habits cause them to travel down this disastrous road? Was this a planned scam from the beginning? Are they hiding out in the United States or in another country?

I don't think I'll ever find out.

The shocking adventure of a
camp owner

WHILE MANY OF US—fishermen, travel agents, writers—like to take the credit for promoting and publicizing new fishing areas, most of the recognition should go to the camp owners. They take the financial risks, which are quite high, especially in exotic or new areas. Sometimes, too, their safety is at risk.

I can cite no better example than what happened to W.E. Lanford II, a Texas sportsman who searched Central America for the "right" spot to build a fishing camp. He found it at Karawala River, on the Caribbean side of Nicaragua. Big tarpon. Some over 150 pounds. Huge quantities of snook. Lots of other species, too. So he set out to build his modest Karawala Tarpon Camp in the mid-'70s, and the initial reports were quite good.

But Nicaragua's politics were not stable. The Sandinistas were organizing the overthrow of General Anastasio Somoza. The former head of Nicaragua fled to Paraguay, where he was gunned down.

The Sandinistas now ruled the country. They promised democracy and new freedoms. W. E. Lanford II returned to Nicaragua to visit and open his fishing lodge for the forthcoming fishing season.

His shocking experience is told below in his letter to me:

September 15, 1979

Dear Jim,

Karawala Tarpon Camp no longer exists.

I arrived in Nicaragua on September 2. It took only three days to renew my permits and licenses and to see the officials of the new government who would be concerned with a tourist business in their country. It all went smoothly. The new director of tourism was very pleased that I had returned and that I was planning to continue my operation. He told me of their plans to promote tourism, and of a new Holiday Inn already under construction. He made phone calls for me that would help to smooth my way, and gave me a letter of recommendation to show to any official I might have to deal with.

In Managua there was a military atmosphere, and even though I had become accustomed to the ever-present soldiers in Nicaragua, this was a new army, apparently without the restraints of training and discipline. It gave cause for caution. The machine guns and rifles, hand grenades and pistols were now carried by adolescents, many of whom were too young to have any need for a razor. And they were everywhere.

Still, I wasn't worried. I assumed that the children would be replaced by real soldiers, or policemen, and that their presence, in time, would be diminished. I hadn't expected everything to be well organized and running smoothly so soon after the revolution. From what I had read in the newspapers here before I left, I assumed that the new government was moderate, that it was protecting private property, and that it would welcome foreign investment and business.

240

Friday, September 7, 1979 I flew to Karawala. The first thing I noticed that was out of the ordinary was that there were no horses or cows on the runway, or visible anywhere, for that matter. Then, as we circled, I saw that the boat shed was gone.

The dock was gone.

The boat house was gone.

The boats were gone.

We landed. In the past, usually the entire village turned out to greet us when we landed, all with smiling faces and laughter. . . happy that I was back. This time not one soul came from the houses. I could see some faces in the windows, and I waved to them.

Then I turned to the camp. The screens were all torn from the windows of the big house. I climbed the steps and stood in the open door. It was all gone. The refrigerators, freezers, stove, tackle. . . all gone. The big house had been converted into a school. Not one thing that belonged to me was left. I walked to the work shop, which was full of tools, lumber and work in progress when I left. It was empty.

I took a deep breath and walked to my house. It, too, was empty. It had even been cleaned, as if someone might be moving in soon. Of all I owned, not one thing was left. Not even a fish hook.

It took less than five minutes to survey the damage. When I got back to the plane, the soldiers were waiting. I was quickly surrounded and taken into the big house, seven machine guns casually pointing my way. Inside, they told me to stand, while they sat in a circle around me. They were all very young, and seemed uncertain as to what to do with me. They had assumed I would never return, and, having returned, I was an unpleasant problem for them.

My papers were demanded. I gave them my passport and the letter from the Director of Tourism. The boy who had asked for them couldn't read, and had to ask his friends if any of them could. Two could, but it took them several minutes, lips moving with each word, to read a half-page letter. When the letter had been discussed, they handed it back to me and said, "This is no good." My stomach felt like I had swallowed hot lead.

"We will have to decide what to do with you," I was told by the boy facing me. He was about 16 years old, and was light in complexion and hair. I wondered where he had come from. Only one of the soldiers was from Karawala. He was one who had been trouble for me since my first visit to Karawala, even before I started building the camp. He had never hidden the fact that he hated me. Now he was dressed as a soldier and held a gun.

A small group of Indians from the village had gathered across the runway, their subdued appearance conspicuous. After a few whispered words, the soldiers began calling them one by one into the big house. I was on trial. My witnesses were cowed, afraid to speak lest they displease their new masters. I stood there in amazement, hardly believing what was happening. My business stood in ruins, the empty shells of the building the only remaining evidence that there had ever been anything there, and I was on trial, my witnesses terrified of my judges. I had seen better days.

Then it was over.

The village parson had said, "He helped us a lot," and I guess that was enough to satisfy them. I was told not to expect to get my boats back. The Sandinistas needed them for transportation. Nor could I expect to get much of anything back. They had scattered it from Puerto Cabezas to Bluefields. But they knew where some of the mattresses were, and a few sheets and glasses, and they'd try to get them back for me.

I was told that I could return to live and work there, but that there would be no more exploitation. I was told not to make trouble for them in Managua, and I was told repeatedly not to involve the CIA or FBI. I was told how much money to bring when I came back to reclaim the mattresses. I was told that I would have to put a camp in each village, and train all the Indians to be guides and cooks so they could all work for me and share the jobs. I was told these things by boys who probably would have shot me had I not come with a pilot. At each demand, I nodded my head in agreement, knowing full well that I would never return to Karawala.

Before I left they asked me to unload the plane, and said they would be happy to take care of my things until I got back. The plane was loaded with tackle, tools, and equipment for the camp, and tucked into a corner of my suitcase was thirty thousand cordobas in cash. I told them I would need everything in Managua, but that I would bring it all back with me when I returned. Evidently they believed I would return and start over. The people in that part of Latin America believe that all Texans are incredibly wealthy. I suppose they thought I hadn't lost much, at least not enough to let it keep me from coming back. At any rate, they let me go with all my baggage.

The flight back to Managua lasted forever. The loss was so absolute that I never entertained the thought of trying to recover anything. I thought mostly about the people of Karawala. The Sandinistas had promised something better when they got rid of Somoza, but times under Somoza were very good compared to what they have now. Now there is no way for them to get flour, salt, sugar, coffee, or any other necessities that once came from Bluefields on the supply boats. The Sandinistas now have the supply boats, and they are not using them to haul supplies. Never again will they get help from the doctors and dentists who came to fish at the camp. Never again will the pilots take the sick and injured to the hospitals. There are no jobs at Karawala Tarpon Camp, and no more fishermen to give away their catches. The only thing the Sandinistas brought was fear, and the people will suffer under them.

Ferlan got a chance to say a few quick words to me over the fuselage of the plane as I was climbing in. He told me he and Eddie had managed to hide my radio and one outboard motor in the bush. I asked him how he was and where Eddie was.

"Eddie not here," he said, and, "Things not good here now." That was all he got to say. He looked to be close to tears when he walked away.

Within a few short months, everything they took from me will either be broken down or used up, and there will be nothing to replace it with. Many of the things they took they will never understand. They will not know what they are or how to use them. I suspect that most of it will rust and rot away without ever being used, but I take no satisfaction in knowing that.

I was told in Managua at the Department of Wildlife that they would no longer try to stop commercial fishermen from catching snook with gill nets. Soon there will be miles and miles of gill nets stretched across the Rio Grande and surrounding waters, and not long after that there will be very few fish of any kind in the area. Gone will be all those snook, and the tarpon will be gone, too, because the nets can't tell the difference between a snook and a tarpon. I have already seen the river choked with the carcasses of dead fish, all killed by gill nets, fouling the air and the water. I got it stopped that time, but my voice will not be heard again.

I am going to miss that camp. I am going to miss being able to go fishing whenever I want to. I'm going to miss the river and the jungle and the people of Karawala, a few of whom were good friends. I had the privilege of living and working in an unspoiled area for awhile, and I am going to miss that. I met many fine people at the camp; people who shared my love of fishing, and nature, and unspoiled places. Now only chance will bring us together again.

I saw people at their best when they came to my camp. They were all doing something they enjoyed, with pressures and problems left behind in another world. Not many occupations can equal that. Seeing people have a good time and knowing I had a part in it was rewarding, and I hope those of you who fished at Karawala Tarpon Camp enjoyed it as I did there. And I hope my next occupation is as pleasant.

And if you should chance upon some new river in an area as yet unspoiled and full of snook and tarpon, please let me know about it. I certainly won't build another camp on it; I'd just like to know it exists. And who knows, I might just see you there some day.

Good fishing!

W.E. Lanford II

Note: This letter was written in 1979. Since that time, conditions in Nicaragua have been vastly improved and many successful fishing trips have taken place in Nicaraguan waters near the Costa Rican border. The *Rain Goddess* (a very comfortable live-aboard houseboat) has been operating in Costa Rica and Nicaragua for many years without incident. In fact, Dr. Alfredo Lopez, Costa Rican sportsman and part owner of the Rain Goddess, is building a world-class resort, the Rio Indio Lodge, in Nicaragua.

My attempts to locate W. E. Lanford II were unsuccessful.—JCC.

The big oak tree at Mirage Bend

IT WAS A BRIGHT, sunny day when I left *Le Shack*, our Wisconsin trout club, to fish a small creek. I wanted to concentrate on Mirage Bend, so called because occasionally you see some very big trout—three to four pounders—but because none has been caught, it almost appears as if they really don't exist: hence Mirage Bend.

As I parked the car, the sun disappeared behind heavy clouds. There was an eerie stillness in the air just before the poplar leaves began their shimmering dance. I knew that the heavens were about to dump lots of water on the very river that I planned to fish.

That's exactly what happened.

I try to look at fishing conditions through my magic mind-filtering system that removes all negative thoughts. It's called optimism.

I had driven to Le Shack, our trout camp in Wisconsin, early on Thursday. I was going to fish until Sunday. Paul Melchior, our vice-president at PanAngling, was planning on arriving Friday afternoon.

"If there is a lot of rain, and the rivers are swollen, give me a call and I'll cancel. No sense going up there if the rivers are muddy."

I half-heartedly agreed to call him.

The river rose and became discolored from the heavy downpour. I got out of the stream and headed for the big oak tree, where I sat down to eat a sandwich and drink some orange juice. I always ate my lunch under the big oak whenever I fished this stream.

The rains continued. There was thunder and lightning quite a distance away, but the tree provided reasonable shelter from the rain. Actually, I was fairly comfortable, so I closed my eyes and nearly fell asleep when I remembered Paul's request to call him in Chicago if conditions were poor.

Conditions were poor, all right. Terrible and getting worse.

Out of nowhere, the two voices began to debate in my head. The angelic voice reminded me that I should go call Paul to tell him that fishing would be poor.

"Baloney!" said the devilish voice. "Why should you call him? You drove from Chicago and took a chance. Why shouldn't he? Besides, you're comfortable and would like a nice, long snooze. Now close your eyes. . . that's it. Doesn't that feel good?"

"Because it's the decent thing to do!" The angelic voice quickly countered. Why should he drive all the way from Chicago and find the rivers swollen?"

"Because that's fishing. You pay your dues and take your chances, dummy."

Back and forth the voices argued. Then the angelic voice made a very good point: "If Paul cancelled his trip, he would stay in the office and perhaps book some fishermen. PanAngling could always use additional business."

"Yeah, but you will have to take off your waders, break down your rod, drive eight miles to the nearest phone, then drive back another eight miles, and who knows? By tomorrow the rivers may be fishable. These trout could go on a feeding binge. Close those heavy eyelids, go back to sleep and forget about calling Paul."

The angelic voice finally won with its "do-unto-others" speech. So I got up, hiked to the car, took off my waders, removed my heavy, rain-soaked trout jacket, disassembled my rod and drove the eight miles to the gas station.

I called Paul at the office.

"Don't bother coming up. It's raining very hard and the rivers are muddy. It doesn't look like they will be fishable for a couple of days."

Paul thanked me.

There was a considerable amount of wind, rain and some lightning in the distance, but I decided to drive back to Mirage Bend. Perhaps I could fool a big trout. I heard that sometimes the big fish are less cautious during or after a storm. Maybe I would forsake the dry fly and cast a streamer with a little lead ahead of it, and bounce it on the bottom, just like Hank Looyer always told me to do. Hank was among the best trout anglers in the Midwest.

The storm increased its intensity and by the time I was halfway there, I almost decided to turn around, drive back to camp, attack the quart of Breyer's ice cream that I'd stashed in the freezer and listen to some Gene Harris and Miles Davis tapes.

But I continued on course. When I arrived at the parking area, the storm had subsided. There was no wind now. The rain had stopped. It appeared that the sun was fighting for position in front of the clouds and the sun was winning.

Hot Dog!

Okay, so the river was a little high. Big deal.

I put on my waders, got everything together and decided to go right to the big oak tree, the start of the Mirage Bend.

"I will use streamers and maybe hook one of those big browns."

Confidence returned.

I quickened my pace until I was within 30 to 50 yards of the tree. I started to walk along the bank softly so as not to alarm any trout which would scoot upstream and alert the big fish. Step by step, closer and closer, my heartbeat increased. Maybe this would be the day.

I came to the oak tree and was stunned!

The storm had knocked the huge tree over in the exact direction where I had been napping. It occurred to me that if I had not left Mirage Bend to call Paul, if I had stayed underneath the giant oak tree and napped, I might have been killed.

Fishing was so-so for the next few days. When I returned to the office on Monday, Paul thanked me for taking the time to drive over to the gas station to call him.

"That was very nice of you to call," he said.

I told him the story.

The fallen oak tree is still there, ten years later, and every time I see it, I am reminded of possibly the most important phone call I've ever made from Le Shack or anywhere else!

Strange encounter

PAUL MELCHIOR came into my office. "I just got a call from a guy, Thomas, in California," he said. "He seems quite nice and wants to fish at Club Pacifico de Panama, but he doesn't have a partner and wants to know if we can pair him up with another single."

"I got a similar call from someone in New York the other day," I responded. "Andrew something was his name. I got his phone number here. He doesn't have a partner either, and wants to try saltwater fishing. Said he can go just about anytime. He seems flexible and appears to be a nice guy, too."

We were very reluctant to put two anglers together who didn't know each other on a fishing trip. To do so was to invite disaster through the front door. One man would want to cast, the other guy to troll. One fisherman would want to target marlin and sails, the other small fish. One guy might like to drink and smoke cigars in the cabin, the other guy might be a health nut.

"Tim Clark called and said that we better improve the financials next month," Paul advised. Tim was one of the original founders of PanAngling, as well as our treasurer.

We decided to put the two singles together. What was the worse thing that could happen? Club Pacifico was a solid fishing destination that surely would satisfy nearly any angler interested in saltwater fishing. Besides, we needed the commission.

We booked them independently and told owner Bob Griffin that if they looked like they would be compatible, he should put them together.

"Work it out," was our final instruction.

Club Pacifico needed the business too, so Griffin said he'd handle any problems.

Andrew and Thomas met for the first time on the charter plane from Panama City to the lodge. They got along very well and decided to fish together. They even shared a cabin.

Fishing was terrific. Each day the sails were more active than the previous day. They caught cuberas, amberjack and many big roosters until their arms ached and their muscles refused to fight another fish. At times, Club Pacifico de Panama was like that.

They joked. They laughed. They got along beautifully.

On the third day of fishing, they encountered pod after pod of sailfish.

"You know, Thomas, I'm really enjoying this trip. I enjoy your company. Why don't we call each other from time to time and get together on other trips? That is, if it's okay with you," Andrew suggested.

"Ahh, I'd like that. I have a lot of fishing friends, but they are all busy making millions and can't get away easily. Actually, Andrew, I was thinking of asking you the same thing."

On the way back to the lodge from Jicaron Island, the two anglers were particularly content.

It was an incredible day.

"Tell me, Andrew. I don't know anything about you. Are you married? Do you have a family? Children?"

"No. I'm divorced. I was married for a few years. We didn't have any children. One day my wife said that she wanted to leave me. She said she loved me. There was no one else, she insisted, but she wanted to be on her own. Pursue a career. It's hard to explain, but I understood it. So she left about four years ago and I never heard from her again."

"That's terrible! What a shame. Have you found anyone else?"

"Naw. I've gone out with a number of women. Somebody is always trying to fix me up. You know how that is, Thomas. Relatives, friends, business associates; they all have *the* perfect woman for you. But I still love my ex-wife very much and I doubt that anyone will ever take her place. I have no idea where she is or how she is doing. That's the way she wanted it and I respect her wishes."

Thomas opened up a couple of soft drinks and handed one to Andrew.

"Well, that's life. With the sweet, there has to be some bitterness, I guess." Andrew continued. "What about you? Are you married?"

"Yeah! To a wonderful person. Met her two years ago in California. We got married last year. A wonderful person, and we both were married before. A beautiful woman, too. Intelligent. Witty. I'm very lucky."

"A good marriage is not very common these days. You're very lucky! So many friends of mine have horrible marriages. One friend described a bad marriage as 'a jail without bars.' "

They laughed heartily.

"I'm sure you'll find someone, Andrew. Perhaps she'll come back one day?"

"Well, maybe, but I'm not optimistic. I don't think so. It's about four years now. I keep busy. Go fishing a lot. I've learned to accept it. Hey, there are worse things in life. My health is good, and I'm financially very stable. Tell me about your wife."

"As I said, she is wonderful. I love her very much. Here's a picture of her," Thomas pulled the photo out of his wallet and handed it to him.

Andrew put down his drink, glanced quickly at the photograph, perhaps as a polite gesture. He was shocked.

Stunned.

It was a photograph of his ex-wife!

Thomas picked up on this immediately. His wife had never discussed her previous marriage.

It was a silent trip back to the lodge, though Thomas tried to comfort Andrew.

According to Club Pacifico owner Bob Griffin, Andrew ordered a special charter plane to take him to Panama City immediately, for his trip back to New York. Thomas stayed at the camp for the rest of the week and fished alone with the captain.

He was very sad.

He understood the pain and anguish that Andrew felt.

Andrew and Thomas never spoke again.

Good fishing partners, like good marriage partners, are hard to find.

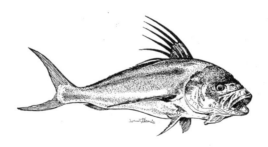

The Bruce Wooksly nightmare

I WOKE UP from a shocking nightmare, terrified but relieved to know that I had not murdered Bruce Wooksly, whoever he was. In my dream I killed this man and buried him in my backyard. The *Chicago Tribune* reporters were asking me leading questions, which convinced me that I was a main suspect.

"Did you or did you not kill Bruce Wooksly?" questioned my father, a military man with a very stern glare.

"I did not! I did not kill Bruce Wooksly!" I lied but I think he knew it.

And that's when I woke up from this outrageous nightmare. I was shaking, because it was so realistic.

That morning when I walked into PanAngling's downtown office, I was still thinking of the nightmare.

"Ursula! Pat! I want you to look through all our records and see if there is a 'Bruce Wooksly' in any of our files. Look everywhere. Look for any spelling variations of the name."

And they started looking.

I went into Paul Melchior's office. "Have you ever heard of a Bruce Wooksly?"

"No. Why?" He continued to type on his computer.

"Cause he is buried in my yard. I murdered him." I said.

Paul spun quickly around with an astonished looked on his face. **"You what?"**

"I mean, I had this very realistic dream. I don't know a Bruce Wooksly. Do you?"

Paul has a great memory. He assured me that he never heard of this guy. Pat and Ursula later reported that they looked everywhere—clients lists, subscription lists, inquiries, travel customers, everywhere.

"No such person as Bruce Wooksly," Ursula insisted.

I felt better. In ensuing days I thought less and less of the nightmare. Yet, it never totally vanished from my memory.

THREE MONTHS LATER, PanAngling partner Tim Clark was hosting a little party at his North Stone Street apartment. He invited a number of fishing friends and their spouses for a barbecue on his patio.

Bill Cullerton, also a PanAngling partner at the time, summoned Paul Melchior and me into Tim's den. Bill had just returned from a Central American fishing trip, and he collected about a dozen names and addresses of fishermen that he met en route; he would turn them over to us and it was our job to try to book them for future fishing trips.

"This guy wants to go to Norton's camp in Costa Rica . . . this guy wants to do an Alaskan fishing trip with his son . . . this man wants to entertain a half-dozen customers in the Bahamas but insists on great accommodations, good guides, money no object."

Paul and I were busy writing little notes on the back of business cards or on the pieces of paper.

"Oh, I got one more."

Bill reached into his pocket and pulled another card.

"I met this guy in Panama. He never heard of 'PanAngling' but he wants to be put on our mailing list. He's interested in PanAngling group trips but has his own fishing friends, too. He's a very serious prospect, I believe."

Paul and I looked at the card simultaneously.

And gasped!

The name on the card was ***Bruce Wooksly.***

I didn't even want to touch the card. Paul put it in his pocket. We tried to explain to Bill about my nightmare and why we were shocked, but I don't think he believed us; he followed his nose to the barbecued steaks.

"What do we do about this card?" Paul was stunned.

"We're not writing him and we're not putting his name on the mailing list!"

"What would you do if you were at a camp and he was there?" Paul asked.

"I'd pack up and leave immediately, if not sooner," I answered with no hesitation.

I've never heard from him or about him, although I've had occasional nightmares about this episode throughout the years. From time to time, Paul and I have discussed this amazing coincidence with others but no one has come up with a reasonable explanation for this paranormal experience.

Note: Bruce Wooksly's name has been altered slightly for obvious reasons.

The $250,000 fish!

I'VE NEVER COMPETED in a "big-bucks" fishing tournament—the kind in which a participant can win several hundred thousand dollars by landing larger fish than his competition—so I can't fathom that special rush that the winner experiences. Nor, for that matter, can I feel the depth of disappointment and despair that unquestionably erodes the loser as he drives solemnly home to deliver the bad news to his anxious family: "Mom, why can't dad get a regular job like all the other dads so we can afford things?"

Both the winners and the losers invest significantly in state-of-the-art boats, motors, vehicles, fishing equipment, entry fees, travel expenses, time and energy. Surely the emotions on both sides of the spectrum, the winners and the losers, must be overwhelming. Then again, perhaps I can begin to understand these emotions to a lesser degree.

As Fishing Director at Safari Outfitters and PanAngling Travel Service for almost four decades, I know the importance of positive fishing results. The pressure to succeed on investigative trips is possibly similar to the pressure felt by the full-time fishing pros on the tournament trails. Allow me to explain.

Contrary to popular opinion, an agent's extensive fishing trips, whether they are exploratory in nature or merely checking on the old reliable places, are not all fun and games. A fishing (or hunting) travel agency survives long term only if it digs up enough new, exciting places to offer its clients. Thus, when a fishing travel agent goes into the field, there's considerable pressure to produce good results, given the high stack of chips at stake. Furthermore, the success or failure can have a fast rippling effect on other agency employees, because their employment and benefits are based on the company's financial health or survival.

When I first started the Fishing Division at Safari Outfitters, Inc., there wasn't any competition from other fishing travel agencies (they simply didn't exist then), so finding new, attractive fishing places to dangle in front of prospective clients was relatively easy. Trout and dorado fishing in Argentina, both coasts of Costa Rica, Belize, Panama (Club Pacifico), Ecuador and New Zealand were almost instant success stories. Today, there are hundreds of outdoor agencies vying to find that new Christmas Island, Tierra del Fuego or Ponoi River. Despite our more sophisticated approaches and increased knowledge, it's harder to strike oil these days, because of the tremendous competition among agencies and more limited unexplored grounds.

Are there still exciting, unexploited fishing places waiting to be discovered today? Certainly, but they are not as plentiful, and sometimes a booking agent goes on a number of trips before finding a good one.

Several years ago, Jay Burgin, co-owner of the fabulous Five Rivers Lodge in Montana, became Carlos Muñoz's partner at Paloma Lodge in Chile. Previously, the lodge had invited several outdoor writers and television crews to help promote its fishing, but from what I was told, Paloma

Lodge had about a dozen *paying* guests during the previous three years.

I went to Paloma Lodge and had a fabulous trip. Carlos has a wonderful operation, but the other Chilean fishing lodges seem to overwhelm Paloma in terms of publicity, marketing and contacts. When I returned to Chicago, I wrote my report for *The PanAngler* newsletter and immediately the phone started ringing and bookings were made.

While I was at Paloma Lodge, I had the good fortune to fish one day with John Randolph, easily one of the most entertaining and astute anglers I've ever met. John, who is the editor of the *Fly Fisherman* magazine, wrote several magnificent articles in this almost biblical publication, which intensified further interest. In fact, his magazine's cover featured Paloma Lodge guide Joel Silverman holding a trout.

The results? Paloma Lodge is heavily booked, a year in advance, and there's talk of opening satellite camps on other rivers to meet the demand. While all this hoopla affected Paloma Lodge positively because the camp's future existence was at stake, it also helped PanAngling's financial status.

However, there's never any guarantee that the outcome of an exploratory trip will always be rosy even at some of the world's best fishing places. Suppose the weather and river conditions had been terrible during the week when John Randolph and I were there? Then what? Chances are Paloma Lodge would not be enjoying anywhere near its present-day success.

To illustrate further the importance of luck in weather: good friend and world-class trout angler Peter Aravosis and his wife Carol returned to Paloma River the next year for two weeks.

"One week was miserable, rainy, cold, windy. It wasn't much fun. Results were poor. The second week was terrific. Good weather and great fishing. What a wonderful week! The difference between the two weeks? Day and night. We anglers are proud of our skill and knowledge and thump on our expanded chests when we do well, but let's face it, weather is the most important determining factor," Peter explains.

So luck definitely plays a very important part, whether it's an exploratory fishing trip or a fish-for-cash tournament.

258

ABOUT SIX YEARS AGO, bookings at PanAngling suffered because of substantial cancellations due to poor winter fishing in Central America during the previous season. If fishing is poor at such countries as Costa Rica and Belize one year, it will reflect negatively on bookings in those places the following season.

We desperately needed a new exciting place for our clients in order to avoid a loss on PanAngling's bottom line. I have an aversion to red ink, and so do my partners and stockholders.

Dick Thomas and his family had started a brand-new tarpon and snook fishing camp in Honduras called Cannon Island Lodge. I decided to fish there because the potential seemed high. Jim Veugeler, whom I had never met before but who had booked many trips through PanAngling, was looking for a fishing trip but didn't have a partner. I explained that I was going to Cannon Island but emphasized that I had absolutely no idea of what it was like. He decided to chance it and came along.

The first disappointment was that my rod case and duffle of clothes were temporarily lost en route. Perhaps the more serious problem was that as we flew to Cannon Island with the small charter plane we noticed that the waters were heavily discolored and muddy.

"Not to worry," said Dennis Thomas, head guide and son of owners Dick and Sandra Thomas. "We'll find some clearer waters and we have some back up plug-casting gear that's perfect for these tarpon."

The first couple of days provided fast fishing for small snook. While our results weren't going to impress any potential clients, Jim and I loved the region. We were the only sport fishermen in the area, and this included the huge lagoon, the mouth to the Caribbean, the ocean itself, and five or six rivers that were barely explored at the time. Once you went up the rivers you were shocked if you saw another human being. It was like turning the clock backwards a couple of centuries.

We finally got into some big tarpon. I hooked one that, according to Dennis and Jim, was more than 150 pounds. It was a bruiser. I felt that it was important to land this tarpon because it could result in many bookings. If I lost the fish, well, bookings would be difficult to obtain. You can describe the flora, the fauna and the magnetic appeal of the rivers, but you need the fishing results, which ideally includes landing and photographing at least one monster fish, in order to attract many clients.

When I was younger, I thought it was fun and exciting to fight big fish for a couple of hours or more because I seldom tired. Not today! They make tarpon much stronger today than they did 20, 30 years ago!

After a few minutes of fighting the tarpon, I knew it would outlast me or something would go wrong because there were plenty of snags and logs in the river. I tightened the drag and fought this fish as hard as I could, realizing that it was imperative to land this tarpon quickly.

Because there was a lot of money in future bookings riding on landing this fish, I believe the pressure was similar to what a bass tournament pro experiences when he needs that one big fish, finally hooks it, and must land it to win. The difference? He can land the bass quickly whereas battling a big tarpon can last an hour or longer and something is bound to go wrong in a long fight.

Applying all the pressure I could, I felt that one of three things would occur:

(1) We would land this fish quickly;

(2) the line would break, which probably would result in my falling backwards into the river; or,

(3) I would merely have a stroke or a heart attack.

After giving my very best, the tarpon was brought next to the boat in 11 minutes and Dennis skillfully was able to gaff the 150-pound tarpon.

Victory.

How sweet it is!

As it turned out we landed several other tarpon of more than 100 pounds. Jim Veugeler hooked an even bigger tarpon—perhaps 170 pounds—in that same river and fought it expertly for about 20 minutes before his giant fish found a snag and broke off.

The upshot of landing the big fish? During the next few weeks, after returning to Chicago and printing my report in *The PanAngler* newsletter, we probably booked $250,000 to $300,000 in business for Cannon Island Lodge and even more for the following year. This ensured profitable financials for PanAngling and was very helpful to the new camp.

In my opinion, the tremendous pressure to produce on fishing trips is one of the disadvantages of making a living based on your fishing results.

So perhaps I do understand that special rush that a pro bass fisherman surely feels when he wins a big cash tournament, and the emptiness when he doesn't win any money.

"The thrill of victory, the agony of defeat!"

And I certainly know all about the agonies through the years.

A feast to remember

IT WAS A HELLUVA TRIP, both good and bad. There was J. C. Campbell, wading near the mouth of the river. By mid afternoon he had caught more than 50 brook trout, and by the time we had to pile in the float plane to return to the main camp he had chalked up about 70. Because we had a heavy *Hexagenia* hatch for most of the day, he didn't have to move more than a dozen yards, and he caught all his trout on dry flies.

Oh, yes. These fish weren't the tiny brook trout we love to hunt in the Midwest at secret rivers and ponds where a 12 incher is considered a bell ringer. On this desolate Labrador river that connected two ponds, most fish weighed between two and five pounds. Maybe six.

The rest of our group—Bard and Ray Higgins and their sons, Drs.

Dan Moos and Dan DeVries, Bob Campbell, Bob Kelly, Art Thrun and a few others—weren't just standing there, gawking at J.C.'s incredible success. We were also busy casting, hooking, fighting, landing and releasing plump brook trout. Robert Traver, the great author from Michigan's Upper Peninsula and a brook trout fanatic, would have flipped his fly-adorned hat, if he had been with us catching these beautifully-marked fish.

Art Thrun and I were taking a break—after all, this was hard work—when a four-pound brook trout wove among the boulders and into the shallows, right where we were standing, in a foot of water, and inhaled Art's dry fly that was carelessly dangling on the surface.

Remember that great Lee Wulff film, *Three Trout to Dream About*, made in Labrador? Lee was fishing with three flies on his leader and landed three big brook trout on a single cast. Seemed almost impossible, right? I'm sure we could have accomplished that feat at least half a dozen times on that day, although our trout would not have been as large as Lee's.

Art mentioned Lee's film. "I wonder if it'd be possible to repeat that here . . . ya know, catch three trout on a cast?" he asked.

"I don't think that would be a problem. I don't like to fish with dropper flies, but let me try something. Give me your fly rod."

Okay, okay. I was going to show off a little, while proving a point.

I held one rod in each hand and cast both rods at the same time, and the flies landed within a couple of feet of each other. Two trout, probably three pounders, gulped the dry flies almost simultaneously. First I set the hook with my right hand, and then with my left.

"See, no problem," I bragged as both trout started to take out yards of line. "Here, Art, grab one of these rods."

"No! No! You show-off! You fight these fish yourself." He and others who had witnessed this silly exhibitionism laughed and teased.

Somehow I managed to land the fish.

It was that kind of a trip.

In addition to the brook trout, there were a few Atlantic salmon in the stream. Norm, a superb angler and camp co-manager, worked over a salmon for about 45 minutes. I stood next to him and got quite an education as he changed fly patterns, casting position, tactics and presentations. He spoke quietly and explained why he was making the various changes. In a way, he was conducting Atlantic Salmon Fishing Class 101 with some graduate and advance studies included.

From where I was standing, aided with Polaroids, I had a good view of the salmon, and its reactions to Norm's various presentations. Sometimes the noble fish would swim close to the fly but suddenly changed its mind. After dozens of casts it looked hopeless, but Norm, exhibiting tremendous patience, retied pattern after pattern. He went back to a Horror—a fly that he invented—and the salmon slammed into it on the second cast and unleashed a couple of spine-tingling jumps before settling in for an underwater fight. Norm tailed it, unhooked it and released it. It was an impressive lesson. What a wonderful classroom! What a superb teacher!

THIS ALL OCCURRED on a special, optional, fly-out charter to some secret spot. We were staying at a modest base camp on Labrador's Upper Eagle River. The accommodations consisted of canvas and plywood living quarters, plus a kitchen and dining area. It provided some of the creature comforts, but because of the advance information no one expected more. After all, this was billed as a *wilderness* fishing trip in Labrador.

The planning for this trip began during the preceding winter at one of Chef Alberto's monthly "Sportsman's Nights." Located on the north side of Chicago, this restaurant provided numerous hunting and fishing films, often presented by various camp owners who came to Chef's to promote bookings.

Janice owned the new fishing camp on the Eagle river and was invited to make a presentation at Chef's. Janice was a stunning beauty, brunette, blue eyes, elegantly dressed. She appeared as though she just stepped out of a *Vogue* magazine ad. Her presentation and delivery deserved top grades, too.

Art and I arranged to go to Janice's camp during the summer with a group of sportsmen from Minnesota. Art, who worked for Air Canada, would check out the camp for inclusion in the airline's *Fin, Fur & Feather* sportsman's program. I would inspect it for Safari Outfitters' Fishing Division.

We flew to Goose Bay, Labrador, which at the time had limited accommodations, but because one of our party had influence, we stayed at the comfortable officers' quarters at a military base. We were scheduled to fly into camp the next morning after breakfast.

The Sunday breakfast served at the military base was fabulous—pancakes, eggs, bacon, the works. I had some coffee and some toast but skipped the huge breakfast.

"Hey, guys! Don't eat a big breakfast because the camp will have a huge Sunday feast with all the trimmings for lunch," I suggested.

"Good idea," someone said.

So we all ate a light breakfast.

There were two float planes assigned to fly our group to the camp. Despite a heavy ground fog and constant rain, we made it all the way into camp without incident.

Upon docking, I realized that there were some problems, because the pilots immediately insisted on payment for the charters from Janice. Usually charter plane companies and other businesses run a tab for the camps they serve and are paid periodically, but this appeared to be a C.O.D. flight.

Was the camp having financial problems?

The paying customers had sent in a deposit and they assumed that they would pay the balances at the completion of the trip. That's how most of the Canadian (and other) camps operated in those days.

Janice, however, insisted that the guests pay the balances immediately. The fellows thought that this was unusual, but didn't mind the slight inconvenience and wrote out checks before our baggage was totally removed from the planes.

We were shown to our quarters, really large tents with plywood floors.

"Hurry up, guys, settle in, because we're ready to serve lunch," Janice, the blue-eyed brunette, announced.

Most of us were glad that we had eaten only a very small breakfast. We were hungry, so we hurriedly made our way to the canvas dining room. It was nice and toasty. There were large soup bowls, glasses filled with water, silverware and paper towels neatly placed on the red and white plastic table cloth.

The first course was soup. Nothing like good homemade soup to get rid of the chill and dampness that is Labrador.

We all started sipping the soup. It was warm but tasted like no other soup I've ever had. It had a few rice kernels and a brown cast. Okay, so the soup wasn't terrific, but it was warm.

"Who would like some more soup," said Janice, the blue-eyed brunette, who looked great even in the Labrador wilderness.

We all passed on more soup.

Bring on the roast. The roast chicken, or roast beef, or pork or roast whatever, with those oven-roasted potatoes and all the trimmings, I thought. There was no sense filling up on more soup when the feast was about to begin.

"Come on, James," Janice, the blue-eyed brunette said, "have some more soup. You'll be working up an appetite when you go fishing after lunch."

I thanked her for her concern but again passed on more soup.

"I bet no one can tell me what kind of soup you ate?" she said.

No one could.

The soup smelled a little like peanuts. Surely, it must be some exotic soup, perhaps made from turtles, or the marrow of moose bones, or frog legs. Or beaver. Something exotic. None of us had a clue.

"Well, I knew no one would guess. It was peanut butter soup!"

Huh? We were astounded.

"What's the recipe?" Dr. Dan Moos inquired. I don't know if he really wanted to know, whether he was being sarcastic or simply wanted to break our group's stunned silence.

Without losing a beat, Janice, the blue-eyed brunette, explained that after she boils the water, she adds one scoop of peanut butter for every serving and then some rice.

266

"You could use noodles, but we're out of noodles, so we used rice. But, and this is important, you must use Skippy Peanut Butter," added the Martha Stewart of Labrador

Okay, so the first course wasn't spectacular. Bring on the roast. I'm starving! We all waited in anticipation.

There was no roast. There was no chicken, or pork, or ham, or turkey or beef. The soup was our Sunday dinner. Period. We passed up a fantastic breakfast at the military base for this? Peanut butter soup? Oops, excuse me: *Skippy* Peanut Butter soup!

We were somewhat stunned as we filed out of the dining tent, to our living tents to put our fishing gear together.

Perhaps if we had caught some salmon during our first fishing session that afternoon, our introduction to this camp would have been tolerable, but we didn't. Kelly *thought* he saw a salmon, but he wasn't really sure. When you are starved, you start imagining things.

Supper time.

Same menu. Peanut butter soup. We're talking about hungry guys, burning up energy fishing up and down the river, in the chilly, damp weather, in need of calories, any kind of calories, and we're served Skippy Peanut Butter soup. Good grief!

The next day was the same. Peanut butter soup. Only worse. Janice, the blue-eyed brunette, ran out of rice, too, so there were only a few precious kernels in each bowl. In all fairness, I should add that we had toast and jam with our coffee for breakfast, and I discovered one thin slice of Velveeta cheese between two slices of bread in my lunch box. And an apple, too.

What was also disturbing was that fishing was poor. Make that terrible. The big runs of salmon never reached us. We all knew that the camp obviously was having a serious financial problem, but what could we do? When someone politely complained about the meals, Janice, the blue-eyed brunette, smiled and said that it was up to us to catch some fish.

"Come on, guys, you seem to be good fishermen. Catch some fish!" She said. "I would surely like to have a salmon dinner. I'm getting a little tired of peanut butter soup."

I chewed Wrigley's Juicy Fruit gum for energy. Thank God, I had bought several huge economy packs. At night when I brushed my teeth, I thought of swallowing the toothpaste, I was so hungry. Maybe it contained some vitamins or some nutritional value. I have a big frame. My stomach and I made a pact decades ago: I was to feed it three times a day, and my stomach promised not to hurt or ache or give me any serious problems. I've seldom broken that pact, but now my stomach was protesting with angry growls.

We were so weak that it was difficult to find the energy to cast, but we knew that we had to cast in order to catch fish so that we could eat. Fishing now became a means to survival. We were that hungry.

Ahh, but the next evening we didn't have the usual Skippy Peanut Butter soup.

"Tonight," announced Janice, the blue-eyed brunette, "we're going to have something different. A special treat."

It was still soup, but it was different.

Sniff. Sniff. We all looked at each other, wondering what it could be this time.

"Okay, James, what is it?" Janice, the blue-eyed brunette, insisted on calling me "James" instead of "Jim."

"Come on, James, don't keep the hungry people waiting. What is it?"

"I've no idea," I said meekly. It tasted sweet. Very sweet.

"Anyone else wants to guess?"

None of us raised a hand.

"It's candy soup! Isn't it delicious?"

I think it was Art who belched. Or maybe it was Bob Campbell.

"What's the recipe?" Dr. Moos inquired. This time I knew he was being sarcastic.

"Well, first you boil some water, then you add the candy," said Janice, the blue-eyed brunette, without losing a beat. "Now I've tried different type of candies but the best is Brach's."

This, my dear readers, is the honest-to-goodness truth! No exaggeration. No skewing the facts.

J. C. CAMPBELL FISHING on the other side of the river hooked a big salmon. It was huge for the Eagle. Maybe it was 15 pounds. The big fish took off and headed downstream, and there was no doubt it would eventually clean out Campbell's reel of line and would escape.

I was closest to J. C. Although I had little energy left, I knew this was our best shot for a meal. I tore-ass downstream, jumping from boulder to boulder, hurdling the occasional log. A fly box of valuable Alex Rogan salmon flies flew out of my pocket and fell into the river. I thought of retrieving the famous flies, but this might mean losing an opportunity to land this salmon. I continued to chase after the fish.

Now I was close to the salmon. It stopped running, perhaps sensing that it had gained its freedom, or maybe, it was also exhausted. The salmon was now in a soft eddy. This was my chance. I jumped into the shallow water, and with sheer determination, I tailed the fish. Soon it was flopping on the bank. J. C. came trudging down the bank.

"Nice job," he said.

We would eat well tonight. I heard that Kelly caught a grilse of about five pounds, so there would be enough for a good meal.

Wrong!

The fish, I'm told, was cleaned and gutted and buried in the ground to keep it cool. The evening meal called for grilled cheese sandwiches. And they were good. They were served with potato chips. But why not the fish? Art and I were non-paying guests, but the Minnesota guys, the paying clients, were too polite to ask.

Or maybe we were all too weak to ask.

Or to complain.

The next morning we signed up for the special charter plane fly-out trip, which, of course, cost additional, and we did enjoy the incredible brook trout fishing described at the beginning of this chapter.

We were allowed to keep a few badly hooked brook trout from that charter trip, and along with the two salmon that J. C. and Kelly caught the day before, we had a feast that night.

In fact we had an overabundance of food. And Janice, the blue-eyed brunette, could cook up a storm.

Then on the last day we had another fantastic dinner. It was a wonderful prime roast beef. I think we had apple pie for dessert, too. Where did that roast come from? The apple pie? There were no charter planes into camp. No one asked. We ate and enjoyed. To this day, I never understood the meals, the camp operation, or Janice, the blue-eyed brunette.

But she was a good looker.

The Parismina mystery

I MET TOM URAGAMI at Camp Manitou, Ontario, in the early 1960s and periodically we met socially. He was a very thorough, considerate person, and I remember that he provided driving instructions to his home in such detail that surely he must have driven from my house to his, for he noted every discernible landmark en route and even warned me of some major potholes along the way.

Tom was an engineer and was offered a very challenging and lucrative position on the West Coast. This would be a major move, because Tom would have to sell his house in the Midwest, buy a home in California and move his family and belongings. After much consideration and encouragement from his wife, they decided to do it. Tom and his family had driven halfway to California when he received a phone call from his new employer. Apparently the company that had just hired him lost a lucrative contract and it would have to withdraw its employment offer. Tom, a very resolute person, turned around and headed back to the Chicago area and eventually found another job but at a reduced annual salary.

Jerry Tricomi, his good friend and owner of Parismina Tarpon Rancho, in Costa Rica, was looking for a responsible person to keep track of his bookings, reservations and payments in the United States. This would be a part-time job, and immediately he thought of Tom Uragami. Tom accepted the job because, not only would it supplement his income, but he could fish at Parismina for free. Since he loved tarpon and snook fishing, this was just as important as the financial remuneration.

"I'm going to Parismina tomorrow," Tom told me at lunch one day. "As you know, the camp is closed for the rainy season except for a skeleton staff, but I like going there at this time, even though it can be very wet. I'm going to fish with Van Smith, an ardent fisherman and a very nice guy. I met him last year. He has a beautiful, big boat—very stable—and he is going to bring it to Parismina."

"Well, have a great trip and let's get together when you return."

Tom, a very serious person, appeared disturbed. " I don't know why, but I don't think you will see me again. I have this strange feeling, but I can't explain it."

"Nonsense, Tom. You'll be fine. I hope you hit the tarpon and snook fishing just right."

We shook hands and as I returned to my office I was concerned about Tom's fear. If he felt that strongly that something bad was going to happen to him, why was he going? I guess I've read too much Greek mythology, for I tend to believe premonitions.

This was in early November. With the fall season completed, lodge owners Jerry and Lorine Tricomi had returned to the States and only a skeleton staff tended to the camp.

On November 12, 1981, Tom and Van were fishing from Van's private boat. Since they were experienced fishermen and knew the waters well, there was no need to hire a guide. Anchored near the mouth of the

Parismina River, they enjoyed terrific fishing as they hooked a number of big tarpon and snook, but the incoming sea was rough and clashed with the outflowing Parismina River, swollen from the tremendous rains that sometimes accompany this time of the year. There were logs, debris and even fallen trees floating down the Parismina to the mouth. The skies suddenly darkened as a fierce storm developed in the Caribbean.

One of the locals who knew the river intimately noted that the current was increasing. He went to the bank and waved them to come in. Tom and Van responded and motioned that they would come in very shortly. The villager went back to his home for a short time, but later sent his son to check on the boat.

The boat was not there, according to the son. Now it was mid afternoon. Surely the boat must be tied up to the camp's dock.

It wasn't.

Four-thirty.

No boat at the camp dock.

No Tom or Van.

The authorities in San Jose were alerted immediately. The weather and visibility was so poor that it was impossible to send small planes from San Jose through the mountainous passages to the coast. Even if planes could be dispatched, it gets dark early in the tropics and therefore it would be impossible to search the seas.

Some of the locals frantically ran up and down the beach, hoping to spot Tom, Van or their boat.

The Caribbean was too angry to send any other boats out there.

When weather permitted, the Costa Rican, Panamanian and American governments joined in a very extensive air search. They combed the beaches and searched the Caribbean, but the boat and the anglers were not to be found. A boat cushion was retrieved from the beach, but was it from Van's boat?

Jerry Tricomi was in the United States, recuperating from major surgery. When he was informed, while in the hospital, he ordered his personnel in San Jose and at the camp to do everything possible to find them, regardless of expense.

"I'm totally sick about this," he said to me on the phone. "Tom was like a brother to me, maybe even closer. I've known him for more than 25 years. We've fished together in Canada, Central America and we even went to Africa together. I didn't know Van Smith for a long time, but we struck up a good friendship. When Tom told me that he was planning to fish Parismina after we closed up in the fall, I tried to discourage him, because the weather can be bad in November, but Tom insisted."

What happened?

The locals advanced many theories. Most felt that perhaps a big, floating tree trunk smashed against the boat, breaking the anchor rope, and the powerful current swept the craft out to sea.

But why wasn't the boat found along the beach? It was considered very stable and unsinkable. True, the strong river current could sweep the boat through the river mouth and into the Caribbean, but then once beyond the mouth, the incoming waves would have forced the boat somewhere along the beach. Why wasn't any of the equipment on board ever found?

Because of these unanswered questions, one Chicago television reporter went on the air and theorized "that perhaps Tom and Van and the boat were victims of an outer space or alien abduction!"

Unbelievable.

I won't forget Tom's parting words when I saw him for the last time and his eerie premonition that something bad was going to happen to him.

Decision: A life for a salmon

W HEN DON DOBBINS walked into a room, he was immediately noticed. He was tall, graceful, commanding and athletic. Unfortunately he had severe heart problems that surgery and a Pacemaker couldn't solve. His heart specialist told Don that
he could live well beyond his 67 years, perhaps ten more, *if* he took it
easy.

"You can continue to practice law and even do some close-to-home
relaxed fishing. You know, still fishing with a bobber, but nothing strenu-
ous, of course."

"And if I don't?" Don questioned.

The doctor didn't answer. He didn't have to.

There was no way that Don would adapt to a sedentary life after being so active in the outdoors. In the late '40s and early '50s he flew his Grumman Seabee on weekends between Champaign, Illinois and his cabin on Bassett Lake, Minnesota His wife Ruth and their four children spent the entire summer at the minimum comfort cottage. At other times, he flew fishing friends to Canada to sample wilderness lakes. Don carried a Link fold-up boat and a small outboard with him on the plane to explore lakes.

He owned and piloted the *River Fox*, a nifty 60-foot houseboat in Florida. Later he financed Casa Mar, the Costa Rican tarpon camp, and previously had helped several other fishing camp owners. Don, who resembled actor Walter Pidgeon, was indeed an extremely active person. There was no way he would follow his doctor's advice.

"Doc, I have two ambitions: I want to fish in Alaska and catch a silver salmon, and I want to take the train across Canada before I die. I'm going to do that, no matter what the consequences are."

The doctor shook his head. He adamantly advised against these goals.

"The choice is yours, of course. I can't stop you."

"I understand. I better do it soon." He began planning.

Don, Ruth, his wife, and I went to Bristol Bay Lodge in Alaska. While at camp, Don became very ill, mostly with the chills, and had to stay in bed for a couple of days, but he didn't waver from his ambition to catch a silver salmon.

Don seemed to gain some strength and, upon his insistence, lodge owners Ron and Maggie McMillan arranged for a charter flight for us to the Togiak River, world famous for its silver salmon run. I can't remember if we were a little early for the run, or maybe the salmon were a little late, but the guides said fishing was slow. Even the seasoned silver salmon fishermen were frustrated.

When we arrived at the Togiak we had a problem getting Don out of the charter plane because he was so weak. I helped to carry him from the plane to a convenient place on the bank where he could cast. During much of my business life, Don carried me on his back, so now it was fitting that I should be able to return that favor in a very small way.

One of the guides, or perhaps it was Ron McMillan, thought he spotted several silvers deep in a nearby pool, within Don's casting range.

We had to hold Don up while he began to cast, he was so weak. We all prayed that Don would hook a salmon, but after the first ten minutes of fruitless casting, pessimism began to grow. Whatever strength Don had earlier in the day seemed to dissipate. One more cast. His voice was very weak, but we could read the determination in his eyes and sense his frustration. He cast again. It appeared hopeless; surely if there were any cooperative silvers in that pool, they would have hit by now.

A guide, trying to be helpful, hooked a silver a considerable distance downstream from us, and quickly rushed up to us to hand the rod to Don. He refused it. He wanted to hook his own salmon. He rested a bit and made another cast.

Suddenly Don's rod bucked up and down and his reel screeched as yards of line shot into the water. He hooked a silver salmon! I wanted to shout with joy, but I didn't. Don wanted to land a silver salmon, not just hook one, and Don was a very stubborn man. He would have to fight a powerful silver salmon, and these fresh-from-the-ocean migrants were fully charged with energy.

Thankfully, the salmon jumped several times, consuming much of its endurance. Don reached deep within himself to find whatever strength he could to fight the salmon. Sensing victory, a discernible smile appeared on his face. Finally, one of the guides tailed the salmon, and soon 12 pounds of thrashing silver was flopping at Don's feet.

We cheered Don. We cheered the fish. We released it. You could perceive an emotional release as Don was now at peace with himself. He had achieved one of his goals: he had caught a silver salmon!

Buoyed by his success, he insisted

on fishing some more and soon he landed a second silver. He was now completely enervated, so we carried him to the plane for the flight back to the lodge where he could rest in comfort.

When our fishing trip at Bristol Bay Lodge was over, we flew back to Anchorage. Don appeared much stronger now, and we went to dinner. He was ecstatic that he caught the two silver salmon. Now he was going to fulfill his second wish: take the trans-Canadian rail trip.

After our lively, upbeat dinner, we headed for our rooms. Don and Ruth would continue to Canada the next day, whereas I had an early morning flight to Chicago.

Ironically, as we parted, Don and I didn't say anything to each other, not even "good night," or "have a great trip," or "see you later." Not this night. Don and I looked at each other for a few more seconds, perhaps we nodded, and withdrew to our rooms.

Silently.

Don and Ruth made the train trip as far as Calgary, where Don became very ill and died.

Don's son, Cam, called me from his office to inform me. I wasn't surprised. I cried and cried. Here was a man who could have extended his life for perhaps a decade if he chose to follow his doctor's orders, but instead he decided to fulfill his dreams: to catch a silver salmon and do the trans-Canadian rail trip.

"Yeah, Don, in a strange way, you won!" I said as I looked at a photo of him holding a huge Costa Rican snook that he had caught on an earlier trip he and I made years ago.

I shook my head but then I smiled, for I admired his tremendous courage in making the most important decision in his life. But then, to Don, that decision may not have been difficult at all.

Fishing with The Greats

Because of my "job," which included researching, developing and publicizing outstanding fishing places for Safari Outfitters and PanAngling, I've been blessed with the opportunity to fish with several world-class anglers. This not only gave me a splendid opportunity to observe these superb fishermen in action, but also to learn about their philosophies. I'm privileged to have fished with the following four highly esteemed persons (presented in alphabetical order):

Stu Apte

I THOUGHT Stu Apte was the biggest B.S.er in fishing. Back in the 1950s, I read about this cat who claimed that he was landing big sailfish—over 100 pounds—in Panama on 16-pound, plug-casting tackle. *16-pound line, mind you!* Heck, we Midwestern anglers were breaking 20-pound lines on muskies that weighed 20 pounds or less. Then later, he landed a 95-pound sail on four-pound test line. What was he doing? Tranquilizing these fish with some kind of a dart?

He was even catching sailfish on a fly rod! Imagine that! I read that he landed a 136-pound Pacific sail on a fly rod using a 12-pound tippet. Then there were all those tarpon, giant tarpon, more than 100 pounds, that he landed on a fly rod. Okay, okay, we fishermen exaggerate a little, but Apte was getting carried away. What gall! Who was this guy anyway and how did he expect to get away with such nonsense?

I later discovered that these feats were true, and soon other anglers were landing billfish on flies because Apte, and other experts, starting with Dr. Webster Robinson, paved the way by liberally sharing their hard-earned knowledge and techniques.

If I were to pick one person as the world's best ***all-round angler*** in the history of fishing it would be Stu Apte in his prime. That's quite a statement, I know, but remember, I said ***all-round***. There are many superb anglers in the world today, but my balance swings toward Apte. There are more experienced Atlantic salmon fishermen than Stu, and certainly more successful permit anglers, or superior bass fishermen and better casters than he is, but I'm talking about all-round. Stu is just as proficient with a plug-casting rod or spinning tackle as he is with a fly rod. A number of famous anglers come to mind, but several lack the "big fish" experience and world record results that Stu has achieved throughout the years, while others fish only with a fly rod. Again, the keyword is "all-round."

If there is a chink in Apte's substantial armor, it might be big-game fishing with the heavy conventional tackle. But wait! In the early 1970s, Stu went to Australia to film black marlin fishing. He was a guest of Mike Levitt, a highly talented big-game fisherman. Stu obtained marvelous footage and even shot a magazine cover of a leaping giant black marlin for *Sports Afield*.

"Hey, Stu," Mike said, "we've all caught lots of big marlin and you've been filming. Why don't you take a turn in the chair?"

Stu put away his cameras. He hooked a huge black marlin and fought it to the best of his ability. In 18 minutes the fish was tuckered out at boat-side! A record time. The next day, the black marlin weighed 996 pounds, and the fish probably lost at least 100 pounds in the tropical heat. Surely, it was well more than 1,100 pounds when he landed it! And, remember he landed it in 18 minutes!

Stu was a Pan Am pilot for most of his working life, and since Pan Am flew to many great fishing countries, he used the opportunity to fish distant waters for a long list of game fish; he bid on certain flights to take advantage of favorable tides or moon phases. When Pan Am furloughed him for several years, Apte became a legendary Florida Keys' guide.

He developed quite a following as a guide. Among his most prestigious guests were President Harry Truman and Bess, his wife.

"One day we were out quite a distance from land," Stu relates, "and Bess had a problem. She had to 'tinkle.' I explained that we could go to a place that had a washroom but we would lose about an hour each way. Or, the President and I could stand on the deck, look the other way, clap our hands and sing "Are the Stars Out Tonight," while Bess used a large pot on board specifically for that purpose. She opted for the latter. What a great sport!"

Stu wasn't exactly popular with some of the other established guides, because he was the new kid on the block and because he insisted on giving his clients more than their money's worth. He was among the first to leave the dock in the morning and the last to come in. At night he rigged and worked on tackle if necessary. If weather conditions for success were impossible, he would postpone his parties ("No use going out for a boat ride").

Stu was fortunate to have several things come his way. For example, he was lucky to meet Joe Brooks, easily one of the best fly rodders of all time, and among the first anglers to fly fish seriously for marine species. They became close friends. Stu guided Joe often, and together they discovered and fine tuned many new techniques applicable to saltwater fishing. They were even featured in ABC's *Wide World of Sports* in a fishing contest against A. J. McClane, who was guided by Jimmie Albright. Stu and Joe won the tournament.

"Joe got me interested in trout fishing," Stu remembers. "At first, I couldn't imagine why anyone would take the time to catch trout that are usually measured in inches, when one could fish for big, powerful saltwater fish. But Joe insisted. I reluctantly agreed to try it and we fished in Montana. Wow! I loved it! In fact, I loved it so much that later I bought a home in Montana for summer trout fishing, and I even considered buying a house in New Zealand!"

Apte did it all. He was featured often in the long-running, fabulous *The American Sportsman,* ABC's national outdoor TV series. (Two separate shows included basketball's great John Havlicek and NFL's all-time best linebacker Dick Butkus: "They were very 'coachable' . . . could have been great anglers") Today, he frequently hosts or is featured on various TV outdoor shows.

He lists guiding Kay Brodney to a 137½-pound tarpon on a fly as one of his biggest thrills. This was back in the mid-'60s when few lady anglers fished for tarpon with a fly rod and even fewer guides would consider guiding a woman.

Stu Apte has had many detractors through the years. Some insisted that he was selfish, conceited, arrogant, egotistical, whatever.

The Stu Apte I know and fished with was quite different. First, he was and is willing to share any information with anyone. I caught my first sailfish on a fly rod in Panama on my very first cast to a sail, but the credit goes to Stu. Prior to my trip, he spent hours on the phone explaining the procedures to me, over and over again, everything from tying knots, to the importance of sharp hooks, where to cast, how to tease up the fish. Everything. Back in the early 1970s, this information was not readily available like it is today. At that time, probably only a dozen anglers had landed billfish on a fly rod, and usually expert fishermen were reluctant to share their hard-earned secrets. Stu invested a great deal of time, researching, testing and reporting his results.

One year he borrowed a $100,000 knot-testing machine from the Du Pont company to test different knots. He invested many hours in research, shared his results liberally, and today many knot recipes are a result of his experimentation.

Conceited? I'd call it confidence. You've watched Michael Jordan in the closing moments of a close basketball game? If the Chicago Bulls were losing, M.J. wanted the ball. Right? Call it confidence, call it arrogance, call it whatever you want, but these super stars know how to get it done, have tremendous faith in their abilities, and may not even acknowledge any personal limitations—if they have any—even to themselves.

One day at Club Pacifico de Panama I was in a very irritable mood, mostly because I was trying to give up smoking and my back was aching because of an earlier fall.

I hooked and was fighting a sailfish on a fly rod.

"I'm going to break it off, my back is killing me . . . " I told Stu as I tried to break that tippet with a few sharp jabs.

"YOU WHAT?" Apte was horrified. "Look. You have to play with those little hurts. No pain, no gain! I can't believe what you said!"

Little hurts? My painful back was telling me how nice it would be to sit down and sip a Coke, so whenever Stu wasn't looking, I would try to break that 15-pound tippet. No dice! I could not pressure the fish, so the fight went on and on.

"I think your sailfish is feeding again. You've had him on so long it's hungry again," he quipped.

"Yeah, yeah, yeah."

Eventually, I landed that sail.

I turned on him. "Okay, Mr. Apte. Your turn! And I'm going to time you." Remember, I was giving up smoking and was cranky.

He hooked a sail, and in the next few minutes I was treated to an exhibition of fish-fighting technique that I've never seen before or since. Apte danced from the stern to the bow with the grace of dancer Igor Yuskevitch, changed rod directions as adroitly as Wayne Gretzky wielded a hockey stick and countered every rush or sudden maneuver with the adroitness of Cantiflas, Spain's famous matador. He knew exactly how much pressure his tackle would withstand. There was that competitive, fierce stare in Stu's eyes, much like when Michael Jordan sank that final basket, the dagger against Utah Jazz for the NBA championship, or when Tiger Woods needs a few almost superhuman final shots to win a close tournament.

All the time, Stu was in total control. It was a wild, wild sailfish and it leaped crazily all around the boat because of Stu's relentless prodding. It was one of the fiercest sailfish battles I've ever witnessed.

Stu landed that fish in an amazing seven minutes. The fish was totally tuckered out.

"Easy fish!" I countered.

"Yeah, easy fish!" He laughed. We both did.

W E WERE IN ICELAND. One of the fellow guests, whom we had never met before, was having problems fly casting. Stu realized that the man's fly line was much too light for his rod. Without hesitation, Stu stripped off his brand-new fly line and exchanged it for the other man's.

"Try it now!" The angler was casting much better and was soon hooking salmon. Stu altered his casting stroke and timing now to compensate for the lighter line.

On another Icelandic river we fished for brown trout near a small village. Soon a group of perhaps a dozen young boys and girls congregated to watch Stu fish. Despite the language problem, Stu showed each child how to fly cast (they had to use both hands) and his goal was for every youngster to catch one trout.

They all did, except for one boy who was having trouble casting and missed the few rises he had. Now it was getting late. All the other kids departed for their homes and supper. Stu and I should have returned to the lodge long ago, but Stu stayed there, helping, instructing and encouraging the young lad. Never mind that there was a language problem. The brown trout were now off their feed, probably because of all the disturbance, but finally the young boy hooked and landed a trout.

Wow, was he happy! Were we happy!

I wonder how many of Stu's critics would have done the same thing?

"You know. It was very important to me that this kid landed a fish. It may seem like a small thing, but experiences like that could influence his life down the road," Stu said, as we headed for the lodge and settled for cold leftovers instead of a sumptuous feast.

I'm sure there were some incidents and some hurts in Stu's youth that later served as a catalyst for his drive to succeed and to be the best, but I didn't ask him. Some things should remain private.

On this Icelandic trip we hit the Atlantic salmon fishing just right. It was so good that we began to experiment with different flies (including tarpon streamers and bonefish patterns) and different methods. Stu hooked a particularly "hot" salmon that tore downstream with tremendous speed. It quickly cleaned out most of his backing, so Stu had only two options, let the fish break the tippet or follow it. Of course he chose the latter. He ran after that fish in the boulder-strewn stream, while Jon Jonsson, one of the lodge owners, and I watched. And cheered. Stu zigged and zagged down the stream like an NFL running back heading for the end zone.

"This is a very slippery section, lots of moss-covered rocks. I don't think he'll get that salmon . . . he'll fall in," Jon said, but soon we both marvelled at Apte's agility.

He caught up to the fish, tailed it and then released it.

We were amazed. Stu tried to carefully pick his way back to his original spot but fell in the river. His waders were now filled with icy-cold water, and the air temperature was on the coolish side. He could have returned to the nearby lodge, (only 15 minutes away) for some warm, dry duds, as we still had a couple hours' fishing time, but he insisted on fishing. Didn't miss a cast. Or a fish!

We ended the trip with an informal contest. Standing on one rock, we were allowed five casts. He hooked and landed four. I think I landed three in the five casts. It was that kind of a trip.

There are two Stu Aptes.

One is very carefree, who can break out in a song, and be all smiles and laughs. Fun to be with.

There is also the other, the serious Apte, the one with that competitive glint in his eyes. He barks out commands to a guide or fishing partner with the unquestionable self-assurance of a general in battle. The latter shows up at a tournament, during the production of a TV film or when there's a real shot for a world record that could help a camp, an area or a country. That's when he is all business. The guide better not mess up. Stay out of his way. Follow his instructions. But, then, don't we all have two sides? Isn't a high-powered CEO different in his office than when he is playing with his kids in the backyard? I like to observe and learn from both Aptes.

Stu is meticulous. No one prepares his tackle more precisely. He ties knots carefully and tests them; if he is dissatisfied with a knot, he reties it. Hooks must be super sharp. Rods? Once when we were fishing in Montana, I borrowed one of his fly rods. On a back cast, a No. 16 dry fly clicked against the fly rod. He took the rod and examined it carefully. Thankfully, there were no nicks in the finish of the rod tip (which I learned could cause a graphite rod to break under heavy pressure). He handed it back to me with a don't-do-it-again look.

Stu Apte's angling philosophy demands the best quality tackle rigged to the best of his ability so that he can pressure a fish to the gear's max or near max when necessary. When he is serious about his fishing, he makes every cast, every presentation, every retrieve as though there is a world record fish ready to hit his lure or fly. He admits it's hard to keep up the intensity, but that's what he tries to do when he is in that "zone."

He knows how to pressure a fish. In some circles, he is criticized for working or fighting a fish too hard. He counters: "Look, if I'm going to lose a fish, because it's poorly hooked, I want to lose it early in the fight and save the time. It's easier on the fish. It's easier on me. The longer you fight a fish, the longer there is a chance for something to go wrong or for the hook to pull out. I like to land a fish fast, revive it and release it. Thus, the fish has a better possibility for survival."

I enjoy and learn from both Aptes.

A. J. McClane

MY FIRST RECOLLECTION of Al McClane was in 1948 in Miss Brabec's English course at Amundsen High School, Chicago. While everyone in class was reading Macbeth—er, at least I think it was Macbeth—I was riveted to McClane's *Field & Stream* article on Parabolic fly rods. I could not believe that anyone could analyze fly rod actions with such scientific and precise detail. I thought a fly rod was a fly rod. Period. What does physics have to do with fly-rod action, I wondered. What also impressed me was that here was a young man writing about fishing for a living! Can you imagine that? Full-time living. Right then and there, I decided I would be a fish-for-a-living guy, too. So much for my becoming a chemist! I wanted to make fishing a career, just like this McClane fellow was doing.

Thereafter my required "what I did on my summer vacation" or "how to" English class themes centered on fishing, while the other guys were writing about how-to change flat tires or build bird houses. I wrote about walleyes being the gold of a lake. And about a mysterious, brightly spotted fish I once saw in Green Lake, Wisconsin. (I don't remember exactly; hey, that's more than a half-century ago.) Miss Brabec, who was very attractive and wore her skirts a little shorter than other young teachers, encouraged me to write more. And I did. I sold some fishing articles to major outdoor magazines while in high school.

I read everything that Al wrote. At my birthday, someone gave me a copy of his *The Practical Angler*. What a wonderful book!

Later on, A. J. and I exchanged a few letters, but I really didn't meet him until 1965 at the venerable VL&A emporium on Wabash Avenue, in Chicago. Later we planned a number of fishing trips. Mozambique. A return trip to Yugoslavia. What a thrill it would be to fish with the greatest of all fishing writers!

Holt, Rinehart and Winston Inc. had just published his prodigious *McClane's Standard Fishing Encyclopedia and International Angling Guide*. Al was on the phone shortly after:

"I can't go to Mozambique and Yugoslavia. Some cat at Holt issued a print order of 50,000 copies of the encyclopedia, and now they're wondering how they're going to sell them. They want me to go on an extensive media tour to help sell the books. Can you believe that? 50,000 encyclopedias!"

Of course, we all know how successful McClane's encyclopedia was during the ensuing decades—over a million copies sold—but at the time 5,000 to 10,000 sold copies of *any* fishing book was considered extremely successful. And his encyclopedia was expensive.

I was deeply disappointed. Heartbroken. Al wanted to know all about Mozambique. When I returned from there I sent him reports, and we talked about doing a fishing travel book together. I was immensely flattered.

We kept in touch, via letters, phone calls, or visits in Chicago or in Palm Beach where he lived. Mostly we talked about fishing, fishing places, fishing guides. He invited me to fish Great Harbour Cay, Bahamas on a long weekend. His wife Patti and Bing McLellan completed the party.

"I can promise you," A. J. was emphatic, "that this is a super place for bonefish."

He said there was a magnificent lodge built next to a 18-hole golf course and the owners wanted to develop its sport fishing business.

We met at his Palm Beach home. He lived across from the Kennedy compound, and I recall that the Kennedy's limo and driver picked us up and transfered us to the airport where a waiting private plane flew us to Great Harbour Cay.

One thing about Al, he knew all about the good things of life. *Bon vivant.*

I can't imagine a place that hosted more bonefish than what we found at Great Harbour Cay. Here you are wading, and you can see a thousand or more bonefish coming straight at you, and then a few hundred to the right of you, and another big school to the left. Just as they come almost within casting distance–KAZOOM! Hundreds of bonefish simultaneously would crash on the surface, leaving you with lots of foam and an experience that is hard to describe but not easily erased. Even decades later.

This happened repeatedly. I wasn't getting any bonefish. When the schools weren't so tightly packed, I could get in a cast or two to bonefish scouring the bottom for tidbits, but invariably other bones milling about would rub against my floating fly line.

ZOOM!

It's fun the first half-dozen times this happens. An incredible, preposterous, zany experience. You snicker, you chuckle or laugh. But then the bonefish's little game becomes less amusing, almost annoying, because you want to hook one of those torpedoes more than anything else and suffering a string of zeros amidst an enormous quantity of bonefish is, well, ego-busting.

McClane, who probably fished the Bahamas as much as any other visiting angler, also flushed a couple of schools, but then he left these crowded bonefish highways for what looked like barren flats. Sensing my frustration, he waved to me to come near him.

"There are too many fish there. You're better off looking for the singles and doubles." Good advice.

I was able to watch a master bonefisherman at work. There were tournament fly casters who could throw a longer line and others who might be more accurate on a platform. McClane was a smooth, accurate caster with the uncanny ability to compensate instantly for any sudden puffs of winds sent his way and his casting distance was more than sufficient for any reasonable angling situation that might arise.

S-m-o-o-t-h was the one word that best describes his casting.

Where he stood, away from the hordes of bonefish, it became a waiting game, a test of patience, waiting for a small school or individual bonefish. Like radar, his head turned slowly back and forth examining every shadow, unusual water ripples, occasional flash or any other telltale sights that could reveal the presence of a bonefish.

And when he spotted bonefish, he unleashed a couple of effortless, graceful false casts. The line would unfurl quickly, and the well-aimed fly would plop quietly on the surface, with just the right amount of "splat" to cause the bonefish to come over to investigate instead of scaring them off to another zip code.

Then Al would make one short strip of a few inches. Perhaps another one and maybe a twitch or two with the rod tip. When a bonefish would hit the fly, Al would first tighten on the fish by stripping in line with his left hand, and if he felt a satisfying weight, he would jab the fish a couple of times. Predictably the bonefish would streak near the surface at awesome (if not impossible) speeds. Rod held high, reel whirling in smooth metallic purrs, McClane's face would light up with amazement.

There was no shouting, no cackling, no laughing, no "Wow! Look at that fish go!" as we often see on our TV screens these days. No showmanship. Here was a man who fully cherished the wonderful species that is bonefish, and it mattered not whether this had been his first or his 10,000th bonefish. The genuine appreciation, I suspect, was and would always be the same.

292

The fast reeling, so necessary to recover dozens of yards of backing as the alarmed bone U-turned from its extended run, was silky smooth. When the fish's dashes were now reduced to a few yards instead of spool-emptying runs, McClane would shift rod positions from side to side, like an expert fencer. At the same time, he exuded the skilled confidence of a matador. He would finish off the bonefish, unhook it, place it in the water and stare admiringly at his opponent before allowing it to slip out of his grasp and back to the azure Bahamian waters. Sometimes he would talk to the fish before releasing it. Surely, McClane must have been among the smoothest bonefishermen ever.

I witnessed Al's performance several times: from spotting, casting, fighting, landing and finally to releasing his finny opponent. But each was a fresh, satisfying adventure. Never mind that he had done this thousands of times before.

That my results were very meager and ego-deflating was unimportant, although I probably hooked the only double-digit bonefish on that trip (I lost it near the end of the second major run because of a wind knot). When you are with a virtuoso and he is performing, this is not the time to show him how well (or poorly) you play the piano or violin. You listen. You observe. You learn. These lessons would prove invaluable in future skirmishes with bonefish.

Until cancer took his life, McClane was always a tinkerer, or more accurately, an experimenter. He was always testing new equipment, new theories, new approaches. When we went fishing in the Bahamas, I noticed that Al had a large bag but no rod case.

"Al, where are your rods?"

He pointed to his travel bag and smiled. When we arrived at the camp, he assembled what possibly was the prototype of the four-piece travel fly rod, now so popular. Though completely avant garde in most of his approaches to life, he turned out all of his wonderful articles and books on a mechanical typewriter equipped with a cloth ribbon even years after computers became the standard.

No one fished more foreign waters than McClane. Many of us associated with the fishing travel biz feel that we've discovered or uncovered new fishing places. Remember, the old "Kilroy was here" graffiti that our World War II soldiers scrawled on buildings and walls overseas? Well, maybe there should have been a "McClane fished here" slogan. We, the self-proclaimed early explorers, or today's "trail blazers," would be stunned to learn that nearly always McClane had fished there first. How many countries did he fish in, 140? With pal Don McArthur, an expert Braniff pilot, McClane practiced his flying along the Chilean coast and Andes searching for new places that still remain "undiscovered!" He fished the Tree River (Canada's Northwest Territories) for Arctic char even before Warren Plummer established his fabulous outpost camp there. He did so many things. And he did them first.

When McClane's health finally spiraled down from cancer, his good friend and outdoor writer Keith Gardner called me one day.

"Call A. J. in Montana. He's very ill." Gardner was sobbing.

The final call.

I composed myself and called him in Montana.

"Hi, Al, how are you doing?" Then I realized how stupid my question was. Here's a guy on his death bed and I ask him how he's doing. *Good grief!*

A. J. handled it well. He had caught a brown trout not long ago from the Madison. And Susan, his daughter, had caught some trout, too. That made him happy.

We swung into fishing talk. I was very much into brown trout fishing then (and still am). I discussed leaders with him. I knew he had experimented continuously on tapers, glint and colors. Is it best if they float and what about George Harvey's theories on tippet diameters? We must have spoken a half-hour on the subject. Just like the old days. Then he said he had a visitor, and we said goodbye.

I wept. No, I cried and cried and cried.

He was the great force in international fishing and I don't know of another man who carried more fishing knowledge in his head.

He will always be a hero of mine.

He died soon thereafter.

Winston Moore

I CAN TRACE my first contact with Winston Moore back to the 1950s when I was struggling with Sportackle International (the rod-making company). We had sold many fishing rods to Kamloops Distributing Company, a tackle wholesaler in Idaho. The economy was very lethargic at the time, and many businesses were having severe financial problems. Simply put, Kamloops could not pay for the rods it had ordered and sold (which was true with several other jobbers), and this put Sportackle International in a perilous position.

Kamloops was almost bankrupt when Winston Moore and his wife Diane mustered enough cash to buy the crippled company. Winston wrote that he was taking over the company and would pay a portion of the bill every month, which he did. I had not met him at the time.

Winston and Diane turned Kamloops Distributing around and it became one of the largest tackle wholesalers in the Pacific Northwest. The company grew and soared, and Winston built distributing centers in Salt Lake City, Utah, Vancouver, Washington and Helena, Montana to meet the increasing demands. He then sold Kamloops and entered the real estate business where he earned a tremendous reputation and eventually helped to reshape Boise.

His addiction to sportfishing started at the age of four. "On my first fishing trip I was 'packed in' to Golden Trout Camp, which was eight hours by horseback," Winston explains. "The camp was on the eastern slope of the Sierras, and the elevation was 9,000 feet. This was good experience because when I became older, I guided there."

He enjoyed fishing for bass on home waters, and later broadened his fishing to include browns in Montana and Idaho and salmon and rainbow fishing in Alaska.

His first major saltwater fly fishing experience was at Boca Paila, Mexico, in the mid-'50s, where he had his first taste of bonefishing. This was followed by tarpon trips to Parismina, Costa Rica, and billfishing gigs in Panama. Today, Winston only fly fished, but he admits that at one time he was a very good plug caster, too.

During the past 25 years, we have corresponded or called each other at least once a month.

The first time we fished together was for silver salmon on the fabulous Karluk River, Kodiak Island, Alaska. We arrived independently at Kodiak the night before and met the next morning for a sumptuous hi-cal, hi-cholesterol, hi-fat colossal breakfast: eggs, bacon, pancakes.

"Hey, can we have a little more butter and syrup, please?" I demanded.

"We've got to get our fishing licenses," Winston said. He had fished at Karluk Lodge numerous times and knew the drill. "Do you like ice cream?"

Huh? Somehow I felt that there must be a connection between obtaining a fishing license and ice cream, but I was puzzled.

After obtaining our licenses, Winston led me to an ice cream parlor. "They open early here. Try the fudge ripple. "

296

Now, I like ice cream as well as anyone. In our teenage years, Cousin Ernie (who later worked at Parismina Tarpon Rancho) and I finished seven pints of ice cream *after* a big supper.

But ice cream after breakfast?

Winston ordered a deep dish of three scoops. Huge scoops they were, and I had no recourse than to order the same. This is the first time in my life I ate ice cream after breakfast.

As we walked out, Winston ordered a triple-decker cone to go.

I passed.

We exchanged ice-cream stories. He said that years ago he hated to go to Belize during March, because the only ice cream maker in Belize City at the time made only one flavor each month. March was tutti-frutti month, and he disliked tutti-frutti. Besides, March was usually a windy month.

I told Winston that Janice Blivas, my wife's friend with the very sexy, throaty voice, told me that one of life's little-known sensual pleasures was to draw a very hot bath, as hot as you can tolerate, and then take a quart of ice cream and sit in that hot bath and eat the ice cream.

"Have you ever tried it?" Winston asked.

"Naw, I'm saving some pleasures for when I get old."

I still haven't tried it.

THE KARLUK RIVER was everything Winston said it would be. There were ten of us at camp in September, and on the first morning I remember Rod Neubert tearing around the bend with his skiff, only to see all nine of us hooked on to silver salmon.

"Where are they? Where are they?" Rod joked. He had to make two casts before he, too, hooked a silver. Fishing was that good!

One day I was to fish with Winston, although he almost always fished by himself. Winston got up very early every morning and he would take his boat up the river to the big pool, just below the weir, to begin his fishing at daybreak. The problem was that Kodiak Island had some of the meanest, biggest brown bears in the world. I read an article in the lodge about how a Kodiak bear mauled one of the camp's guides. He required more than 200 stitches and facial reconstruction. The guide was lucky to survive, but, understandably, he had frequent nightmares of the attack.

Winston was aware of this, but a bear was not going to deter him from his silver salmon fishing. The rest of us would still be in our sleeping bags, when we would hear Ikbuk, the camp dog, bark as the undaunted Winston made his way to the boat.

"Ikbuk accompanied me in total darkness to my skiff, about 200 yards from the camp. Several times he chased bears away," Winston explained later.

I got a ride to Winston's boat at a more civilized hour, after breakfast. I think he had already landed more than 20 silvers by the time I got there. Heck, many anglers don't land 20 silvers in a *week's fishing* at deluxe fly-out camps in prime time!

Winston is a very strong caster, can double-haul big flies long distances even in strong winds. He enjoys every fish he lands—as though it was a brand-new adventure or his first experience with that species—and invariably talks to the fish before he releases it.

"Come here, sweetheart. My, what a beautiful, strong fish you are! Now, keep swimming upstream and make some babies . . . " He thanks every fish and wishes them a safe journey. He didn't take a lunch break; for energy he would grab a handful of M & Ms, stored in a pocket in his trout vest.

We both caught lots of salmon, and by the week's end our group landed more than 1200 silvers on flies. Each evening, Winston would report fewer salmon than he actually caught.

"What do you do in Boise, Winston? For leisure?" I asked him at dinner time.

Well he tied flies and hunted pheasants with his dogs during the season, and then he mentioned jazz, one of my favorite pastimes. We talked about Stan Kenton, the Jazz at the Philharmonic concerts, Slim Gallard (we both were probably shocked that the other knew of him), Dodo Marmaroso, Wes Montgomery and June Christy. All of them.

"There is a fabulous jazz pianist in Boise. Gene Harris. Have you heard him play? He's terrific. Seldom leaves Boise."

"You got me there, Winston. Never heard of him."

"You have to hear him. He is going to Chicago with Ray Brown, Milt Jackson and a few others this winter. "

Later Winston informed me when Gene was coming to Chicago (my hometown), and, of course, my wife Sally and I went to the Jazz Showcase to hear him. Awesome! Never have I heard any jazz pianist stir up an audience to such an emotional pitch or frenzy as Gene Harris could. I've heard Oscar Peterson, Lennie Tristano, Bud Powell—all the cats. Harris quickly became my favorite. Gene and Janie, his wife, were gracious enough to accept our invitation to have lunch at our house. When I drive to my favorite trout streams in Wisconsin, I play Harris all the way. Unfortunately, Gene Harris died in February 2000, but his music will always live.

Winston, Chico Fernandez, the superb fly fisherman, writer and instructor, and I were at a sport show discussing jazz and how it relates to fishing.

"Maybe because both jazz and fishing feature improvisation, but at the same time there is structure and both are played within certain parameters. Creativity plays a very important part in jazz and in fishing," Chico said, and I think he is absolutely right.

A FEW YEARS later I joined Winston Moore on a fishing trip to El Pescador, Belize. This resort was more of a fun-in-the-sun resort than a fishing place. Yeah, some of the guests would go to the Barrier Reef, five minutes from the dock, and soak some bait for snappers, jacks, cudas and other species, but it wasn't known for its tarpon fishing. Bob Cazort, a subscriber to *The PanAngler*, tuned me into the good tarpon fishing available at El Pescador. Bob Miller, a well-traveled angler, read about El Pescador in our newsletter and took a chance. He experienced very windy conditions but thought the potential was very high. Winston Moore also went there and had such success that for a couple of years, he fished there two weeks every month from late spring until early fall. Winston hooked over 300 tarpon and boated and released 77, including several 100 pounders, during one year (seven trips). Bear in mind that this is visual fishing, not chuck-and-luck fishing practiced elsewhere in Latin America. He asked me to join him.

"This is something very special." Winston eyes lit up as we flew the charter to Ambergris Caye. "We need good visibility—fairly calm, clear waters, plenty of sunshine—as this is visual fishing like in the Keys. If we have those conditions, well, you won't believe what can happen. Keep your fingers crossed."

I had fished Belize, many years ago, when Vic Barothy built his main camp on the Belize River and had just completed his Turneffe Island Lodge, but I had never fished Ambergris.

It was one of those trips that you dream of, but seldom experience. Sight-fishing for tarpon on the flats was incredible. And what was great is that Winston, his good friend Sam Clements and I had all the flats to ourselves with no one else in sight. We each had our own skiff, guide and motor and we seldom saw each other. It doesn't get any better than this.

How good was it?

"Let's go somewhere else, get away from these tarpon, and eat lunch. I'm starved," I told Pancho, my guide.

Of course, I wasn't hungry, My God, it was only 11 A.M., but I was exhausted from fighting tarpon all morning. I just didn't want Pancho to know that I was whimping out.

After a ten-minute run, he stopped the skiff and assured me that we could eat in peace here.

"No tarpon ever come to this spot," Pancho insisted; nonetheless I tied on a fly-rod popper since this is not a favorite lure for big tarpon. If any tarpon were foolish to come near us, I thought, I'd just flick the popper at them and they would laugh and go away and not bother me.

I was that tired.

Of course, they came. Two from the left, one from the right, all 60 to 80 pounders. Coming slowly up at center court was the biggest of them all, a bruiser that was probably more than 100 pounds. While still sitting down, with a pork chop dangling in my mouth, I made a lazy cast with the popper, which landed a good distance from the big fish. The tarpon must have been starved, because it swam slowly to the surface and inhaled the popper. The hook set.

Back to work. Sore arms. Tired back. I lost him soon thereafter.

"Geez, first time I've ever seen tarpon here!" Pancho sort of apologized and fired up the engine looking for a more peaceful place to lunch.

Meanwhile, Winston was racking up tarpon after tarpon on the flats.

One early morning he even went into a lagoon for some "fun fishing" while waiting for the right light conditions for the big tarpon. If I remember correctly, he landed 16 small tarpon.

Former El Pescador owners Juergen and Kathleen Krueger told me that Winston caught more tarpon during his five or six trips in a year than all the rest of the camp guests put together during the year-round season!

"And as you know, we are often playing to a full house and there are a lot of good rods fishing here," Juergen added. "Some very, very famous guys."

On one of those trips Winston hooked a huge tarpon while being accompanied by his son, Jeff, and guided by Romel. The fight lasted six hours and ten minutes and took them more than 22 miles away.

"We hooked that fish at 6:30 in the morning and didn't get it to the boat until 12:40 P.M. When we saw that big fish next to the boat, we were amazed by its size . . . we taped the tarpon and after applying the usual weight formula, it was 212 pounds!"

Even though it would have easily surpassed the fly-fishing record for tarpon, the great fish was released at boatside. For years Winston never kept a fish, including many potential world records. He caught a measured 49$^+$-pound permit while fishing from Ascension Bay Bonefish Club (Mexico) and returned it. The fish was 50 inches long, and undoubtedly was the largest permit ever caught on a fly at the time.

At Club Pacifico de Panama, he hooked and could have landed a 400- to 500-pound black marlin with a fly rod (16-pound tippet) if there were a large gaff on board. Winston fought the marlin to exhaustion. The great beast jumped more than 60 times!

The captain radioed another nearby camp boat to bring over a big gaff. "We've got a huge marlin on a fly rod all played out. Hurry with the gaff!" But just before the other boat arrived, Winston's great fish recovered and broke off.

"Maybe I would have kept that marlin. *Maybe*." Winston said later.

At the time of this writing, Winston has caught and released 103 permit and 138 Pacific sails. He also has caught two striped, two blue and two black marlin via fly fishing! He has landed more than 7,000 bonefish. He has caught huge rainbows, browns, salmon and other species. Winston prefers to concentrate on one species at a time rather than practice grab-bag fishing.

When he was on a bonefish kick, he went to Los Roques, Venezuela. On one trip, he landed 308 bonefish in 13 days for an average of 24 bones per day! His score would have been much higher, except that Winston often passed up schools of bones—which are easier to fool— in order to concentrate on the larger singles and doubles (the bigger fish seldom school up).

While fishing at Los Roques, Winston noticed a scrawny dog on the island. He found out his name was Polvo and he immediately befriended the dog. He would feed it, give it water and each night Winston would bring lonesome Polvo into his room. When Winston would get in his skiff to go fishing each morning, Polvo would dive into the water and swim to the skiff. Winston would haul the dog into the boat.

"Polvo was a wonderful companion. He brought good luck, too."

On a trip to Belize, Winston was disturbed to hear dogs howling during the night. He found out that some lobster commercial fishermen would bring dogs to the various islands to guard their traps and catches. When the lobster season ended, some of these heartless commercial fishermen would abandon the dogs, leaving them on the islands without food or water or anyone to take care of them.

While fishing from live-aboard cruisers, Winston and his crew did their best to feed the dogs and provide drinking water. When he returned to the United States, Winston, Fred Keller (former resort owner) and I embarked on a crusade to save these dogs by contacting the Belize tourism department. Now the commercial fishermen can be heavily fined if they abandon their dogs on the islands, so the inhumane treatment of these dogs has subsided.

What I find remarkable about Winston's angling accomplishments is that he lives in Boise, Idaho, hardly the epicenter for the exchange of saltwater fishing information, and yet he is one of the greatest saltwater anglers of all time.

As I write this, Winston is strongly addicted to permit and just about all his trips are targeted toward this most elusive of all game fish. He usually books ten-day permit trips and concentrates entirely on this species. Do you know how tedious it must be to stand in a skiff for ten days, with your head turning slowly like a radar antenna, probing every square yard of flats for the elusive permit? I don't know of another fisherman who is that dedicated. Mind you, this takes place in the hot tropics, usually under a bright, blazing sun, where anglers and guides stare for hours into revolving mirrors of shiny, reflecting waters. Winston is the first to leave for fishing in the morning and the last to return. He seldom drinks water while fishing, but allows himself a quart or two of fresh orange juice when he returns to camp or a live-aboard boat at day's end.

Of course, I am impressed with his dedication, skill, patience, and mind-boggling results. No one comes close to him in these attributes. That he is one of the finest fly fishermen of all time is certain, but my admiration for him extends well beyond his fishing skills. He has helped many people financially in a private way, and yes, he has become a very successful business man. But what impresses me the most about Winston H. Moore is that he came from a dysfunctional family and was raised by another friend's parents. After a stint in the Navy, he received about $500 mustering-out pay. He gave all of it to his insisting father, except for about $50, which was the seed money for his great business success.

Winston works hard at staying in shape. He exercises daily and that's why today, in his mid-70s, he could outlast most fishermen, regardless of age.

Lee Wulff

I**T WAS A HOT**, sweltering August day and we were all busy at PanAngling's office on Chicago's Michigan Avenue. The office door swung open and in entered a tall, lean figure with shocking white hair. It was Lee Wulff! He was probably 78 or 80 at the time, at the height of his popularity, among the most famous fishing icons of all time, and although he wasn't feeling well and the heat was oppressive, he wanted to say "hello." He was in Chicago for a speaking engagement at a private club.

This was one of the most flattering things that ever happened to me. The great Lee Wulff visited me: the guy who tamed all those huge salmon and trophy trout on bantam-sized fly rods; the man who subdued giant bluefin tuna on light conventional tackle; the angler who explored and popularized fishing in Labrador and Newfoundland and invented the fishing vest, and once dove off a bridge in waders to demonstrate that belted waders would not cause an angler to drown. The conservationist who preached catch-and-release, when many of us were loading Coleman coolers with fish fillets. Many things. It was indeed a flattering experience.

The first time I met Lee Wulff was at the Executive Club in Chicago more than 35 years ago. He spoke at this prestigious club every year, and while the cavernous room at the old Sherman House could accommodate more than 1,000 persons, Lee's annual visits were very popular—the toughest ticket to obtain—and easily he outdrew every dignitary, including past U. S. presidents.

Lee's stunning fishing movies, which he produced, and his riveting live narrations were part of the big draw. His rich, wonderful voice and his relaxed but mindful script and style were presented with such precise timing and spacing that surely Lee's delivery was the envy of many TV or radio announcers. Amazingly, he told me that at one time he was a very poor speaker and lacked confidence but overcame this deficiency by long hours of practice. Lee would speak into a tape recorder while driving between engagements. He was sort of a modern-day Demosthenes. Lee always drew a standing ovation at his annual visits to the Executive Club and everyone left the huge room feeling much better about the world.

The rest of the angling world would come to know Lee through his wonderful appearances on such TV programs as *ABC's Wide World of Sports* and *The American Sportsman*. His charismatic personality, his tall, statuesque physique, his voice and delivery, his great skills as an angler and his penchant for adventure provided a complete package that TV media gurus loved.

I saw Lee several times briefly through the years and we once had lunch arranged by our mutual good friend and fishing companion Bus Duhamel. We stayed in touch and sometimes he sent me new innovations in fly patterns and constructions to try. I've learned that famous personalities are pestered constantly by well-meaning fans, so I never bugged Lee or other famous personalities. We exchanged letters from time to time, but that was it for the most part.

I was invited to New York to celebrate Lee's 85th birthday at the posh Waldorf Astoria. Lee and I greeted and hugged each other warmly. Then he said: "We have to fish together soon."

Sure, I thought. So many people say, "Let's have lunch sometime," but it never happens. Lee's fame, despite his age, was increasing every year and he was busier than ever, but he called and he wrote several times.

"Let's fish together," he insisted on the phone. How flattering! I jumped at the chance.

"What would you like to do?" I asked.

He wanted to try for a sailfish on a fly rod, so Lee, Joan, his wife, and I flew to Quepos, Costa Rica to fish with Tom Bradwell's Marlin Azul fleet. Prior to our trip, angling great Winston Moore said, "Find out what Lee uses to keep so active and so energetic. Let's bottle it, save some of it for ourselves and for our friends, and sell the rest and retire."

On the first fishing day, Joan picked the right straw which earned her the first shot at a sailfish via fly fishing. Joan Wulff is known for her fantastic casting skills, and her columns in *Fly Rod and Reel* are classics. Years ago she competed in the men's division and won a national distance fly casting championship with precise timing rather than brawn.

We teased up a sail, the captain shifted the engine into neutral and Joan delivered a perfect cast. She stripped the popper a couple of times, and a big sailfish inhaled the surface lure but the hook didn't set. Darn!

We teased another sail, up-close-and-personal, and this time everything worked to perfection and Joan was hooked solidly to a sailfish. Cool and calm, she parried the fish's best efforts, and in about ten minutes the sail was billed, photographed and carefully released. This was her first sail landed on a fly rod. Very few sails are landed in ten minutes on a fly rod by any angler, including the most experienced, so Joan's accomplishment was incredible.

Now it was Lee's turn. Whereas Quepos' sailfishing had been spectacular during the preceding weeks, Murphy's Law kicked in with a

306

vengeance during our fishing time (March 5 to 7, 1991). Sails were very scarce, reluctant to follow teasers, and not at all aggressive.

"Lee, do you think these sails would take a dry fly? Just floating on the surface?" I don't know what possessed me to ask that question. Just to fill in a lull in our brisk conversation?

That night, Lee apparently thought about my question and fashioned a huge dry fly from the little material he was able to find. The fly was about six inches long but very light.

The sea was rougher the next day so I thought the chances of taking a sail on a dry fly were nil. Surely, Lee would switch to a more conventional fly—a streamer or a popper—and move it on the surface, but, no, Lee was going to use a dry fly.

"How else are we going to find out?" he questioned.

"Well, yes, Lee, but these are tough conditions, and there aren't many sails around."

"Then this is the time to try something new, whether it's a method, a lure or fly. Try it under adverse conditions and if you succeed, it means something. If you try something under great conditions, when fish will hit everything, what does that prove?"

I nodded politely, but I was mad at myself for asking about dry flies for sails the day before. There was virtually no chance of succeeding, and I wanted Lee to get a sail on this trip. Who knows? It might be his last chance at getting a sail. I wanted to be part of this historic catch. So there were also selfish motives involved from my perspective.

The second sail we teased plucked the motionless dry fly from the surface. Just like that! And Lee Wulff was attached to one of the most tenacious sailfish I've ever witnessed. He hooked the sailfish shortly after noon. Whatever breeze that had existed before subsided. The perspiration poured down Lee's thin face. Joan tried to wipe it off, but he shooed her away. I found some shade under the bridge, sipped several cold drinks, placed ice cubes under my hat, and I still found it unbearably hot. There's Lee, now 86, in blazing sunlight, fighting the sail.

The fish was unyielding. It didn't jump itself silly at first and therefore use its energy; it sounded, taking yards of line from Lee's fly reel.

Somehow, some way, Lee worked the fish back to the surface, where it would promptly unleash a series of dramatic jumps before sounding again, and resting.

One hour passed.

Lee worked the fish in closer. He was sitting on the bait box next to the transom. In his younger days he'd have been standing up, fighting the fish hard and tough, giving up line only when it was absolutely necessary. Now aged, Lee had to conserve his energy, for this battle was developing into a very long fight. The sail dove for the deeper waters again.

"Of all the sailfish in this big ocean, we have to meet this one," I thought to myself, greatly paraphrasing Humphrey Bogart's line in *Casablanca.*

"Do you think Lee is okay?" I asked Joan.

"He's okay. His intensity and dedication are his strengths."

"I'm amazed." I told her. "Here's a guy in his mid-80s, fighting that fish as best and as hard as his strength allows, on this hot, humid day from a rolling boat. I often see a baseball pitcher in the prime of life needing to rest because he just ran 90 feet to first base. Or a football player bursts for a 35-yard run and he points to the coach that he needs to come out for the oxygen mask."

Joan laughed and agreed.

She brought Lee a cup of Coke. He took a couple of swallows and then said he wouldn't need any more. Almost two hours passed. Lee was stubborn; it was important to him to land this fish. The fish was stubborn; it was fighting for its life. Just when the sailfish seemed to be tiring, it dove for deeper water where it recovered its strength.

Round Four.

"Why don't you go to Lee and talk to him? I think he'd like that."

"Are you kidding?" I asked. "While he is fighting that fish? What if he loses it?"

She insisted. So I went and sat next to Lee. We talked about how that sail hit a dry fly and what a strong fighter it was. Lee wondered what the sailfish took the dry fly for? "Perhaps a baby albatross?" Perhaps.

"Lee, I bet you can't wait until this is over. I bet you're thinking about how nice it will be when we go back to the air-conditioned hotel, and have a couple of chocolate sundaes? Right?"

"**Absolutely not!** That's the worst thing you can think about. It would be self-defeating because then you would want to get this battle over with so that you could enjoy the air-conditioning and ice cream. It would be a terrible mistake."

"Then what do you think when you are fighting this fish for a long time?" I had to know.

"I think what a splendid, strong fighter this buck is . . . but then I think I have years of experience and that I have patience. As I get older, I lose more strength, but on the other hand I gain experience and I have confidence in what I'm doing. It's youth against experience."

He was absolutely right. The encounter between Lee and the fish was almost a Hemingway confrontation. I noticed his unique fly reel.

"What kind of reel are you using?"

"It's custom-made. Stan Bogdan made it for me. Actually he made only two and gave them to me," he replied.

Whoa, only two reels of this model made by a famous reel maker, and Lee was fishing with one of them?

"Aren't you afraid of losing this rare reel, overboard?"

"So?" he replied. "Many people have good tackle and other equipment and never use it. Stan made these for me for fishing, not to sit in a drawer and collect dust. If I lose a reel overboard, I lose it. "

I felt a little sheepish. I have some unusual, valuable fishing rods and reels, but I hesitate to use them for fear that they will break or be damaged. I learned this from my grandmother, who used to save China dinnerware and linens for special occasions that never materialized.

"Are you okay, Lee? You've been in the hot sun out here? Would you like some water? Some ice? Anything? "

"No. I'm fine. I'm okay."

I left him to fight his fish. Two and a half hours. Just when you'd think this fight was hopeless, Lee worked the sail to the surface where it uncorked a volley of spectacular, somersaulting flips. There was hope.

The jumps tired out the fish, but then it sounded in deep water again, where it rested and recuperated.

Three hours.

The crew was getting antsy. All the other boats had gone in for the day. We were a helluva long way from the shore. I drank a couple of ice-cold Cokes. In the shade.

I remember that the previous trip to Costa Rica, Lee fought a blue marlin for six hours at Golfito Sailfish Rancho before the eight-pound tippet broke. Years ago, Wulff was among the first to land sailfish on a fly rod, and he even subdued a 148-pound striped marlin on a fly for *The American Sportsman* television cameras. It became obvious to everyone on board that it was very important to Lee that he land this fish. There was no doubt that he was ignoring tired, aching muscles and battling almost total exhaustion.

The break came. The fish flushed to the top and slashed all over the surface, right next to the boat. On one jump it looked like the fish was coming into the cockpit. Raphael deftly maneuvered the boat and Carlos sprung like a cat into action, so fast that I don't know what really happened. I think he fended off the fish with a small gaff as it was about to come in. The fish was stunned. Carlos grabbed the bill. The fish was landed after three hours and ten minutes.

Hurrah! It was a great trip back to the docks. Bradwell's crew (Raphael and Carlos) deserved tremendous credit. It was one of the greatest fishing moments I've ever experienced. Moments? It was an epic! Lee at age 86 had used a dry fly on a fly rod to conquer a tough sail.

After dinner we discussed many things. Lee had a very noticeable limp. I asked him about it. He had injured his foot while playing football at Stanford University. He played fullback. It didn't bother him before, but now in his 80s it did.

"Fullback? Why'd you play that position?" Lee had the physique of an end or wide receiver. He was much too thin to play fullback, especially in those days of power football.

"When you're young, you do dumb things. You think you're invincible."

"Like that wild sailfish that came up to take a dry fly? Perhaps mistaking it for something else?"

"Like that." He smiled. "Of course, we'd like to stay young and vigorous but that's impossible. But there are some advantages to old age."

"Like what?" I needed to know, as my birthdays were flying by.

"Well, you can say just about anything to anyone, and they'll dismiss your comments because of your age. Say the same things when you're young, and you could get a bloody nose or a broken face!

"The one disease I fear is cancer. Slow death. Painful for you and others . . . you degenerate like a Pacific salmon that has returned to a river to spawn and then the dying process accelerates. "

At this point, I brought up the first day of our fishing trip. Our captain had to let us out at the end of the pier because of the unusually low tide. There was a circular, rusty metal staircase without handrails that wound its way up for about 20 feet. The dark water swirled ominously underneath the pier. Joan and I weren't particularly fond of going up this staircase, but we said nothing. Lee grabbed his rods and even with his bad foot he didn't hesitate. He went up first. Whoa!

Naturally, I had to do it, and so did Joan. I asked him about this.

"You know, Lee, I didn't like climbing that circular staircase. It just didn't look safe, not having any rails, but you didn't hesitate! I climbed the stairs, because you did it."

"It's all mental," Lee said. I'm sure he had sensed my reluctance to go up the staircase. "Many people defeat themselves mentally, when physically they are capable of doing a task without hesitation. Let me give you an example: Let's say you had a wooden board that was four feet wide and say a dozen feet long. Anyone who can walk would have no problem walking across the board. Right?

"But now place this board high, say ten stories up, between two buildings 10 feet apart. Most people would have a terrible time going across the board. Most wouldn't even attempt it."

"You're absolutely right!" I said. "One time I was fishing in Argentina for trout. George Wenckheim, my guide, and I were returning to our tent camp in the dark. He suggested a short cut and I remember we walked across a big wide log. George told me to be careful and had only a small flashlight. No problem.

"The next day he wanted to use that shortcut again. When we came to it, I was shocked to notice that the log bridged a boulder-infested river. I think the log was 40 to 50 feet above the river. No way was I going to go across that log again, although I did that at night. You're right. So much is mental."

We talked about Charles Ritz, the tackle industry, a book that he was writing (*Bush Pilot Angler*), Yellow Bird (a plane he owned), catch-and-release, advances in tackle and so many other things.

I found his spirit, enthusiasm and discussions a very necessary example. As I age and find myself not as agile as 30 years ago, and aches and some pains begin to take over, I often recall Lee's words of wisdom.

"This summer," Lee continued, "if all goes well, I'll fly my plane to Labrador for brook trout." He talked about putting floats on his plane and using a "dolly-like" contraption to take off from his landing strip. He explained that he would land on floats on wet grass. "It's been done before but you have to be careful . . . want to come along?" he asked me.

"Huh?" I was flattered. But I'm not a fan of little planes under the best of circumstances.

"Think about it. Great brook trout fishing."

Soon after, Lee Wulff crashed in his plane near his home in New York while renewing his flying license; apparently he suffered a heart attack while landing. The instructor, Max Francisco, suffered compound fractures, broken bones in his feet, facial lacerations and was lucky to survive the crash.

Before he died, Lee Wulff tied two flies for me without using a vise: A No. 12 and a No. 28 Royal Wulff. Thoughtfully he even included letters of authenticity. (He also tied a revolutionary sailfish fly for friend Peter Aravosis who was going sailfishing.)

The sail was the last big fish he caught, and these may be the last flies Lee tied.

I am honored.

PART SIX

Regrets, hope & dreams

Le Shack—close-to-home fishing;
aging stinks, it really does;
Fishing then and now
(were the "good old days" really <u>that</u> good?);
what about the future of fishing?
(We better wake up! The anti-fishing campaigns aren't going away).

Le Shack

W HEN I FIRST visited Le Shack 35 years ago, I wasn't impressed. Le Shack—a private trout fishing club located in central Wisconsin—was a two-story converted farmhouse with a dozen beds and assorted chairs and furniture of unknown vintage scattered about. There were two bedrooms, kitchen, dining room and a screened-in porch on the first floor. The upstairs was designed dormitory style and slept eight, but capacity was usually about 14 if one included the half-dozen resident bats that soared about at night; however, they were no major problem since there were no vampires reported among them. Actually, some of us welcomed the bats, because if a mosquito dared to enter our sacred house through the Swiss-cheese window screens, a bat would quickly hone in on it. *Slurp.* Dead meat.

There was no running water, of course, but a squeaky, cranky hand pump delivered pure ice-cold water. Well, not exactly "pure." Occasionally, we'd pump water and a cute, little frog would plop into our pail. I named him Jessie. We'd release him, of course, and somehow he would make his way 25 to 35 feet below, to the source of our water supply. I don't know why he choose to live down there; perhaps he liked being pumped up through the pipe. Once we sent a member's son to fetch water and he was stunned when Jessie came up the pipe and belly-flopped in the pail. He never drank water from the pump again and brushed his teeth with Pepsi or Coke.

City slicker!

For bathing? Well, most guys didn't bathe if they stayed for only for a few days. For those who insisted on a daily bath there was a small creek about 70 yards from Le Shack. The mosquitoes at the creek hid in the trees or grass until we removed all our clothes, and then, on an indiscernible signal, the mosquitoes swooped on us from all directions and our only escape was to dive into the ice-cold waters of Frothy Creek. The mosquitoes always won these skirmishes, because they knew that we couldn't last long in that frigid creek.

Since there was no running water in Le Shack we didn't have an indoor toilet. We had an outhouse. A two seater. Hey, company.

A dozen or so old battered fishing hats hung at the entrance of the dining room. These hats belonged to deceased Shack members. It's an eerie feeling to know that one day our fishing hats would also be displayed there.

While everything was run on a very casual, come-when-you-can, leave-when-you-must basis, we observed a ritual every morning if there were five or more members at camp. The ritual was called *Sol Er Uppa*.

At sunrise everyone filed outside, and each member was handed a glass of rye and orange juice, usually prepared by Freddie Leu, Carl Johnson or Dick Korsgard. The rye, we were told, covered the orange juice and "protected its vitamins from escaping."

Everyone lined up, faced east, and held his glass with his thumb on top and little finger at the bottom, while the remaining three fingers curled in. Don't ask why. Tradition, I guess.

Bus Duhamel, a transplanted Canadian, bellowed *Sol Er Uppa*, a Norwegian fish poem, while the rest of us, in assorted stages of dress or undress, repeated each Norwegian line in unison. At the completion of the poem everyone had to finish his drink in one swoop. Chug-a-lug, we used to call it in college. If someone didn't do it right, or if someone developed the giggles during the poem—and this was often the case because nearby farm dogs barked or howled in protest—then the whole procedure had to be repeated. Duhamel was a hard taskmaster and once he was not satisfied until the fourth try. After that ritual, most members

had difficulty tying a tiny Adams to their wispy leaders, but since early morning fishing was not considered good, no one felt shortchanged.

The hefty breakfast of blueberry pancakes, eggs, bacon, coffee cake and other goodies prepared by the members steadied everyone. Except for one morning. Art Thrun insisted on preparing a special breakfast, which was so ghastly we termed it, "Thrun's Tragedy," or "Thrun's Trash." He was abolished from ever cooking another breakfast at Le Shack for at least five years and was ordered to sleep on the porch for the remainder of the year.

The ringmaster of Le Shack's circus was Hank Looyer, a character right out of Robert Traver's *Anatomy of a Fisherman.* Looyer had just about perfect attendance at Le Shack for more than 40 years. I am talking about every weekend during the entire trout fishing season. Only a serious business problem or a scheduled fishing trip out of the country had kept him away. Did he take his wife fishing on their honeymoon?

Of course not! Trout season was closed, so Dorothy had to settle for a duck-hunting honeymoon.

There were other characters, of course: Russ Gaede quickly comes to mind. Built close to ground ("God made me small, so that the trout don't see me good"), Russ was a living copy of Ed Zern's trout fisherman illustrations.

Russ was assigned to take me fishing on my first evening at Le Shack, and since he had fished these waters as much as anyone, I welcomed the opportunity.

"We gotta check on the hatches and fishing reports," Russ announced.

He drove to a tavern.

"The bartenders know what's happenin' on the cricks. Fishermen come in, drink too much and spill out all their secret fishing information, ya know," Russ explained while he drank a couple of martinis and I polished off a root beer-on-the-rocks.

Suddenly Russ decided which creek we should fish that evening, but how he determined it escaped me because he never asked the bartender about fishing or hatches.

"The bartender didn't know nothin'," Russ concluded as we walked to his car.

He drove and drove for a while and then seemed perplexed.

"Tell ya, Jim, this place looks like a foreign country. This looks like nothin' I've seen before. I think I'm lost. I've fished this area for 30 years and know it like the back of my hand, but this is all different."

Russ didn't blame the martinis.

I spotted several people up ahead on the desolate dirt road and suggested that we ask them for directions.

"Pardon me, can you please tell me where we are? What road this is?" I inquired.

"*No hablamos Ingles*," was their response in unison.

"What'd I tell ya, Jim? We're in a foreign country!" Gaede retorted. "We've driven all the way to Mexico!"

Obviously, I had asked some migrant crop pickers for directions.

I JOINED THE CLUB in the 1960s. It was certainly affordable. Six dollars a night. We put the six dollars in a little money purse in back of the front door. The six bucks not only covered the daily rate, but also essential groceries. If we were out of eggs, bacon, coffee, bread or other staples, we'd take the money out of the purse and go to the grocery store.

"Yeah, but this doesn't cover any steaks or fancy stuff," Hank warned us. "Just essentials. And put the receipts in the purse."

I wasn't impressed with the fishing. It was (and is) the toughest brown trout fishing I've ever experienced. I did my serious trout fishing in Yugoslavia, Ireland, Argentina, New Zealand and elsewhere. I went to Le Shack to visit with the guys and because it was fun.

Dick Korsgard, the "Silver Fox," as I called him, used to sing the praises of Le Shack's fishing.

"Jim, where are you gonna find trout fishing like this? Dozens of streams all around us. *Wild* trout. None of this planted stuff."

Oh, he could get excited when he talked about Le Shack's fishing.

"Yeah, Dick, this is the best," I wasn't going to spoil his enthusiasm for these streams by telling him about some of my results on foreign rivers.

Dick Korsgard was in the commercial floor covering business. Once he invited one of his best customers up to Le Shack. Don, the customer, had never fished in the area before; nonetheless, Dick took him to his favorite section, the notorious White Rag stretch. Most fishermen avoided this place because you had to know where to step, on land or in the water, since there were many oozy, muddy places that sucked your legs down. Some of the club veterans insisted that there was quicksand and that you could get into very serious trouble. No doubt there were sink-holes and quicksand, but I suspected that they used scare tactics to discourage other anglers from fishing their favorite stretches.

It was a perfect evening when Dick and Don arrived at the river. After putting on their waders, Dick forged ahead, down the faint trail, and got into the stream, forgetting all about his valued guest who lagged slowly behind him. Don somehow wandered off the path and walked into a soft, muddy spot. He struggled to pull himself out, but his legs were stuck, and he was sinking.

"Dick! Dick! I'm stuck. I can't pull my legs out of the mud!" Don shouted. "I need your help."

There was silence. But only for a moment.

"Crissakes. Cut those f- - - - - - legs off! The trout are out," was the echoing response. Dick seldom swore.

He continued to fish.

"W-i-l-d t-r-o-u-t," he'd yell in his high pitch voice every time he hooked a trout. Don finally worked himself out of the oozy spot by slipping out of his waders, which he surrendered to the mudhole. He found the river and waited at the bank in his stocking feet until Dick finished fishing. He waited a long time.

"What the heck are you doin' on shore?" Dick asked, noting that his very important customer was in stocking feet and swatting mosquitoes. "And what happened to your waders? Oh, never mind. Tell me later. Wait'll ya hear 'bout the big trout at the third bend."

Don still gave Dick a big share of the floor-covering contracts, but I don't think Don ever fished at Le Shack again.

W E, THE NEW MEMBERS, weren't very successful in our fishing attempts at Le Shack during the first few years, and suffered many failures before we were able to catch trout. Hank McRoberts caught some fair-sized trout at Alfred's on hoppers, and one night he made a killing at the Leapin' Beaver stretch. Then Chuck Mitchell, Art and Bus and I began to take a few trout at dusk provided that there was an evening hatch. Occasionally we succeeded in the daytime but our catches were always modest.

The veterans—Looyer, Gaede, John Johnson and others—told us what to do, but we weren't very good listeners. We wanted to do it our way. We had to learn the hard way. Hank Looyer's most important advice was the necessity for extra careful wading.

"When you come to a good lookin' pool, wait at least five minutes before you make a cast. Let the trout settle down. Look around a bit. Enjoy nature. In these small, deep cricks you push water upstream and the trout know you're there, even if they can't see you," Hank advised us.

But no, we were impatient. We'd cast after pausing for a few seconds. No rises, so we'd conclude that there were no trout at this pool and moved to the next bend.

Slowly we learned. As

my scores improved, I started going to Le Shack more frequently because I loved the fishing, the challenges, and that special elation that I received whenever I succeeded in catching a 15-inch brown in the daytime. Once I caught three 20-inch trout in a 24-hour period in the dog days of August when nothing was moving. Wow, that was almost an orgasmic experience!

At the time I was learning how to fool Le Shack trout, I was also fishing some of the world's best trout streams as part of my job at Safari Outfitters and PanAngling. I enjoyed these foreign trips tremendously, but catching trophy trout at these incredible places wasn't that difficult if one could cast reasonably well and listened to his guide.

I wasn't going to kid myself. I knew that these international rivers were among the best wilderness places in the world. I'm sure that some of the trout I caught never saw a fisherman before. The guide selected the fly, tied it on my leader, positioned me in the stream, spotted the fish from his vantage point, told me when to set hook, how to fight the fish and even netted it. Of course, this was fun, even ego-inflating and I loved it, but I wanted a more active, personal involvement in decisions.

The ultimate trout fishing challenge was clearly at Le Shack, because it was not only tough fishing, I had to make my own decisions: where to go, what to use, where to cast, many things.

Why were these Wisconsin browns on these *specific* streams so difficult to fool? Until recently, catch-and-release was unknown. For decades, the locals considered it almost a sin to release a fish. Some of them felt that the main purpose of fishing for trout was to help feed their families, not for sport. Most locals worked very hard, jobs were low paying and limited in this rural area and many Catholics were supposed to eat fish on Fridays. What better fish to eat than freshly caught trout from nearby ice-cold streams? Even the anglers who traveled long distances from other states to fish this area wanted to bring home a limit of trout.

Year by year, most of the "dumb" brown trout were caught, not only by the fly fishers but also by bait and hardware fishermen, and because there were no hatchery plantings in these streams, a special, extremely wary brown trout strain evolved through the years. Sure, there are a few big trout landed now, but most of them are caught at night usually during a heavy *Hexi* hatch. Today, most giant trout die of natural causes rather than at the hands of some fisherman.

These streams are quite deep and narrow and you need to wade in them because it's impossible to fish from the banks, which are lined with heavy vegetation. As you progress upstream, no matter how carefully, you alert the smaller trout along the undercut banks. The spooked

trout initiate a chain reaction as they frantically scoot upstream to the safety of the deeper bends. This frenzied behavior alerts the larger trout that an intruder is advancing. At European chalk streams and some of our eastern streams, you can fish from banks, and if you tread lightly and stay low, you won't scare the trout.

I FISH ALONE most of the time. I pack my car trunk with food and cold drinks and off I go, making all the decisions myself, from which stream to fish to what fly patterns to use. I'm self-sufficient and I don't have to meet anyone at a specific time or place. I eat when I'm hungry, fish as hard as I want to, change streams as often as I'd like. Sometimes, I don't fish for long periods of time. Instead I'll position myself on a knoll or high ground and watch the stream. Occasionally, I'm amazed at what I see. There are some very big trout in these waters, but you have to pick your point of observation and patiently remain statue-still.

My approach to daytime fishing is generally the same, regardless of where I fish. I wade slowly up to a river bend, all the time fantasizing that there's a huge trout in that undercut bank or below that sunken log waiting for something to eat. I find that I need to fire up a positive fishing approach in order to maintain my confidence and enthusiasm.

Sometimes a big trout will come out slowly from under the bank to inspect the fly, its snout only inches away. My pulse quickens. Should I move the fly a bit, make it quiver, make it appear like it's alive or let it float naturally? Before I can decide, the trout usually drifts back under

the bank where it evaporates into the darker, deeper water.

"Didja see that? Didja see that?" I might yell out loud even though there's no one there to hear me. That's usually the scenario with big trout in the daytime. Occasionally a big trout actually hits the fly and the fun begins because I'm using very light tippets in the daytime. There are lots of sunken logs and obstructions in the waters I fish and these browns know how to use them.

When I enter the sacred waters of Le Shack, my thoughts are locked in to trout. Period. I don't think of any extraneous problems, certainly not business, and I find this very cathartic. Some people go to shrinks, others practice yoga, I go trout fishing to clear my head. The Dow-Jones, Nasdaq, bills, payments, problems; who cares! They all disappear when I'm fishing.

I'm addicted to this area. I've passed up Atlantic salmon trips to Russia's Kola Peninsula, a blue marlin gig to Madeira, Alaskan fishing, and once even a scheduled trip to Greenland with Al McClane and his pals because I wanted to fish the waters of Le Shack. That, my friends, is a real addiction.

Or insanity.

W E HAD A PROBLEM, a serious problem, in 1990. We really didn't own Le Shack; Hank Looyer had leased it through the decades from a local family. We lost the lease because the family's teen-age son wanted Le Shack for himself and his friends. You know, parties.

We had no place to stay.

Member Art Thun learned that a small brick house across the river, not far from Le Shack, was for sale. It was a converted schoolhouse. He bought it, we christened it Le Shack II and Art saved the club.

Compared to the old one, Le Shack II was the Ritz Hotel at Place Vendôme! We didn't have to go to Frothy Creek for a bath and fight the mosquitoes. This place had a shower, hot and cold water, inside modern plumbing, wall-to-wall carpeting, overhead fan and no bats. We moved the fishing hats of the deceased and a few other memorabilia to the new place. John Johnson, Russ Gaede, Dick Korsgard, Ray Sauvé and Ole

Johnson had died and new members joined the club.

Through the years, the daily rate "soared" to $12 a day and this didn't include buying groceries. Le Shack was not immune to the inflation. Only strong protests—mostly from me—kept Art from raising the daily fee to a hefty $13. We settled for $12.50.

I LOVE FISHING these streams at night. It's great to have the entire river to yourself, but this is rare on a warm summer night with the promise of a heavy hatch. Usually there are other anglers on the water, but after 11 P.M., they begin to leave for home.

You hear car doors slam and engines started as one by one the cars depart. Finally, I have the whole stream to myself! This is my most joyous time at Le Shack's waters. I look at the heavens and I'm overwhelmed that some of the stars that I see, may not exist today; they are so far away that it takes thousands of years for the light to reach us. Hard to believe.

'Round midnight. The witching hour. It's almost silent now. Occasionally the drone of an overhead plane breaks the silence, but mostly I hear frogs and crickets. I try to filter out their croaking and chirping, as I need to zero in on the sounds of big trout feeding on the surface. Sometimes they'll feed so quietly that the noise isn't audible, while at other times they'll crash the surface and scare the heck out of you. It's important not only to hear the trout but also to know its exact location.

Sometimes, at night, I hear a slurp or sucking noise, much like a plumber's plunger, a sure sign of a big fish inhaling a floating insect. That plunging sound is rare, and the lower the resonance, the larger the trout. As in my daytime fishing, I fantasize about big trout at night, too, but at night my imagined trout are huge. Twice as big.

Perhaps this incredible trout is around that bend. Or the next one. Or under that big log that can only be fished successfully with a bow-and-arrow cast at night. For more than 25 years, I have been convinced that my imagined giant trout actually exists, that one night I'm going to hook it and I better be ready for it. These fantasies remove negative thoughts from my mind, especially on nights when I do not hear or hook trout for long intervals. They serve to recharge my enthusiasm.

One night, I hooked many big trout in a 50-yard stretch and landed four or five that were more than 20 inches in length, the largest being a 24-inch trout. That was an incredible evening on these waters, where a 12-inch brown is considered a good-sized trout, but I was convinced that there were bigger trout than that 24 incher and I'll continue to hunt for these rare fish.

SEPTEMBER 4,1999. I went to a favorite stretch. I met "Jack" from Hancock, Wisconsin who had just completed his nocturnal gig.

"It's slow," he said. "I thought tonight would real good. Conditions are perfect, right water level, but nothin's working. One small trout."

He was discouraged.

"No one's on the river now," he added as he disassembled his fly rod. "I'm driving home tonight."

I'd have the whole river to myself!

Once I got in the water I moved very slowly. I was in no hurry. It's important to minimize noise and motion because even at night the trout are wary. Especially the big ones. Periodically, I sat on the bank at various strategic places, observing what I could in the darkness but mostly listening. I have a severe hearing problem, but on the creeks I have no problem hearing even a small trout take a fly from the surface many yards away. I have problems driving at night because oncoming headlights tend to blind me, but on these streams, I'm able to easily distinguish land and overhanging brushes from water. I don't fight the darkness, like many novice night fishermen do. Instead I accept it. I allow it to surround me as I become part of it. I surrender to it.

It was a warm September night. The moon was in its last quarter phase. At times it was shrouded by slow-moving puffs of clouds, while it shone softly on the dancing waters. Perfect conditions, I thought. On this particular night I decided to fish a stretch that I've been observing during the day. I'd only spotted a few trout here, but somehow I was convinced that the giant brown that I'd visualized for decades might live in this vicinity.

I attached a giant Disco Trout, a huge, heavily hackled downwing fly that's similar to a Rio Grande, and tied on a No. 4 or 6 hook. Big and bushy. I cast it perhaps 50 times without moving my position more than a few yards. For some inexplicable reason I was positive that I would hook my imaginary trout.

It happened! It was one of the most explosives strikes I've ever heard in all my years of trout fishing. Even with only a partial moon I could see the huge waves roll from the center of the strike. But the fish missed the fly or at least I didn't feel it. This was my fantasy trout. I'm sure it was. The fish I've searched for during the past 25 years.

I was trembling. I was literally shaking.

Why was the strike so explosive? Why did it expend so much energy when it could have plucked the fly from the surface with a minimum of effort? Perhaps a little trout had come to the fly, I reasoned, and just as it was about to take the fly, the enormous brown struck the smaller trout. That made sense to me.

Maybe the little trout escaped from the big brown and the giant fish was furious. And still hungry. Since I didn't feel the trout, I didn't think it was alarmed.

I switched to the largest surface pattern I had and kept casting to the same spot. Over and over again. I wanted to aggravate or tease that fish to a point that it would strike again.

I tried different techniques. Lots of motion on some retrieves, dead drift on other casts. There was no doubt in my mind that this monster trout would hit again.

I cast the big fly dozens of times.

There was a tremendous swirl.

The huge trout exploded on the surface again, just as dramatically as the first time. Maybe more so. This time I was able to set the hook. I was on to my dream fish; the trout of a lifetime. Adrenalin shot through my body. This was it! The fish that existed in my mind for 25 years. My fantasy fish solidly hooked. I could feel the fish shake its head trying to get rid of the fly.

Let the fight begin. *Mano a mano.*

The trout stayed on top, churned the surface with heavy body rolls and by shaking its powerful tail. Then it torpedoed to the deeper water.

That's when everything went limp. The rod lost its beautiful arch, the line was slack, the whirling reel was silent again.

Damn!

The great brown trout that I thought about every night I fished was gone. I stood in the center of the river, quivering. I felt as though my clothes, my waders, my vest, my body and mind were all still there but something from within me had left my body. For lack of a better term, I'll call it the "fishing soul." The fishing soul had left me.

Elsewhere, I've landed my share of outstanding trophies of various species through the decades and I've lost many impressive fish, but none of the lost monsters ever caused such despondency, such depression as this fish.

I was in a catatonic state. Several minutes passed by before I finally reeled in the line to examine the leader. The 12-pound test tippet seemed chafed and cut in the middle. At night it's customary when hunting big fish to use heavy tippets because of all the brush and sunken logs and because it is difficult to cast big, air resistant flies on light tippets.

The great trout apparently rubbed the tippet against a rock or a log and broke off. I don't know how big it was. Somewhere between eight and 12 pounds, I'd guess. Maybe it was a ten pounder.

In the recent years, a 31-inch,10-pound brown trout was the largest caught in this area. Garry Erdman was fishing at 1 A.M. during a *Hexi* hatch when the giant hit. It took him 20 minutes to land it.

Oh, one could go to Lake Michigan and hook and land much bigger brown trout, but that's a different game. We're talking small-stream fishing here. Resident trout. This was my opportunity to catch the giant trout that, at times, I thought only existed in my mind.

I had not been able to understand the traumatic reaction I experienced when I lost this fish. Sometimes I think that perhaps subconsciously I hoped that the elusive giant would never be hooked, that it was fun to pursue a dream but not necessarily attain it. Other times I feel that in a lifetime, a dedicated angler has one opportunity to catch his dream fish.

330

He or she lands it or loses it. I also wonder if losing this fish was symbolic of real-life pursuits. Most of us, have a dream, we chase it, we come close to attaining it, but something goes wrong at the last minute and it eludes us.

I don't have the answer.

I love the waters of Le Shack as much as before. I've gone back to Le Shack many times since that experience, and hopefully one night I will catch that big fish, or one similar in size. Maybe then I can recover that inexplicable "fishing soul" or maybe it's a "spirit" that seemed to have left me on that special night on a certain stream on September 4, 1999.

Note: Originally, the club was composed of six members: Al Long, Earl Pease, Al Hopkins, Jimmy Thurmond, Parky Parkinson and Hank Looyer. At least three of the above are deceased. The club was known as *The Shack*. Later another generation of anglers formed a new club, and Bus Duhamel named it *Le Shack*. We pointed out that it really should be called **La Shack**, because in French a house takes a feminine pronoun.

"Nonsense," said Ray Sauvé, of French descent. "There's nothing feminine about this place. We'll call it, **Le Shack**, and let the French call their homes by feminine names if they want to. . . "

Aging stinks

... or it's hard to grow old gracefully

WHEN I WAS in my late twenties and guided at Camp Manitou, in Ontario, Val Perrault, one of the premier fishing guides, challenged me to a canoe race around the island.

"Let's see how good ya are. We don't use paddles," Val said. "You stand on the gunnels, like this, and by bouncing up and down you go forward. See how easy it is? Race ya around the island. Loser—that's you, of course—buys the Cokes for all the guides. Ya willing to try or do you jus' wanna buy the Cokes and save yourself a dunkin'?" It was an initiation, of sorts.

I raced him. Of course, he beat me. I bought the Cokes. I felt accomplished because I didn't fall into the water and I did make it part of the way around the island.

A few years later at Costa Rica's Parismina Tarpon Rancho, I had to fish the river mouth from a cayuga (dugout canoe) because there was a shortage of boats. Trouble was, the cayuga leaked water. Rather than get my sneakers wet, I balanced myself on the gunwales by placing one foot on each side. I found it relatively easy to keep my balance and I was able to fly fish even though there were some waves.

In Mozambique, I fought a huge hammerhead shark for many hours. Sure, I was tired, but after resting for a few minutes and drinking some orange juice I recovered.

333

In Costa Rica, I battled an enormously strong tarpon for three hours under a scorching tropical sun without anything to drink, but I recuperated quickly and even tried to hook another tarpon.

In Ecuador, I landed seven marlin and one sailfish in one day after only three hours' sleep because of a late flight.

I took these and other events for granted in my younger days, but not now. When I see younger people nonchalantly accomplish similar feats today I admire their agility, balance and confidence.

Hey, I used to do that many years ago, I remind myself.

Today I find it difficult to stand on a skiff's deck in choppy water. I'll fight a big fish hard for about 15 minutes or so; either I'll land it or the hook will pull out. My hiatal hernia kicks in and I tire quickly. The long fights are a thing of the past.

Aging stinks. There's no other way to put it.

I do a lot of wading at night in deep, narrow Wisconsin streams, booby-trapped with sunken logs or huge boulders. In the inky darkness I must rely on a memory of the stream bottom that I mentally programmed during my daytime fishing forays. When I've misjudged an obstruction, I've come close to falling in and ruining a pleasant evening of fishing, but so far, I've recovered my balance at the last instant and have avoided the baptism. It's just a matter of time.

Night fishing was absolutely no problem in decades past, but today I'm not as cavalier about it. I fish easier streams at night and for some rivers I even carry a collapsible wading staff. This is annoying to me not only from a machismo standpoint, but because I waste a considerable amount of time probing the stream's bottom with the staff when I should be exploring the surface with a dry fly. Surely the *clickety-clack* noise created when my staff scrapes against rocks, gravel or logs must alarm the trout

Aging stinks.

Years ago Art Thrun and I would fish these same streams during most of the day, take a supper break, and then fish the night shift. We'd meet back at the camp 'round midnight, polish off a pint or two of ice cream, and often return to the river for a couple hours of fishing. Today,

334

we don't do that as often. Art complains of arthritic knees and takes a Feldene, and I grumble about a pinched nerve or other aches and pains, some real, some perhaps imaginary, and swallow an Extra-Strength Tylenol or Aleve.

There are about a dozen streams that surround our Wisconsin camp. One of my favorite, the Devil's Tail, requires a 12-mile drive and a half-hour hike through woods. I used to fish there almost every night, because few anglers fished these waters. The land was owned by a hermit who had three vicious dogs that had an acute sense of hearing and smell. He thought that since the waters ran through his land, the stream was also his private property, completely disregarding Wisconsin laws. There was a sinister sign at one end of his property. It read, "SURVIVORS WILL BE PROSECUTED." And to make sure you got the message, he riddled the sign with bullet holes. The hermit and the dogs are gone now, but his notorious reputation lingers on, so fishermen avoid it.

The Devil's Tail is almost like my private beat at night.

But during the last three years I've seldom fished it. The long walk and drive back to the camp late at night are the main reasons.

I've become soft. Aging stinks.

I've "discovered" some potent waters closer to the camp and this is where I'm fishing most nights. It's easy to get there. It's convenient. Never mind that sometimes there are five or six cars of fishermen crammed in the little parking lot!

As years whiz by, I've become increasingly cautious. In my younger days there was no place that I wouldn't fish. Day or night. I fished a wilderness stretch that was swampy and log infested. If you got stuck in a silty section and didn't have very strong legs, you could be there for a long, long time, because very few anglers fished it. I haven't been to that stretch in years. Nor do I go to the Bald Eagle's Roost because I would have to climb over and under many logs at night to get there.

Today, I'm always thinking ahead. What if something happens? What if I twist an ankle? How do I get out? What if I get lost in the woods, which is easy to do on a moonless or foggy night? These thoughts never entered my mind before. They do now.

A few years ago, I fished El Pescador in Belize with Pancho, a favorite guide. We hadn't fished together for about ten years.

"Man, you've gained weight." He was never very diplomatic, but he was right. I had gained weight. Meanwhile, Pancho was proud of the fact that he had lost about 25 pounds since we last fished together.

We went to a favorite tarpon place.

"Get on the deck and be on the lookout. We're in tarpon country," he told me.

I stood on the platform for a few minutes, but was constantly losing my balance.

"I can't stand up there," I told Pancho. There was a resignation in my voice. It was a sad experience.

"Whad'ya mean? Last time you were here, it was choppier and I was runnin' the motor and you'd be standing up there. Doncha 'member?"

"Yeah, I remember. That was ten years ago! I can't do it today."

So Pancho took me to some inside lagoons where we had great fun fishing for small tarpon, but it was another defeat served by the aging process.

I've joined a health club, exercise three or four days a week and maybe that will help.

I'll take a page out of Bus Duhamel's book. Bus belongs to our Wisconsin trout camp and at 90 he wades streams even at night. He falls in occasionally, but gets up, "dusts" himself off and goes right back to fishing.

Bus won our club's Angler-of-the-Year (2000) plaque!

Yeah, I'll carry a wading staff on some rivers, and hold on to a guide when we cross a boulder-strewn western river. And I'll put markers on trees to guide me through the woods and back to my car at night.

Maybe I'll carry one of those cell phones. Maybe.

But aging stinks. It really does.

Fishing then and now

THE GOOD OLD DAYS. Those of us who have vigorously pursued sportfishing through the past half century are quick to recite how great the quality of fishing *used* to be. We drift into a dreamy, somewhat hazy zone when we describe all those great angling experiences of decades past.

Immediately a very powerful, magical filter springs into play. This filter tends to enhance, emphasize, even magnify the numbers and the size of fish that we caught or lost then. At the same time, this remarkable filter minimizes the many angling failures that everyone experienced regardless of the decade he or she fished.

The more skilled raconteur purposefully cites a few failures, because, by contrast, they serve to heighten the intensity of his successes and to

337

sprinkle a dash of reality. After all, his audience would soon lose interest if all fishing accounts were an endless string of successes.

No doubt about it. Fishing in general was better then than it is today. Rivers flowed cleaner and civilization and industry had not encroached on our lakes, rivers and oceans to the extent that they have today.

Fishing at many of the popular foreign waters was also better then than now. Today, as fishing quality in the United States diminishes, anglers with time and money fly to Argentina, Chile, Bahamas and elsewhere for a more ego-satisfying lift. Consequently, some of the foreign waters are feeling the effects of increased fishing pressure.

On a 1968 Argentine fishing trip to the fertile Patagonian trout waters, Count George Wenckheim, my guide, was stunned when we saw eight or nine anglers during the *entire* trip.

"The place is going to hell! Too many fishermen," the Count grumbled periodically.

Because there were few accommodations near most of the Patagonian streams we wanted to fish, we camped out in tents. Today there are deluxe inns, resort hotels and probably a couple hundred fishing guides in that same region. Many of the experienced guides have clients booked for most of the season. Result? Fishing is still good in Patagonia but only a fraction of what it was. Quality and quantity have diminished.

Today there are more than 300 fishing camps in Alaska, but in the early 1960s I can only think of Bob Curtis TikChik Lodge, Northern Consolidated Airlines' camps and a few fishing safaris offered by hunting guides to tide them over between hunting seasons.

The same proliferation of fishing camps and lodges and increased fishing pressure has occurred in Baja California, Costa Rica, Belize, and many other countries. Businesses that cater to sportfishing have prospered, but the quality of fishing at popular fishing centers has suffered.

When I fished Costa Rica before most of today's camps existed, one could catch almost as many tarpon in the freshwater jungle lagoons as out in the Caribbean. Today? Nearly all outstanding catches take place in the Caribbean, because the fishing quality of the inside lagoons has greatly decreased. Anglers fishing the beaches of Costa Rica often caught snook weighing more than 25 pounds. Big snook are rare today.

Bonefish are not as plentiful nor as large in Latin America as they were decades ago. One reason is that commercially caught bonefish occasionally end up at local fish markets, even though this is illegal.

Dorado fishing in Argentina has greatly diminished due to the construction of dams.

Atlantic salmon fishing? It's criminal as to what has happened to this noble species. Norway, Ireland, Iceland, British Isles, eastern Canada and just about everywhere else have experienced a dramatic decline in salmon stocks.

The biggest disaster of all takes places on our oceans where state-of-the-art longline ships put out 25 or more miles of lines with a baited hook every few yards. The destructiveness of these longliners is incredible, and our oceans are fished every day by huge fleets.

However, there are many places that produce marvelous fishing today. Some of these waters are relatively new, while others have only been lightly fished in the past because these regions were difficult to reach, lacked sufficient accommodations or hadn't been greatly publicized. Examples:

• The Tierra del Fuego rivers at the southern tip of Argentina are producing sea-run browns that weigh more than 15 pounds on a very con-

sistent basis, and just about every prime week yields a 20-pound-plus trout. Occasionally a 30 pounder is caught!
• The tremendous Atlantic salmon fisheries on Russia's Kola Peninsula may have saved classic Atlantic salmon fishing. Until the Kola discovery, the number of Atlantic salmon streams had shrunk to a point where few anglers were attracted to this species.
• The spectacular fishing for giant peacocks in Brazil and the fabulous payara fishing opportunities at Venezuela's Uraima River are on many anglers' wish lists.
• The newly discovered Seychelles bonefish flats (Indian Ocean) have only been fished for a few years, but I'm sure that the final verdict will be very positive as soon as some of the flats are more fully investigated and logistical problems are solved.
• The relatively new Pacific sailfishing off Guatemala continues to be probably the best in the world.

Give the fish biologists lots of credit, too, for they have made numerous creative fish plantings, including the stocking of salmon and steelhead in the Great Lakes. At one time, Lake Michigan contained only a few small species. Today Alaskan-sized salmon, giant steelhead and huge brown trout and other exciting species can be caught in the shadows of Chicago's skyscrapers.

The comfortable new camps that are sprouting up in wilderness areas is another plus for modern day angling. When A. J. McClane first started fishing for peacocks in South America's Orinoco basin decades ago, he slept on huge rocks near the water, for the jungle was often impenetrable, to say nothing of the countless critters that hunt at night. A. J. told me that these sun-baked rocks were so hot, "that my brains seemed to turn into jelly." Today you can fish for South America's precious peacock bass from luxurious accommodations, some with air conditioning, enjoy wonderful meals, and cast flies or plugs from state-of-the-art bass boats, powered by four-stroke engines that whisk you to fabulous waters and back in minutes. The peacocks in these new areas are also considerably larger than what A. J. caught.

While the "olden days" in most cases produced superior fishing, today's angler need not feel shortchanged.

Hank Looyer and I frequently discuss our favorite Wisconsin trout streams. I've fished these waters for about 35 years, but Hank, who celebrated his 91st birthday in 2001, fished these rivers 60 years ago.

"Yeah, we caught many big trout then," Hank fondly recalls. "These rivers had lots of rainbows and huge browns. On many weekends, someone in our party would catch a brown of about four pounds or so, and sometimes several and even much bigger trout. The hatches were heavy then, but the fishing pressure was light."

William Phillips showed us some of his grandfather's photos of rainbow trout caught from the same river that Hank and I fished. The photos were of proud fishermen with six-, seven- and eight-pound rainbows! You would be proud to have caught these fish in Argentina or Chile.

Today, a 12-inch brown trout from these Wisconsin streams is considered a good catch. The rainbows are all but gone except in a few isolated, pathless waters. There are big browns, huge browns, in some of the rivers, but because of fishing pressure they are very difficult to catch, even at night.

"The fish are much spookier and not as many today. The hatches aren't as plentiful," explains Hank Looyer, "but there are lots of advantages that today's fisherman has and probably takes for granted. I'm speaking particularly of tackle. Take leaders, for instance. Today you can buy 5X tippet material that tests five pounds. Back then, anglers didn't have nylon leaders. They 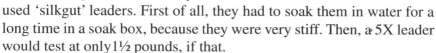 used 'silkgut' leaders. First of all, they had to soak them in water for a long time in a soak box, because they were very stiff. Then, a 5X leader would test at only 1½ pounds, if that.

"You have the tremendous improvement in fly rods. When the fiberglass rods came out, we couldn't believe their lightness and durability.

Then graphite rods were introduced. Another important item was the fly line. We used silk lines then. The best were the King Eider silk fly lines, made in England. The silk lines were thinner than our nylon fly lines of today, but because they weren't good floaters, we had to dry and dress them constantly, usually after a few hours' fishing, so we carried two lines or two reels. What a nuisance.

"We had to learn many things on our own. Today, there are hundreds of books, television programs and video tapes that teach everything from fly casting to releasing fish. A person can go to one of the fly-casting schools and become a good caster fairly quickly. So the young angler of today has it pretty good. I wish we had today's tackle and knowledge back then."

Yeah, there are trade-offs. I treasure my exploratory fishing trips in past decades, for there is a special thrill in testing new waters, but the modern angler is not shortchanged. Reliable flight schedules even to remote areas, comfortable accommodations, better tackle, state-of-the-art technology and the periodic discovery of new fishing grounds are some of the advantages that should excite the younger fishermen.

A worldwide fishing federation

I FEEL VERY FORTUNATE because I've made a living through sportfishing. It's been an enriching, exciting career and I've seldom been bored because of the unique challenges and new experiences that constantly presented themselves. The intriguing people, magnetic destinations, incredible episodes and the fascinating species of fish are poignant cameos in a continuous ribbon of fishing adventures.

Periodically, I step back to take a look at the future of angling. What are the major problems facing sportfishing? Are there solutions?

On the surface, it appears that angling is doing extremely well. Take a look at the lavishly designed mail-order fishing catalogs, surf the thousands of web sites, view the many television fishing programs or check out the video tapes and CDs that teach us how and where to fish.

There are more than a thousand fly-fishing books, and dozens of new titles are printed each year. Women are not only attracted to fishing, but they are also guiding, operating fishing lodges, writing books, teaching, lecturing, designing and recommending tackle! Twenty-five years ago, there were six international fishing travel agencies; today there are more than 600, if one includes the major fly shops and tackle stores that also sell fishing travel. Bass fishermen are paying thousands of dollars for fully equipped, state-of-the-art bass boats, and fishing tournaments are paying huge cash prizes to the winners.

The most important change in the past 25 years is that fishermen understand the importance of catch-and-release policies. If only we had listened to Lee Wulff when he preached release fishing decades ago!

So all is going well for sportfishing? Not exactly.

There are major problems and some of them are so crucial that we must address them immediately with short- and long-term strategic planning. Band-aid solutions will not work. Let's look at just a few important issues that threaten sportfishing:

The enormous demand for fish

Today there is a tremendous shortage of seafood, not only because of the growing population, but also because we have become a health-conscious world and know the nutritional value of fish. This huge demand skyrockets the price of fish to such a point that the commercial fishing companies are willing to make enormous investments in huge boats equipped with deadly, ultra-sophisticated gear. We are harvesting four times as many fish as six years ago, and, at the same time, we're continually losing fishing grounds.

It's estimated that there are enough commercial nets and

longlines in the Pacific Ocean alone to circle the earth at its equator. A longliner can put out 25 miles of line with baited hooks every six to 10 feet. Imagine what damage these nets and longliners can do in a day? In a month? Several years?

Aggressive commercial fishing in the Pacific has decimated marlin, sails and other pelagic species and has greatly depleted anadromous fish including steelhead and salmon.

Similarly, fish stocks in the Atlantic and other oceans are being destroyed. The overharvesting by commercial interests almost knocked the Atlantic salmon out of the ocean and on to the endangered species list. Bluefin tuna has virtually disappeared from many waters. We are destroying our oceans at an unbelievable rate because of the insatiable demand for fish and the efficiency of the sophisticated commercial fishing fleets.

It's not only the oceans that are being destroyed. In Latin America, locals and immigrants have netted many bonefish flats, and strategically placed monofilament nets can quickly ruin prime bonefish flats beyond repair. Remember when giant snook were so prevalent along the east coast of Costa Rica that 25- to 30-pound snook earned only a polite "nice fish" comment? Heavy netting, especially at or near the river mouths, has depleted the snook population. Thankfully, something is being done about the netting on the east coast and the big snook are coming back slowly.

Officially, the swordfish is not on the endangered species list, but commercial fishing has reduced its populations at such an alarming rate that in many waters this storied species no longer exists. Commercial fleets from the United States all the way to Brazil are capturing juveniles.

Freshwater fish are also affected. Check a fish counter at a supermarket and you'll see northern pike, lake trout, walleye, whitefish and other species for sale at skyrocketing prices.

Pollution and acid rain have destroyed thousands of lakes and rivers that, at one time, provided good fishing. There are no fences in the air that prevent the clouds of pollution from drifting from country to country. We think of the Scandinavian countries in terms of pristine environments, mountain lakes, rushing rivers and winding, pastoral streams, but they have suffered massive losses. Norway, for example, has lost total fish stocks in approximately 5,000 lakes! More than a third of her rivers have critical loads of acid rain! And more than 90 percent of the acid rain that falls on Norway *originates in other countries.*

The symbiotic effect of pollution, commercial fishing and disease has destroyed many of the great Norwegian salmon rivers. Years ago, I enjoyed fishing Norway's Driva River, famous for its huge salmon. Sadly very few (if any!) salmon are sighted on the spawning beds today because of a parasitic disease (*Gyrodactylis salaris*). Other rivers are also tainted with this parasite and recently the Norwegians reluctantly poisoned the classic Laerdal River with the hope that in five years this river will recover sufficiently to support healthy Atlantic salmon.

The United States and Canada are no less vulnerable to acid rain despite the North American Clean Air Act that was implemented in 1990. Nova Scotia claims that "the salmon runs of 14 rivers in Nova Scotia's southern uplands have been killed by acid rain and another 50 rivers have been seriously impacted. These number will grow unless the Canadian and U.S. governments adopt stricter emission laws . . . "

It's estimated that in another 20 years the demand for seafood will be increased by 700 percent! Aquaculture or fish farming may to be an answer; however, serious problems are associated with oceanic fish farming. They include the spreading of parasitic diseases, polluting the water from feed and fish wastes and the genetic dilution of wild fish. "Farmed" salmon, escaping from damaged pens or cages, breed with the wild fish and their offspring are not capable of surviving the rigors of migration.

346

Aquaculture is big business. One report estimates that more than 100 million people in the world make their living through aquaculture. In the United States fish farming (in freshwater ponds) is a huge industry and its potential is enormous. Some experts predict that it will eventually surpass cattle ranching.

Unquestionably, aquaculture could be a valuable solution, but it is up to the angling community to insist on stringent controls and the reduction or elimination of the known problems.

The anti-fishing campaigns

The People for the Ethical Treatment of Animals (PETA) has been actively involved in anti-fishing campaigns in Europe, because it considers angling cruel. In recent years, PETA brought its "trunk show" to the United States, to stop sportfishing at all costs. PETA—which claims a membership of more than 500,000—has mapped out numerous PR strategies and has established a network of protesters that is unbelievably persistent and testy.

But they cannot win. Or can they?

In the 1960s and early 1970s big-game hunters publicly discussed their safaris and shikars and even non-hunters admired them. Hollywood produced more than a dozen movies with hunting safari themes. Fashion and "shelter" magazines featured lavish pictorials of hunters' trophy rooms. When the antihunting people stepped in, we chuckled at their initial awkward attempts, but today, a big-game hunter is reluctant to discuss his successes except with other hunters.

Can't happen to angling? Ever hear of Pisces? Headquartered in Bristol, England, we knew this organization as Campaign for the Abolition of Angling (CAA), but in 1994 it changed its name to Pisces. Whereas PETA is a "horizontal" organization for the protection of all "animals" including fish, Pisces concentrates on fish and fishing, and among its goals is to ban angling everywhere. It has attained remarkable success in outlawing fishing on several European waters.

Pisces' tentacles reach beyond sportfishing. As mentioned earlier, aquaculture or fish farming is an important food source that helps to feed the world's population. Pisces strongly opposes fish farming for entirely different reasons than the spreading of parasitic diseases, pollution and genetic dilution. High on Pisces' agenda is a long-term project of brainwashing young students. Here are a few paragraphs from *Freda the Fish,* an essay that Pisces widely distributes among young students (while most of it relates to fish farming, Pisces doesn't miss the opportunity to slam angling and anglers):

"It was only the wire netting of the cage that separated Freda and her friends from the sea . . . When she was younger Freda would swim her way over to the netting and gaze longingly at the sea, dreaming, of swimming freely. . . . "

Later Freda and Felix escaped from the fish farm.

" 'Owww. Help!' Felix suddenly cried. His lip was caught on a hook. He thrashed around in agony and Freda could only watch as he was dragged out of the water. . . .

"She vaguely remembered being told about anglers . . . the only way she could console herself was with the thought that at least Felix had a few wonderful days of freedom before he had been so brutally killed."

By the way, how did Freda escape from the fish farm? There was a hole in the net, but she was too big to fit through it. So she thought it out. She quit eating for days, lost weight and escaped.

Anthropomorphism at its best. Hello. Bambi is back!

Pisces recommends that its members disrupt angling by any means, including throwing rocks in the water near fishermen, using scuba divers to cut lines in tournaments and other devilish tactics.

While in England a few years ago, I came across some Pisces members who were trying to disrupt a fishing tournament.

"Aren't you afraid that one of your members could be killed?" I asked a group of Pisces members. I was pretending to be an innocent bystander.

"Oh, but that's what we want! We need a martyr to carry on our work," the leader explained. Suddenly his eyes beamed with joy.

Other problems, other headaches

In the United States and Canada there are never-ending problems with the Native Fishing Rights. Illegal netting of salmon on both North American coasts have been well chronicled. In Minnesota and Wisconsin, Native Americans and sportsmen have clashed fiercely through the years. In Alaska, Native Americans were temporarily successful in closing several important fishing areas to visiting sportsmen. Every year there are violent conflicts—some resulting in bloodshed—involving Native Fishing Rights and sportsmen. While Native Fishing Rights were initiated in North America, the problem is spreading to other countries, including in New Zealand, where aboriginal tribes are disregarding fish and game laws.

Another important concern is that our young people are not taking up fishing at the same proportional rate as in previous generations. The competition from other activities plus the tremendous interest in computers and electronic devices are blamed. But what are we—the older generations—doing to interest our youth?

"I've never found any young person in serious trouble who had a strong interest in fishing and the outdoors," says Dr. Ronald Trunsky, Michigan's eminent psychiatrist and an ardent fisherman.

There are hundreds of other problems that confront sportfishing and fish on a regional, national and global basis.

Okay, so what do we do . . . take up golf?

One of our real problems is that the sportfishing community is fractured. We do not have a common voice. There are lots of clubs and associations, such as Trout Unlimited, Fly Fishing Federation, B.A.S.S., IGFA, The Billfish Foundation, Walleyes Unlimited, Muskies Inc., Atlantic Salmon Federation, American Museum of Fly Fishing, The National Fresh Water Fishing Hall of Fame, American Sportfishing Association, Izaak Walton, North American Fishing Club and hundreds more! Each, on its own, tries hard to solve its problems but, except for B.A.S.S., does not have the numbers that impress the politicians and governments.

We desperately need an umbrella organization or federation composed of the above groups, associations, clubs and anyone who has a stake in sport fishing.

Let's use **International Congress of Sportfishing (ICS)** strictly as a working title for this mythical federation.

In addition to the previously mentioned fishing clubs and associations, the strength, influence and success of the ICS lies in a multitiered structure of the various sportfishing segments.

Consider the outdoor/fishing magazines. *American Angler, Salt Water Sportsman, Field & Stream, Sports Afield, Outdoor Life, Fly Fisherman, Marlin, Sport Fishing, In-Fisherman, Fly Fishing in Salt Waters, Atlantic Salmon Journal, Gray's Journal, Fly Rod and Reel, Bassmasters, Florida Sportsman, Flyfishing & Tying Journal* and all the rest of the fine angling publications would gain tremendously from the success of ICS. In many cases, ICS might be the most logical and perhaps the *only* road to survival: Could these publications survive if PETA, Pisces and other anti-fishing organizations achieve their goals? If commercial fishing destroys our oceans? If pollution continues to poison our lakes? If acid rain sterilizes our rivers? I don't think so.

The outdoor/fishing magazines would be a very important tier to ICS's success and, at the same time, protect their own existence.

What about the outdoor writers? The Outdoor Writers Association of America (OWAA) has about 1,700 members who write books, articles and newspaper columns. They host outdoor TV and radio programs, photograph and lecture. If we were to hire the best PR firms with a multi-million-dollar budget, it could not begin to compare with the job that all these outdoor writers could do for sportfishing.

How about the fishing tackle manufacturers? The giant mail-order tackle suppliers? Boat and outboard motor companies? The retail tackle stores? How about the fishing camps, and the fishing travel agencies? All should be encouraged to join. Again, their future is at stake.

Consider the enormous power anglers could have if these well-meaning but fractured, faint voices combined into one booming, ear-deafening, brain-rattling roar. Then, and only then, could we flex our muscles and get things done for sportfishing.

Let's look at two examples where the ICS' huge membership would make a substantial difference:

1) Facing a severe shortage of swordfish, The Billfish Foundation started a campaign years ago to persuade restaurants to discontinue serving swordfish because this species is fighting for its survival. Right now, most of the swordfish served are juveniles that have never spawned. Despite limited PR efforts and letter writing, swordfish are featured on many restaurant menus and sold in super markets. Sure, The Billfish Foundation made a dent, but if members of the proposed ICS supported a Save our Swordfish (SOS) campaign, the general public would become aware of the shortage and quit ordering it. It would not matter whether the protesters in the SOS program are bass, trout, salmon, pike or tarpon fishermen; it matters only that we present a powerful, united angling front. Many feel that the swordfish's future is doomed and that efforts should concentrate on saving the marlin and sailfish.

2) Recently, Perrier—the giant bottled-water company—came close to establishing a plant at the Mecan River, one of Wisconsin's famous trout rivers. As an enticement, Perrier pointed out that this would mean lots of local jobs. It claimed that the water it would take from the Mecan would not damage the river or its fishing. ***Ha!***

Thankfully, Friends of the Mecan, an association of several hundred sportsmen and naturalists, was quickly organized, and campaigned so vigorously that Perrier is prospecting elsewhere. If the ICS were in place and a membership alert was sounded, I'm sure that Perrier would have been so overwhelmed by the huge number of protests that it would have immediately looked for other waters to tap rather than conduct a long, bitter fight. Again, it wouldn't matter that we may not be trout fishermen or that we may never fish in Wisconsin. We are all anglers; we differ only in methods we choose, the species we seek.

The above are just two reasons why we need to lock arms and walk together.

Governments and politicians only pay attention to big numbers. Look at what the controversial National Rifle Association (NRA) accomplished in past decades. Very few candidates considered running for an important political office without "endorsing" the NRA. Why? Because the NRA has numbers. So why can't we apply the same "numbers" philosophy and make it work for fishing? There are twice as many fishermen as hunters in the United States. Just imagine the political power that angling would have through the International Congress of Sportfishing.

The beauty of the proposed ICS is that every segment of the sportfishing community stands to benefit from its existence. The fishermen. The writers. The magazines. The tackle manufacturers. The retail stores. The fishing travel agencies. And, most important, the fish!

But why would competitors in the outdoor/fishing fields join hands? The answer is simple: SURVIVAL! Let's look at the magazine segment for a moment. If the anti-fishing groups, like PETA and Pisces, convince the advertisers to cancel their ads, some angling magazines—if not all—would be out of business.

Ludicrous? Remember *The American Sportsman* (national TV series) hosted by Curt Gowdy? Every Sunday, sportsmen would gather around their television sets to watch Curt and Lee Wulff, and Stu Apte and Bing Crosby and others hunt or fish at some of the world's great destinations. The antihunting groups protested to the advertisers and soon *The American Sportsman* gave us hang gliding, cliff diving, surfing, mountain climbing and other non-hunting and non-fishing sports. *The American Sportsman?* Rest In Peace.

It is vital that we band together, that is, if we want to protect our waters and pass on fishing to future generations. **It's a win, win, win proposition.**

The Save our Sealife campaign, which limits marine net fishing in Florida state waters, is a great example of how angling groups and individuals can work together. The Save Our Sealife committee conducted a very effective petition drive on November, 10, 1992 by collecting 201,000 signatures outside the polling sites in Florida. This might be the most successful one-day petition effort ever in America. *Florida Sportsman*, its publisher Karl Wickstrom and the Florida Conservation

Association were the important players in this fight, but they received tremendous assistance from many outdoor writers, numerous associations and federations, such as the Florida Wildlife Federation, Tropical Audubon Society of Miami, Sierra Club, Legal Defense Fund and others. The result: An overwhelming victory on November 8, 1994, when 72 percent of the people voted to ban the nets. The formula for success included sportsmen, magazines, outdoor writers, grass roots campaigners and associations working together. While this worked to solve a regional problem, a similar model could be applied for national and international issues.

Once the ICS has been established in the United States, it must become international in scope because pollution, acid rain, overharvesting of our oceans, anti-fishing campaigns and other problems are global issues. Going international would be relatively easy because nearly all the countries that offer fishing have associations or angling clubs in place and share similar concerns.

Until recently, the formation of ICS would have been extremely difficult, but today it can be activated quickly and inexpensively because of the Internet. There are thousands of fishing sites available right now that could be quickly linked but at the same time protect each site's sovereignty.

So what are some of the things that the International Congress of Sportfishing could accomplish via the Internet? Obviously, it would instantly open communication among all the fishing clubs, associations and members. Just think of the potential: fishing clubs around the world could chat on the Internet. The ICS could be in touch with millions of anglers without spending any money for printing and postage!

Another great advantage of the ICS/Internet is that anglers could easily communicate with local, state and federal governments. We all have good intentions to write to our representatives regarding various issues but we tend to put it off because writing a letter requires effort. With a few clicks on the computer keyboard we can instantly inform the government of our position on various sportfishing issues.

Who owns the International Congress of Sportfishing? Obviously there has to be a council or officers that gives the ICS direction. But we can take a page from the Internet: computers are linked together world wide but there are no owners of the Internet. Similarly, all fishing groups (associations, clubs, writers, tackle, etc.) could be linked together with no particular owner. And while solving sport fishing problems is the most important *raison d'etre* of ICS, there is the fun aspect, too. Fishing information could be exchanged between anglers from around the world.

How about holding an annual International Congress of Sportfishing World Symposium in a different country each year? That would surely be a wonderful dream come true.

If world organizations, associations, and individuals could not physically attend the ICS World Symposium they could participate—even vote on issues—via the Internet.

We need imagination and dream weavers in sportfishing.

We certainly have the talent in the United States and abroad to make this happen. We have highly successful business people who have built huge empires and know how to put the modules together. Some of them claim that they want to be "difference makers" in the environment. Well, here's their opportunity. There are giants in television, Hollywood and in the entertainment field who love to fish. We have outstanding writers, artists and scientists who care what happens in our ocean, lakes and rivers. We have the expert anglers, such as Stu Apte, Lefty Kreh, Winston Moore, Billy Pate, Steve Sloan—hundreds of them—who can advise us. Great communicators like Bob Stearns, Mark Sosin, Bob McNally, Joe Doggett, Joan Wulff, John Randolph, Mike Leech to name a few. We are fortunate to have two former presidents, Jimmy Carter and George Bush, who are passionately involved in sportfishing (and wouldn't they make wonderful presidents of the International Congress of Sportfishing?) The talent, the brains, the dream builders are all there. We need to develop an ICS concept: for the sake of fish, for the sake of fishing, and for the sake of future generations.

This chapter is based on the December, 1996 issue of *The PanAngler* newsletter.

Last days at 180 North Michigan

IT WAS AFTER FIVE and the PanAngling employees had left for the day. I had to finish some work and make a few calls before I could leave. As was my custom for many years, I'd walk to the train station, board the 6:35 commuter, get off at the Rogers Park station, get in my car and drive home.

That's about 1½-hours' travel time each way between the office and my home. Three hours a day, round trip. I reached for the calculator and discovered that I had spent almost a thousand hours a year and more than 30,000 hours commuting during the past forty years. By dividing that number by 16 hours—I deducted eight from 24 hours for sleeping—I realized that I had invested the equivalent of 1,875 days or about full five years' time traveling between home and work. Five precious years!

Bummer.

When I was younger, I wouldn't have concerned myself with such trivia, but after celebrating my 65th birthday and realizing that the meter is clicking faster than ever, there is cause for alarm. I want to conserve as many of those "golden hours" as I possibly can.

Commuting to and fro is not my idea of quality time.

I didn't bother to finish my work or make the calls. I left the office. I

355

was depressed. Life was passing me by in a wicked, fast-forward mode. As I walked to the train I felt older, tired. Was I burned out? Years ago I worked a 12-hour day plus Saturdays and sometimes even Sundays, but lately I was taking it easy. Five days a week. Eight hours a day.

I think I had walked past the Picasso sculpture when I came to an important decision: I had to sell PanAngling. But how? I asked for divine assistance: God, I need to sell PanAngling. I need help. I am not into formal religion, but through fishing and being outdoors I've developed a simplified but strong spiritual philosophy. I am a strong believer.

The following day when I returned to the office after lunch Jessica Del Real handed me a note.

"This man called while you were at lunch and left his phone number. Wants you to call him back."

The caller was Pat Galyan. I had only spoken to him once before, on conservation matters, but I know that PanAngling had arranged two trips for him and the fishing was terrible. Disastrous.

As I began to dial, an inexplicable message shot through my mind. Actually, it was more like a voice than a thought.

"Jim, this man is going to buy your company," the inner voice seemed to say. Never before was I more positive about a premonition.

Pat Galyan came right to the point. He was interested in the fishing travel agency field and wanted to know if PanAngling was for sale. He had made lots of money, spent a couple of years hunting and fishing, and I think he missed the challenges of the business world. After all, he was only in his mid-40s, and much too young to retire permanently.

I told him that I was considering selling PanAngling, but I warned him that the outdoor travel agency field was not lucrative. Competition was very keen and if I were he and anxious to get back into business, I'd consider other fields. I couldn't possibly be more truthful. I broke every rule in salesmanship. I even told him that it would be cheaper for him to start his own agency rather than buy an existing one.

My comments didn't scare him.

He lived in Indianapolis, so we decided to meet halfway at a restaurant in Merrillville, Indiana in a few days.

356

I learned that he was a very successful businessman and had transformed the family-owned Galyan's sports stores into huge successes. He had recently sold Galyan's to Limited, the giant conglomerate, for a lot of money.

"Before we proceed, Pat, I would like to make something perfectly clear. There have been several very wealthy potential buyers interested in buying PanAngling in the past, and they came up with these business formulas, you know, seven times the average profit for the past five years and other mumble jumble. This has to be an *emotional* sale."

He seemed puzzled by the term "emotional sale."

"Look, some anglers will pay more than $2,000 for a Jim Payne split-bamboo fly rod. Right? Is it worth $2,000? Of course not. But people want to own one and they buy it on an emotional basis."

To make sure he understood, I explained that recently a business group was considering buying a major league baseball team that had been losing millions for years and didn't even own the stadium.

"Now if we follow the logic of these business formulas, the interested group shouldn't have to pay a dime for the team, right? I mean, the team lost many millions during the past five years and virtually has no assets except the major league franchise. Actually, the club is loaded with huge liabilities—player contracts that total over $60 million a year, and some are for many years. Yeah, they own a few bats, equipment, uniforms and a logo. A lousy logo, at that. And you know what the asking price for the franchise is? $300 million!"

Pat finished his coffee and said he had to leave but would be in touch.

I made my point. PanAngling would not be sold based on some business formula but rather a fair, equitable price. I thought about all this as I drove back on the Dan Ryan Expressway, trying to stay out of the way of 18-wheel trucks honking and blinking their lights because they wanted me to speed up even though I was traveling at 75 mph!

I OPERATED PanAngling more like a family than a corporation. The next day, I explained to the employees that I was tired, perhaps burned out, getting up in years and that the business might be sold to an interested buyer. They seemed to understand.

A few weeks later, Pat Galyan came into the office, pulled out a sheet of paper from his pocket and handed it to me. It was his purchase offer.

He had examined PanAngling's financials and obviously gave good consideration to my "emotional sale" comments. It was a very fair offer, very close to the price that I thought would be good for both parties. After discussing it with my partners, we agreed to proceed with the due diligence and all the other irritating but necessary steps that are involved in selling a corporation. There was virtually no squabbling on price.

There was only one stumbling block. Pat wanted to move the company to Indianapolis where he and several key people, that he planned to hire, lived.

I could work out of my house for a year or so, he said, and all the other employees could move to Indianapolis. Paul Melchior and Lee, his wife, agreed to the move. The other employees could not because of family and other issues. I felt very badly about this, but as it turned out all the other employees found other jobs almost immediately.

THE LAST DAY. It was Friday. Jay Burkert, who had worked for Pat at Galyan's for many years, was now PanAngling's vice president in charge of operations. He and Pam, his wife, drove from Indianapolis to oversee the packing and moving.

Mounted trophies and paintings were removed from the walls. Books, brochures and office supplies were packed. File cabinets were sealed. Desks and chairs were stacked up against the wall. Computers were placed in boxes, except for the IBM Displaywriter, our first computer that cost more than $22,000! No one wanted it, because today for less than $2,000 you can buy a PC that would run circles around the Displaywriter. We had to pay to have it hauled away! There was no joy in the office, and yet we all knew the sale was necessary and the move to Indy was inevitable.

At day's end, it was befitting that we should have a drink in my office. There was Linda Hoffman, our accountant. Jessica. Martha Porras. Frank Wergin, Paul and a few others.

We opened one bottle of wine. Martha almost choked on it. It tasted sour. I got another bottle of wine with a fancy French label from the store room. This time, Linda was our official taster. This bottle also was spoiled. It tasted like vinegar. Then a third one. All the wines were sour. I realized that these bottles were given to us 15 to 20 years ago and they were not stored properly.

We laughed about it. Geez, we can't even muster one good bottle of wine for a going-away drink. Perhaps this was befitting of our moods.

It was a sad day. I looked at Martha and her sister Jessica. Before they were hired, their sister, Dina Del Real, worked for us for a number of years. All of them were fabulous employees. Frank Wergin was manager of our travel department, loved to fish and thought nothing of flying to Bangkok or London over a weekend to earn mileage. Linda Hoffman, our accountant, was always very cheerful, except if a month wasn't profitable and she had to tell me about it. She was sadder about it than I was. Paul Melchior had been with us more than 20 years and I had relied on him tremendously, especially in the past few years.

The employees had to finish packing and now, alone in my office, I had a little time to reflect on the past. I thought of Ursula Grzesik, Pat Rice, Versha Deshmukh, Bill Cullerton Jr., Al ("the Legend") Schaefer, Claudia Levy and dozens of employees who had given their best through the years, even if they were underpaid. Al Trungale and John Tianis, our graphic designers, were big contributors to our success.

I recalled the "coffee breaks" we used to have years ago, when all employees would gather in my office to discuss whatever they wanted, except office work. Wow, did I get an education on modern dating and single life! These breaks became an institution and sometimes employees from other offices would come in for the 3:00 to 3:30 symposium.

I thought of partners Bill Cullerton Sr., Tim Clark, Don Dobbins, Cam Dobbins and Ken Gould and directors Don Edelmann and Mike Love and their valuable contributions.

The good times. The sad ones, too.

The sharing of problems, whether business or personal.

Yeah, it was a good, long run. Almost 25 years at PanAngling.

No regrets.

It was time to close up and leave the office. We said our goodbyes, promised to stay in touch, wished each other luck and filed out of the office for the last time.

It was over.

Someone flicked the light switch and the offices were suddenly dark. Gloomy. Ghostly. Quiet.

Paul Melchior and I stood outside of the office at the door for a few seconds.

"You lock it up, Paul. Close this chapter, and begin a new career in Indy." He locked the office for the last time.

It was time to move on. PanAngling belonged to someone else now. We had nurtured it long enough.

Paul walked slowly to the elevator and punched the button. He was emotional, more so than I'd ever seen him before.

I went back to the office because I forgot to tape a sign to the door. It announced that PanAngling was moving to Indianapolis.

"Good luck, PanAngling. We certainly had some great times together, ehh? Have a good life."

I think I said that out loud, but I'm not sure.

PS: On September 28, 2001, 17 days after the terrorists' strike on New York and Washington D. C., PanAngling filed Chapter 7 and closed its doors. Dean Langton purchased its assets to reactivate the company.

360

Index

I

J

K

L

Cover Painting:

Charles B. Mitchell

Illustrations:

Charles B. Mitchell

John Tianis

Cover and Book Design: All That Matters Graphics

For comments, information or additional copies:

AnglingMatters P.O. Box 4938, Skokie IL 60076-4938 ●847.673.3915

email anglingmatters@ameritech.net